My Brother's Voice

**How a Young Hungarian Boy
Survived the Holocaust:
A True Story**

Every time Stephen Nasser speaks to an audience, he reminds them that he, like every human child, was born into a culture that he did not choose or design. He was born a Jew, just as each of us was born into our own culture. Nasser asks us to understand that, and to value our diversity.

The atrocities perpetrated upon the Jews by the Nazis during World War II are hard to think about. If we permit ourselves to grasp the horror of the Holocaust, then we must confront the dark recesses of our own natures and question our own priorities. It is painful to believe that such horrors could ever happen, let alone be repeated. Denial relieves the pain of disillusion, so there are some today who claim that the history of the Holocaust is some sort of bizarre fiction, conveniently made up for political purposes. It is more comfortable to believe that man must be incapable of such evil; otherwise, how could anyone have survived?

Somehow, miraculously, some people did survive. Stephen Nasser survived. He was there. He wrote this account not to ask for pity or retribution, but tell the truth that could allow us to save ourselves from ourselves. He simply asks us to listen to his painstakingly unembellished story, so that we will know what happened. What gave Stephen his courage? How does he manage the nightmare images that have been seared into his memory? What philosophy allows people like him to go on living, having lost so many loved ones and friends to violent death?

Nasser leaves the answers to those questions up to his readers. *My Brother's Voice* simply tells the unvarnished truth, without preaching or moralizing. It is a tribute to Nasser's brother, who died in a Nazi concentration camp, but it is also a reminder that each of us can find the strength to survive.

Edwin Silberstang, Editor
Laura Brundige, Copy Editor
Evan Fields, Designer

Nasser, Stephen.

My brother's voice : how a young Hungarian boy survived the Holocaust : a true story / Stephen Nasser with Sherry Rosenthal. — 1st ed. — Las Vegas, Nev. : Stephens Press, 2003.

p. ; cm.

ISBN: 1932173102
1932173102 (pbk.)

1. Nasser, Stephen. 2. Holocaust, Jewish (1939-1945)—Personal narratives. 3. Holocaust survivors' writings. 4. Holocaust survivors—Biography. 5. Holocaust victims. I. Rosenthal, Sherry. II. Title.

D804.196.N377 N37 2003
940.53/18/092—dc22   CIP

Stephens Press LLC

A Stephens Media Group Company
Post Office Box 1600
Las Vegas, Nevada 89125-1600

Printed in Hong Kong

My Brother's Voice

How a Young Hungarian Boy
Survived the Holocaust:
A True Story

Stephen Nasser
with Sherry Rosenthal

Stephens
Press LLC

A Stephens Media Group Company
Post Office Box 1600
Las Vegas, Nevada 89125-1600

Foreword

For over half a century my memories of all that took place between May, 1944, when my family and I were deported to Auschwitz, and April, 1945, when I left Muhldorf, stayed buried within me. My goal, after all, was to get on with life. I'd come to know many concentration camp survivors whose lives were never again normal, and I vowed not to become one of them. I married, raised a family, and enjoyed several successful careers. As the wounds of my adolescence healed, though, I yearned to tell my story.

One obstacle remained. My beloved Uncle Karoly (my late father's brother) was still alive in Budapest, and I had a terrible secret from Auschwitz to keep from him.

In 1996, Uncle Karoly died, at 92. Only then was I free to tell my story. The secret that kept me silent so long is finally revealed within these pages, since it can hurt him no more.

I dedicate this book to the memory of my parents, and above all, to the memory of my older brother Andris. They, together with so many mothers and fathers, brothers and sisters, sons and daughters, were innocent victims of human history's worst genocide, the Nazi war machine, within whose path millions were ground to death.

In recent years, it has become popular in certain political or even intellectual circles to refute the existence of the Holocaust altogether. As has often been said, however, those forgetting history are doomed to repeat it. Make no mistake: the Holocaust *is* history.

I know. I was there.

Stephen "Pista" Nasser
Las Vegas, Nevada
May, 2003

Now he is dead, wherefore should I fast?
Can I bring him back again?
I shall go to him, but he shall not return to me.

II Samuel 12:23

Chapter One
On the Train from Hell

Clackety-clack—clackety-c-l-a-c-k. . . The cattle train in which I'm riding through the Bavarian countryside suddenly slows down. I wonder where we are, exactly, and why we're stopping here. I'm halfway dead from hunger. It's been that way for months: over a year, really. I'm 14 years old by now, I think. My given name is Istvan (Hungarian for "Stephen"). But everyone calls me by my nickname, Pista. Our family name is Nasser, and I come from a long line of Hungarian Jews. Before the Holocaust, we Nassers had lived in Budapest, the capital, undisturbed and prosperous, for many generations.

I think I smell Mother's paprikas potatoes. But. . . no. . . it can't be. . . It's just my imagination. I'm still in Bavaria, somewhere outside Muhldorf, the concentration camp where I've done slave labor for over a year, courtesy of Hitler and his men.

Rubbing sleep from my eyes as best I can with such skinny fists, I squint into the sunlight toward a tiny window in our crowded boxcar. From what I can glean as I sit on the filthy wooden floor, jammed against 80 or so men (all older than me, some in better, some in worse condition) it seems we're approaching a town. A prisoner standing up and looking out the window reports that he can see whitewashed houses, green farmland, and storage sheds.

Now the train enters a tiny station and jerks abruptly to a halt. With all my strength, I force myself wide-awake. I'm weak as a newborn baby. But I'm alive. Yes.

Our comrade, peeking out the window, informs us that he sees the stationmaster dart from his office, his arms upraised, yelling, *"Alles frei,"* or "All free!" God, I hope it's true.

Now the strongest among us stand up and stretch, try to jump for joy, and embrace each other. Eagerly, these lucky souls prepare for their first taste of long-awaited freedom outside our boxcar, and, more importantly, away from the forced labor facility from which we've just been evacuated. I'm too weak and sick to stand, much less join them, so I can only look on in envy.

Healthy or sick, no one aboard our train from Hell carries any belongings but the clothes on his back. I *have,* however, managed to bring my diary out with me. The diary is written on sheets of cement paper (that was all I could find), and bound with wire.

My friend Joska, (who, before deportation, was a professor of psychology at the University of Budapest) is another Muhldorf "veteran." Though 12 years older, he's closer in age to me than anyone else at Muhldorf. Now he comes over to where I sit and embraces me. "Pista, the war's over! We're free!"

"Thank God!" I reply.

When Joska stands up again, I notice, for the first time, that he's still wearing his awkward canvas prison shoes, although they've nearly fallen apart. Then I observe my own feet. I wear no shoes; the ones the Nazis issued me are long gone. Pus and blood ooze through the tattered wrappings around my ankles. The trousers and jacket of my striped prison uniform are worn thin. I haven't the strength to kill the lice that crawl all over me.

Now I see some of my other fellow prisoners climb down from inside their boxcars and begin walking toward the village to celebrate their new freedom.

"Pista," Joska instructs me, "you stay here!"

I smile, involuntarily. As if I had a choice. "Sure."

"I'll go into town, find some American soldiers, and bring them back here to help get you to a hospital."

"Thank you," I say, wearily. As he climbs back out, I call after him "Joska, be careful!" I still can't imagine people like him and me just walking around freely in what must still be southern Germany. I don't know why, but I have a feeling we're not out of danger. Not yet.

"I'll be careful," Joska calls over his shoulder. I watch his scrawny back, and his joyous stride, as my friend pads happily after the others, still wearing his own baggy zebra-striped prison uniform.

Will I ever be glad to get out of this one and never see it again!

I nod off until various familiar, but unpleasant, noises jar me awake again. Gunshots! First I hear just a few, as sharp as fire crackers. But more soon follow. I sit straight up, craning my neck to see outside. What on earth is happening? Where is Joska? Now I wish he'd never left my side.

Soon I see groups of terrified prisoners, the same ones who'd just jumped down from these boxcars and hugged each other so happily, rush frantically back to the train, with uniformed Nazi SS troops in hot pursuit.

Unfortunately, this doesn't surprise me. The Nazis may realize they're about to lose the war, but even so, I doubt they want Jewish concentration camp "scum" like us already contaminating their pristine Bavarian villages. Also, any remaining SS around here have probably been ordered to continue picking off as many Jews as possible, in order to help cover up evidence of the camps and their overworked, underfed prisoners.

Many of the prisoners now scrambling up inside my boxcar bleed visibly from fresh wounds. I lie down flat, trying to avoid being hit by any stray gunfire. I see Joska crawl back inside. Thank God! But the fingers of his left hand look a bloody mess. Why did I ever let him go for help?

More shots pepper the train. I'm not hit, yet. But Joska is. He's barely inside again when he tries to stand, but then teeters, spins crazily around, and falls back outside, a fatal bullet through his head. To come all this way, only to be killed now, while seeking help for me! How can I forgive myself? And when will this madness end?

When we were all first herded onto this train, on SS orders that the camp be evacuated, a rumor circulated that we'd be taken up into the Bavarian Alps to be shot. But then we heard otherwise.

Before the train actually started up, one uniformed guard told us that, although the SS (Hitler's elite uniformed officers who ran the camp) had indeed ordered us shot, they couldn't stay around to see the order carried out. They themselves had to flee for their lives from the advancing Allies.

This left us prisoners, luckily, in the hands of the remaining, uniformed *Wehrmacht* guards (the enlisted men of the German army), many of whom actually disapproved of Hitler's tactics.

After the SS all cleared out, the *Wehrmacht* commander of our camp then ordered his men to begin taking us by train up into the mountains, as originally instructed, but to then abandon the train someplace below the mountains, where the Allies could find us easily.

Clearly, this is what whoever is driving our train just tried to do, but obviously, he chose the wrong spot. Wherever the Allies are, or are headed, they're nowhere around here just yet.

Finally, someone manages to shut the boxcar door. The shots subside, our Nazi pursuers having achieved the goal of killing as many of us as possible, and running the rest of us off. At last our train gathers steam and begins to chug out of the village.

At some point, I fall asleep again. This time, though, I wake to the whining sounds of fighter planes directly overhead. It must be the Allies! Unfortunately, though, all they can see from up in the air is a German artillery train.

Actually, the artillery at the end of this train is a decoy, or so we've been told. It doesn't even shoot (according to the same guard who told us earlier that we wouldn't be killed). But how would the Allies know that? Oh, God, help us! I didn't come all this way, and survive against all the odds, just to be killed accidentally by the Allies themselves!

"*Wrrrmm. . .*" One of the fighter planes makes a low pass.

I hug the floor as bullets rip through the wooden roof of our boxcar, cascading onto our helpless bodies like heavy, lethal raindrops.

Someone lying on top of me starts bleeding profusely. I feel warm blood dripping onto my jacket and the skin beneath my threadbare prison uniform. Next, I feel a sharp sting, and find myself groping frantically for my kneecap. I've just been hit right in the knee, and it hurts fiercely! I want to reach for and clutch at my damaged knee, thinking that it might help ease the pain. But I can't even move. I lie trapped beneath the weight of numerous others, lots of them probably dead by now.

After half an hour or so of this particular misery, the train suddenly halts again. The weight atop me lessens a bit, as those who can still move struggle to their feet to flee our flimsy coffin on wheels. I hope they make it. Weaker than ever, I can only remain lying here, mingled amongst numerous bodies in what has turned into a freezing cold night. Arms, legs, and torsos of various others, mostly dead, provide me my only blankets and pillows.

I close my eyes again, drifting in and out of consciousness. My handsome older brother Andris smiles at me from Heaven. I'd like to join him now. **"No, Pista,"** Andris insists, silently. Firmly, my brother sends me away from him again. I'm sad. I want to be with Andris. I miss him so. . .

Asleep awake asleep awake. . . finally, I slip into a genuine slumber. As I drift off, my diary drops from my hand. I'll retrieve it later, I tell myself. I'm too sleepy to find it now amongst all the bodies. Besides, I can hardly move.

When I wake again, the train remains stopped, in the same place as before, as least I think so. I'm not sure how long we've been here, wherever it is, but at least I don't hear any gunfire. Forcing my gluey eyelids apart again, I peer out the boxcar as best I can. I can't see much in the darkness, but from what I can hear, there are no signs of life outside.

An American poem by Emily Dickinson I once read in school starts reciting itself inside my mind. I remember a line at the end of it about someone nearly dead who could not "see to see." I never understood that line before now. At this moment, though, I do.

"Andris, I see you. I want to come to you."
"Not yet, Pista."

I could be dreaming, but I think I just heard a faint hum coming from somewhere outside the boxcar. I *do* hear it! Now the hum builds steadily to a roar. The sound reminds me of jeeps in American movies. I can even picture a caravan of them, full of uniformed Yankee soldiers, speeding to the rescue! In my mind's eye, the jeeps' powerful headlights slice right through the soupy fog, like Moses parting the Red Sea. Maybe, just maybe, someone's coming to save me.

There's Andris again, still smiling. Ah, Andris! To be with you! It's lovely where you are.

"Not yet, Pista."

Just then, the humming noise stops. I hear dozens of heavily shod feet hitting the ground, clomp-thud-clomp. Someone climbs up inside my boxcar. Another person follows. Now I hear *two* sets of footsteps stomping around, right near my head. I'm still too weak to open my eyes much, but I manage to move my left hand enough to yank at a hair on my right arm. It hurts. Now I know I'm not dreaming.

Voices. Two men are standing very near me, speaking American-accented English.

"My God!" says one. "Some of these fellows look like they're just kids!"

"They're probably young Jews from a concentration camp near here," says the other. "Damn Nazis. How could they do this to people?"

"However they did it, most of these guys are dead."

"Shit!"

Then one of the men notices *me* amidst all the heads and bodies. I feel him place a finger gently on my forehead.

"Look!" This boy's still breathing! C'mon, Sergeant, let's pull him out of here! We need to get this poor kid to a hospital right away."

"Yes, sir!"

Now I hear other American soldiers climb up inside the crowded boxcar and begin combing the heaps of bodies for signs of life.

At some point, I'm picked up, lifted down from the boxcar by several sets of strong hands, and carried to a waiting jeep. Before blacking out again, I feel the same pairs of hands place me gently on my back inside the vehicle. Someone covers me with a wool blanket.

But I've left something behind. . . I can't quite remember what it is now.

But something important remains in the boxcar. . .The jeep's engine starts up with a roar. It's too late to go back now.

Opening my eyes, I squint hard against the light. A burning pain has installed itself firmly inside my eyelids. Somehow, I'm in a bright white room. White-clad women bustle around. Angels! Ah, I'm in heaven! But where are the wings of all these beautiful angels?

I pull at a hair on my right arm. It hurts. That means I'm still on earth, darn it! But where on earth could I be?

Where are the hard wooden bunks of the Muhldorf concentration camp?

What has become of my fellow prisoners?

Why all these white coats on everyone, and that disinfectant smell? Is Mother cleaning *again?* With effort, I work a bony hand beneath an unfamiliar sheet, and pull another hair, this time on my leg, just to make sure. Ouch! I'm definitely not dreaming.

Now a doctor with a stethoscope snaked around his neck bends over me, peering, with blue-green eyes, into my stinging brown ones. My tired lids snap shut in protest. The doctor pries them back open.

"Hello, son." I recognize an American accent, speaking German.

"Where am I?"

"You're in Seeshaupt, Germany, outside Munich. This is an American hospital. I am Dr. Popper."

"Is the war over?"

"As of a few days ago."

"Who won?"

"The Allies."

"I'm free?"

"You're free, yes, but you're extremely weak and very sick. What's your name?"

"Istvan Nasser. I'm called Pista."

"How old are you, Pista?"

"Fourteen, I think."

"When were you born?"

"February 17, 1931."

"Yes, you *are* fourteen. This is May 13, 1945. Where are you from?"

"Budapest, Hungary."

"You've been talking in your sleep to Andris. Who is Andris?"

"My brother."

"Where is he?"

"In Heaven. I saw him."

"When did you see him?"

"I think yesterday. I wanted to go with him but he wouldn't let me."

The doctor nods. "Lie back, Pista. Rest."

Obediently, I lie back. "How did I get here?" I ask. "How long have I been here?"

"Some American soldiers found you near here in an abandoned boxcar, almost dead. You've been in this hospital about five days."

I recall none of those days.

Now my bed is cranked up, and I'm brought a cup of warm chicken broth. Slowly, I sip it through a glass straw. It isn't much, but compared to the prison food I'm used to, it tastes wonderful. But the mere effort of drinking exhausts me.

After eating my soup, I lapse again into restless slumber, this time punctuated with horrific nightmares. German tanks roll into Budapest. . . I am deported. . . I see the glaring twisted lights of Auschwitz, the creepy fog. . . at the Auschwitz selection point my baby cousin Peter is murdered before my eyes, and then Andris and I are separated from Mother and our Aunt Bozsi. . . Andris and I escape to Muhldorf, where we're then starved and beaten. . . here, now, is Andris again, dying in my arms inside the Muhldorf camp.

"Don't go, Andris! Please don't go!" I wake up, sob-screaming at the white wall. Nurse Erika, a fresh-faced beauty with braided blonde hair, whom I met earlier today, rushes in.

"Easy, Pista, easy," she coos, patting my shoulder. "You've had a bad dream."

"Yes Nurse Erika, just a bad dream." I try sounding manly and nonchalant, like American men in movies.

"I'm going to give you an injection to relax you."

I force myself to take this news like a man. "Yes, Nurse." I roll over and she gives the shot. When I'm on my back again, I force a smile. "Thank you, Nurse Erika. You know," I gulp, "I just want to tell you, I'm not a sissy. I. . . I'm not a. . . sissy, Nurse, or. . ." I begin to cry.

"Pista, we all realize how brave you are."

"You do?" I'm surprised and warmed by her words. I'm used to being a number, not a human being anyone talks about.

"We've spoken of it already: how brave you are, and how remarkable it is that you're here, after all you have endured. It's a miracle."

I grow bolder, something like my old self. "Would you like to sit down? If you sit down awhile I'll tell you all about my brother Andris." This I say as if offering her a huge, important favor.

"All right. But only for a few minutes, Pista. We're not supposed to let you get worked up."

"I promise not to get worked up."

Nurse Erika settles into a chair beside my bed. "But before you start, Pista, I have a favor to ask you."

"Of course." I can't imagine what favor I could possibly do for her, in my wretched condition.

"Please, Pista. Speak Hungarian to me!" This she says in perfect unaccented Hungarian.

"How do you know my language? It's kind of an unusual one."

"My mother was from Budapest, like you. I visited my grandparents with her every summer as a child. When I was twelve, my grandparents both died within a few months of each other. I haven't been back since, but I miss it."

"Me too," I reply, softly.

We're silent for a moment.

Then Nurse Erika folds her hands in her lap and closes her eyes. "I'm ready for you to start now, Pista."

I begin speaking in my native tongue, the first Hungarian I've spoken to anyone other than a few inmates inside Muhldorf in a long long, time.

"My brother Andris was three years older than me. That would have made him seventeen now. He was brilliant; he planned to be a doctor. He was handsome as a movie star, blond and blue-eyed. He was the best soccer player at school, and. . ."

Chapter Two
Mother, Father, Andris, and Me

It's sometime in 1940. I'm nine years old and I've just finished my Hebrew class at the Jewish elementary school near home. Twenty-four boys and girls, myself included, wait for Mrs. Steinberg to give us our homework assignment so we can leave. Finally, the assignment is on the board. I copy it. At 3:05, the buzzer sounds, and I'm free!

I gather my books, jamming them into my backpack. I wish it was next year already and I attended the same school Andris does, the *Konyevs Kalman Gymnasium*. He has a leather briefcase for his books, not an ugly backpack like we "babies" have. He's eleven. Next September, I'll go to *Konyevs Kalman*, I hope. The school only accepts about two Jews a year. I've studied hard to get in, and should find out any day if I've made it.

Outside the classroom, I wave good-bye to my schoolmates and run through the open doors onto the street. As always, Mother waits outside to walk me home. Even at my age, I'm aware of how beautiful Mother is, slender, graceful, and always impeccably dressed, with light brown hair and blue eyes. I can't help but notice the many admiring glances she receives whenever we're out. Her name is Georgia. There are only four of us (Mother, Father, Andris and me) but Mother herself is one of seven children, with four brothers and two sisters. My Aunt Manci, her oldest sister, is my favorite.

Today, Dad comes home early for the weekend. In addition to owning and helping his younger brother manage the big jewelry shop on Istven Street, he's the Hungarian representative to the Alpine Gruen Swiss Watch Company. Its headquarters is in Biel, Switzerland and he's been there all week. I'll be glad to see him. It's common for him to travel, but I wish he weren't away so much.

Like Mother, Dad is an impeccable dresser. They look sharp together. For work, Dad always wears a three-piece suit, and funny looking things on his shoes called "spats." He's dapper, clean-shaven, and well groomed, with a high forehead, strong jaw, and a cleft in his chin. His name is Dezso.

I know a secret about my father. Beneath his jacket he wears a gun in a holster, behind his back. I once asked him why, and he said his licensed gun is for protection when he travels.

"Your father and I have some important things to tell you when we get home, Pista," says Mother.

"Good things?"

"One of them is very good."

"Tell me now, then."

"I promised Dad and Andris I'd wait until we were all together."

"All right, then," I reply, walking faster.

"Pista, slow down! I can't keep up with you!" When I glance back at her, though, she's laughing.

Minutes later, I arrive at the front entrance to our big pale yellow multi-level building. I run up six flights of a marble staircase to the floor where we live. When I get there, I'm panting hard, my tongue hanging out like a dog's on a hot summer day. Tired, I lean my whole body against the doorbell.

Anna, our live-in maid, answers the door. "Hi, Anna," I shout, slipping past her. "Dad, where are you?"

"Relax, Pista," calls Mother, from somewhere on the stairs. "Dad's probably in the living room with Andris waiting for us."

I race toward the living room. She's right. There they are! I run to my father and give him a hug.

"Dad!" I shout.

"Hello, Pistukam!" He hugs me back.

"Dad, what is it?" I ask him anxiously, as soon as we break our embrace. "Mother said you have something good to tell me."

I climb onto the vacant chair between my father and brother.

Our living room has a shiny parquet floor, with scattered oriental rugs stretching toward the big balcony, which offers a commanding view of all of Arpad Street. The street we live on is one of the main thoroughfares of Ujpest, an upscale Budapest suburb. On our living room walls is pale gold flowered wallpaper, bordered by raised white molding. The large black piano, covered with white lace, looks impressive in the afternoon daylight. (Mother and Andris both play piano; I am learning the violin.)

A Victorian sofa and matching chairs, with gold flowers on white upholstery framed by delicate, scrolled ebony wood, tie the room together. In the corner stands a gleaming white, curved-tiled, freestanding fireplace. Across the wall hangs a large Venetian mirror, shaped like a kite, with laced mirror trim. It sparkles in the sunlight, like a tiara.

Mother soon enters, slightly out of breath, having overheard my questions to Dad. "He tried to pry it out of me on the way home, Dezso, but I wouldn't let him."

My father laughs. "Very good, Georgia. That must have been a challenge."

Mother sits down gracefully on the sofa, completing our circle.

"Andris," Dad asks, "how would you like to be the one to give Pista the good news?"

"Sure, Dad." My brother's blue eyes sparkle as he clears his throat. "It just so happens, little runt . . ." He pauses, dramatically, then repeats, "It just so happens, little runt, that. . ."

"Come on, Andris. Tell me!" I'm about to burst. They all laugh.

"Okay, okay," says Andris, clearing his throat again. "I'm pleased to inform you, little brother," he intones, with mock solemnity, "that you and I will be schoolmates next year!"

"You mean I'm accepted to the *Gymnasium?*"

"That's right, Brat! Congratulations!"

I look at Mother. "When did you find out?"

"The letter came Monday. But Andris and I decided to wait to tell you until Dad came home."

I shake my head in disbelief. Imagine! They'd known about it all week, but I hadn't suspected a thing! I give Andris a hug, then Mother and Dad. All my endless studying has paid off, finally!

But after I sit down again, I notice that the light-hearted mood has abruptly turned serious. My parents and brother stare at me intently, their earlier smiles gone.

"What's wrong?" I ask.

My father clears his throat. "Pista," he begins, "Now that you will be a student at the *Gymnasium* next year, there are certain matters we all need to discuss."

"Oh?" I can't imagine what will come next. In all my life, my father has never spoken to me in such a grave tone.

"Just last weekend, Pista, Andris told Mother and me that some of his classmates call him "Jew Boy" and tease him about being Jewish.

"Yes, Dad. He's told me about that, too."

"And do you remember awhile back, when your Uncle and I first opened up the jewelry store? How someone right away painted Star of David symbols all over it, and wrote "Jew Pigs" on the windows?"

"I do." How could I possibly forget?

"Pista, you've just been admitted to a very prestigious school, one that accepts very few Jewish students, sometimes none."

"Yes, Dad."

"That means you're mature and smart enough to know that there are signs of serious trouble here in Hungary. The Nazis have taken over Germany. Hitler's goal is to exterminate every Jew in Europe. Rumor has it that the Germans have built concentration camps in Poland, where they're housing political prisoners. Next it will be the Jews' turn."

"Do you think those rumors are true, Dad?" I asked.

"Let me put it this way. The last time we heard from your Uncle Poldi in Warsaw was three months ago, and not a word since. That isn't like him."

I nod, solemnly. If this is what being a grownup is like, I don't care for it.

"Pista, I've already told Mother and Andris that I've been trying, through my Swiss employer, to get us all out of Hungary, but so far to no avail."

"But Dad! Hungary isn't Poland! What about all our friends? What about school?" I look at Andris, hoping he'll second my objections.

Instead, Andris lets out a big sigh. "Quiet, Pista," he says. "Just listen. We're trying to give you some facts. Right now you go to an all-Jewish school. Next year, though, you'll be at the *Gymnasium.* And let me tell you, it can get pretty tough. A lot tougher than I've ever let on."

"How?"

"Certain kids will try to beat you up."

"But you'll be there." No one messed with Andris, or with me, for that matter, whenever Andris was around. He was too big, too formidable. My brother never starts fights, but if dragged into one, he always wins.

"I can't be with you every minute, Runt. We're three grades apart, you know."

"I'll be okay, Andris. I can take care of myself." If only I felt so sure.

"Oh I'm not worried, Brat. I know you can be tough when you have to be."

With that, my family falls silent awhile. I wish for the whole conversation to end; I want to go off somewhere and be alone.

But Dad continues, having saved the worst news for last. "Boys, just last week, Prime Minister Imredy stripped all Jews of Hungarian citizenship. This makes us all extremely vulnerable to Hitler's jurisdiction. Our own government no longer protects us against trouble from the Germans. With signs like that everywhere, we all need to be very careful, and stay ready for anything."

Chapter Three
Getting Well

The next morning sun streams through my open window. Nurse Erika appears with my breakfast. As usual, she wears her crisp uniform and lovely smile. She places my tray before me, then cranks up my bed. "Eggs, milk, juice, toast, porr. . ."

"My diary," I interrupt her, almost rudely. "Have you found it?"

"What diary?"

"It's got to be here somewhere. I brought it out of Muhldorf with me."

"Pista, please. You had nothing but the clothes on your back when they brought you in. Calm down and eat your breakfast."

"I don't want it."

"You *have* to eat it."

I obey, but taste nothing. As I eat, Nurse Erika sits beside me, occasionally helping me steady my shaky hand.

"I don't know how my diary could have been lost. I've taken it everywhere with me. . ."

"Listen, Pista. The American liberators pulled you out of that boxcar from among hundreds of dead bodies. When you first arrived here, you had typhus, pneumonia, and sores all over your body. You were scarcely alive. Probably, you dropped the diary when you were still lying half dead inside that boxcar, without knowing it."

Realizing her words make sense, I'm overcome with sudden sadness. Stoically, I force myself to finish breakfast. My makeshift diary, "bound" by hand with cast-off wire, has been my steady friend and confidante. Now, like so many other friends, it has vanished mysteriously.

Later that day, as I recognize the tinny, clattering sounds of lunch being served, I wriggle my way up into a sitting position in bed, take in an experimental deep breath, and discover, to my surprise, that I'm strong enough to hold it. Slowly, I release it. Then I part the top of my pajamas and inspect my chest, a task I've been curious to do, yet avoiding. Upon examination, I see that my chest cavity looks much as I've feared: a skinny barrel of bones covered by a taut, nearly transparent layer of pasty-hued flesh. Next, I try to inspect my legs, but lack the strength to wrestle off my pants.

Half an hour later, a tall, dark-haired young orderly named Helmut arrives to bring my lunch (for which I'm not hungry), and to help me use a bedpan. With his help, I eat as much as I can of the soup, bread, and potato salad. Afterward, as Helmut assists me in removing my pants, I glance down at my bare legs. They are worse than I imagined. Before deportation, my thighs and calves had bulged with the strong, well-formed muscles of an active young athlete. Like all kids my age, I'd run, bicycled, and swum. I'd played soccer too, not as well as Andris, but not badly.

Now my legs have become mere sticks, my thighs scarcely thicker than my calves. My bony right kneecap resembles nothing so much as a lopsided knot at the center of a skinny, bleached out tree limb. My left knee, the one that was shot, is wrapped in gauze.

Having gone this far, I wish, now, to view the rest of my godforsaken body. But my hips are also wrapped in gauze, as are both ankles.

"Helmut, how much do I weigh?" I ask him, after I finish using the bedpan.

"I'm not sure, Pista. We'll weigh you soon. Right now, you're still too weak to get out of bed."

Five days later, I'm carried to a scale. I weigh a grand total of 72 pounds, pajamas and all.

"I weighed more when I was 9 years old!" I tell Nurse Erika and a couple of the orderlies.

"What did you weigh in school? Before the Nazis took you away?"

"About 140 pounds."

They all shake their heads in disbelief. "Pista, someone up there must be looking out for you," says NurseErika.

"Yes, it's my brother," I answer. "He told me I must not die, and I promised him I wouldn't."

The next week, Helmut and Ernst (who is another of the orderlies in his mid-fifties, with a large gold front tooth) walk me around the hospital floor, giving my limp muscles their first taste of exercise in many weeks. At first, I can hardly put any weight at all on my legs. But with steady encouragement, I grow stronger daily.

Soon I'm walking, with crutches. And now, when I eat, Nurse Erika no longer assists me, though she still visits me regularly.

One evening, as she sets my dinner tray before me, she says, "You seem a lot stronger now, Pista. Much more cheerful, too."

"Yes, Nurse. I'm thinking about going home."

"You will go home, Pista, just as soon as you're well. When you do, though, we'll miss you around here."

"I'll miss you, too, Erika, and I'll never forget your kindness."

"By the way, Pista, now that you're feeling better, I've been wanting to ask you about what really happened in those camps. If you don't mind telling me, that is."

"I don't mind, Nurse. At first, when I lost my diary, I thought I'd forget everything, and maybe that was just as well. Now, though, I realize I *can't* forget *any* of it. Not even the parts I'd like to."

"It might do you good to share the memories."

"Perhaps."

I begin to eat. The meal tastes good tonight, pork loin with noodles, and applesauce for dessert.

"This food sure is better than what they fed us at either Auschwitz or Muhldorf."

"What did they give you to eat?"

"Breakfast was coffee and a hunk of bread made from sawdust, and a tiny speck of butter, if you were lucky. Lunch and dinner were meals of this hideous stuff, *gemuse*. It was stew, if you could call it that, made from the worst leftover parts of everything: potato skins, tops of carrots (the green parts, that is) turnip stems. Sometimes, we even found pieces of the field rats that ran all around mixed in, their tails, feet, and whiskers. The guards always claimed this was by accident, but we had our doubts."

"Your father had already passed away when your family was deported?"

"Yes, he died the previous year. Maybe he was the lucky one in our family."

"What did he die from?"

"Complications of a liver disease he'd caught when he served in World War I. He was a Hungarian Army officer."

"Were you and your brother close to him?"

"Quite."

"How old were you when he died, Pista?"

"Twelve."

"He must have been just a young man himself."

"Forty-four."

I lean back on my pillow. For the first time, I'm close to tears for my father. I've scarcely grieved his loss; I've had too much else to do. Yet the hole in my heart remains right where it had lodged the day of his funeral, fresh, and unhealed, as if he'd died only yesterday. My convalescence here has allowed me, finally, to reflect.

"What are you thinking about now, Pista?"

"I'm thinking about my dad, and Andris. Maybe they're in Heaven, watching over me. And, and. . ." I choke back tears.

"Yes, Pista. Tell me what else you're thinking."

"I'm thinking. . .God knows,. . . that. . . by now Mother may even be with them. Why, Nurse Erika? Why did this happen to us?"

"Nobody knows, Pista. But it shouldn't have."

I clutch for the handkerchief I now keep handy beneath my pillow for when I wake, sobbing, from bad dreams. Dabbing roughly at my eyes, I try to hold back a flood of tears, but fail. Erika leans over me, helping me wipe my eyes.

"Pista, Pista, Pista," she singsongs, in a lilting voice. "Sleep, now, *Pistukam*. We can talk more tomorrow."

"Yes, Nurse Erika." I blow my nose into the damp handkerchief. Then I lie down again, and manage to stop crying long enough for her to leave. I watch her back until she disappears down the hall. Then I bury my head in my pillow and sob myself to sleep.

Chapter Four
Father's Death and Afterward

Dad was quite athletic; I'm sure that's where Andris got his talent. He was proud of both of us. We loved him dearly. Dad must have been sick for quite awhile, but he always made light of it. He never wanted us to worry. I remember the day Andris and I first realized our father was gravely ill. It was a shock.

Andris and I had just returned from a soccer game at our school, where my brother had led his team to victory, single-handedly. On the soccer field, a Jew could still be a hero. But on the streets, we already had to wear yellow stars on our outer clothing and endure constant harassment.

I lean back against my pillow, close my eyes, and remember.

It's 1943, early spring in Budapest. I'm 12; Andris is 15, and at this point we're still all at home together: Dad, Mother, him, and me. Nothing really bad has happened yet, though the Hungarian government now gets its orders directly from Nazi Germany. As a result, we Jews have lost many freedoms. But my brother and I still attend school, and the daily rhythm of our lives is the same as always.

This morning, as we all eat breakfast, Dad remarks, with forced casualness, "Doctor Biro ran some tests on me the other day. We expect the results back tomorrow. It's probably just that liver thing of mine from the first war acting up again."

Too preoccupied with our upcoming soccer game to think much about Dad's words, Andris and I rush through breakfast, and then head off to our school's soccer field, where today's game will be played. The weather is crisp, clear, and cool: perfect for a soccer match. By the time we arrive at the field, the sun has melted any lingering overnight snow from the ground. A good-sized crowd is gathered. Today's match is crucial; the winning team goes to this year's finals.

"Good luck, Andris!" I call to my brother as he runs onto the field to join his teammates. Minutes later, the referee blows his whistle and all the players immediately surge into motion. I stand on the sidelines, cheering my brother on. He's tall, fast, and strong—a champion.

For the first half, though, our rivals lead.

"Come on, Andris, *run!*"

Andris moves away from the centerline, kicking the ball in short bursts.

Now he arrives at the sixteen meters line. He turns sharp left, shifts his weight to his right leg, and makes a terrific shot that lands smack in the upper right corner.

Goal! *Bravo, Andris!*

My brother's just tied the game.

Now the players line up for the center kickoff. Fifteen minutes left! The ball is changing positions in mid-field as the referee blows his whistle; the other team is offside.

Following the penalty kick, Andris is at it again. Sprinting hard, he brings the ball down with his head, setting himself up. He wastes no time dribbling through the defense.

"Go, Andris!"

He doesn't let us down.

The goalie runs out, but my brother outmaneuvers him, leaving him sprawled in a heap on the field. Now no one can stop Andris! Our team's ahead, two to one.

Only minutes remain.

Then it happens. Deftly, my brother dribbles the ball down the field and kicks it squarely between the goal posts. Victory, thanks to Andris!

I'm about to burst with pride.

Suddenly, though, I hear a big commotion. At first, I think it has to do with our team's triumph. But no. . . the crowd is shouting about something else entirely.

Students from both schools run about crazily now, in all directions. "The Germans are coming!" everyone shouts, our soccer game instantly forgotten.

The sight of Nazi tanks rolling down our streets gives all of us hollow feelings inside our stomachs, but especially Andris and me. Like all our schoolmates, we love our country and hate the Germans. For us Jews, though, the increased German presence represents a unique danger. Lately, we've been cautioned by our parents to avoid encounters with the Hungarian Arrow Cross, the uniformed thugs who are equivalent, in our country, to Nazis, especially when we're out alone.

Before he can even begin savoring his team's victory, Andris grabs my arm and barks to me, "Pista, let's go!"

We make our way home, like frightened, hunted prey, through various back alleys. All the Jewish families have been hearing nasty rumors lately: in many

Nazi-occupied countries Jews are being forced by German soldiers into isolated ghettos, deported from their native countries, and then, finally, killed abroad. We've assured Mother and Dad we won't take any chances with our own safety around here.

Finally, we reach *Arpad Street*, and our house, Number 42. Directly outside the big front entrance to our building, the street is packed. Curious onlookers line both sides of the avenue, all of them gaping at our unwanted foreign "guests," whose leather jackboots click rhythmically against the cobblestones of our lovely, tree-lined street.

The two-story house where we live has a soft yellow tint to its stucco-covered brick exterior. Our building entirely dwarfs the surrounding single story tenements. To enter it from the street, a solid oak door must be wrestled open by pushing one's shoulder against it, which in turn makes its hand-hammered hinges squeak in protest.

Now, Andris pushes the door open with extra determination. Preoccupied, we scarcely even hear the hinges squeak as we race up the marble stairs to our floor.

On the balcony outside our living room, we see Mother leaning out, watching for us, a pained expression distorting her beautiful features.

Seeing us, she runs to open the front door, ushering us quickly inside.

"Andris! Pista! Listen to me," she says insistently, closing the door hard behind her. "From now on, make sure you both keep off the streets, away from those Nazi soldiers."

"Why, Mother?"

"I've heard of them doing bad things to Jews."

"Like what?"

"Please, boys. Just stay away from them."

Now all three of us stand outside on the balcony, gazing down onto our once peaceful, but now Nazi infested street.

"By the way, who won the game?" Mother asks, her voice artificially cheerful.

"Andris," I reply. "He scored both goals himself. . ."

"Hush, Runt." Andris, though pleased, muzzles me before I can finish.

"Mother, how is Dad feeling?" I ask.

Andris gives me a little shove. "Pista. . . "

"It's all right, Andris," Mother says. "I should tell you boys. . . your father started hiccuping badly again today. Dr. Biro stopped by to check on him.

Then, right away he arranged for a bed at the hospital tomorrow."

"Where is Dad now?" Andris asks.

She points toward their bedroom. "He's resting. Don't disturb him."

This afternoon and evening, our mood is glum. We need to keep the house quiet so Dad can rest. Today, though, this is not as difficult as usual.

The next morning, Dad goes to the hospital. Our house always feels distinctly empty when he is away, but now it's as sad as a funeral parlor. Somehow, I have a feeling my father won't live much longer. I'd never thought it possible to feel this sad.

A few days later, with Dad having grown worse, I visit him at the hospital. Dr. Biro has told us Dad's condition is grave, but even that doesn't prepare me for the sight of him now, wasted so quickly by his illness. Entering his room, I see him lying in the semi-darkness, a thin rubber tube attached to his mouth, draining poison from his liver into a surgical dish.

His once robust, healthy body has become skinny and shriveled. Between painful hiccups, he manages to open his eyes. Approaching his bedside, I bend down toward him, kiss his forehead, and take his cool, bony hand in mine. His eyes open a bit wider when he recognizes me. This alone, though, seems to challenge his remaining strength. Then his lips move, whispering something. I lean closer, placing my ear near his mouth.

"You're a good boy, Pista. Remember to always love Mother and Andris."

"Yes, Dad." I want to cry.

I wish this were just a bad dream. Where is God, anyway?

Dad's lips stop moving. He tries to wet them with his tongue.

Dr. Biro enters, requesting in a hushed tone that I leave now. I gaze once more at my father's face, trying to memorize it, seeing all his love for me reflected in his pain-filled eyes.

Once outside his hospital room, I let go and weep, shamelessly.

Two weeks later, my father dies.

Gentiles and Jews alike attend his funeral; hundreds of people are there, in fact, from all walks of life. The Hungarian nation has given Father, like many Jews of his generation, previously unequaled opportunities for education, success, and friendship. All this is reflected by the crowd gathered today.

Having been a Hungarian Army officer in World War One, Father receives a full military funeral, replete with uniformed soldiers standing at attention, their swords drawn. Today I'm proud of my father and the life he's lived; yet

I've never been so sad. It's a sadness beyond description, a dull, ache that fills my heart, nearly overflowing.

Andris and I must be brave, though, for Mother's sake. During the funeral, the two of us actually hold her up, physically, one of us on each side of her. We then walk, together, toward the open casket.

At the casket, I gaze down at my father, handsome in death, as in life, and dressed splendidly in full military uniform, just as he would have wished. Throughout his days, he'd been a patriot, to the core, always first a Hungarian, and then a Jew. Without hesitation, he'd have given his life instantly for Hungary, that same land that had now turned against him and his children.

For the final time, I take my father's hand in mine, and kiss his stiff, cold lips. "I love you, Dad," I whisper. "I'll always love you." Then, for Mother's sake, I choke back my tears.

In the following weeks, I nurse my pain and watch in amazement as Mother somehow wills herself onward with a strength I'd never dreamed she possessed.

Though I hide it, especially from Mother, I feel extremely depressed. Often, I experience a real physical pain inside my chest and, when no one is around, burst out crying uncontrollably, like a baby. I know Andris feels the same, though he bravely says nothing. More than ever, we depend on each other, just to get through the days. As if our own grief is not enough, we are now reminded daily of the growing anti-Semitism among our own countrymen. Here in Hungary, anti-Semitism has always existed. But now it's been stirred up anew by our unwanted German "guests."

A few days after Father's death, Andris and I walk to school as usual. It's 7:30 by the clock outside the bakery we pass each morning, always savoring the sweet smells of freshly baked breads and pastries. I'm nervous about today's Latin test. My personal world is topsy-turvy from Dad's death, and the world outside our sad household is none too stable, either. I stay focused on school, though, as best I can. That is what Dad would have wanted.

Busy Arpad Street bustles with activity as always, this time of morning. Multitudes of people rush to work. As we saunter along, we hear the usual sounds, like bicycle bells and the hum of streetcars.

Suddenly, four or five tough-looking characters appear from nowhere and stride toward us. Andris and I try our best to avoid them, but can't. With his index finger jabbing at the yellow star sewn onto my jacket, the tallest one yells, "Hey, Jew boys!"

"Walk close to the wall," my brother instructs me.

"Hey, Jew boys!" the tall one repeats. Now he's walking backward, his face only a few inches from mine.

"These stinking little Jew bastards are scared! Just look at them, standing against the wall," our tormentor continues.

Another man from the group shouts, "C'mon, leave them alone."

"What are you?" yells the tall one. "A Jew lover?"

Andris holds my arm tightly, pulling me along, purposefully ignoring the insults. Eventually, the thugs disappear. As we soon learn, though, this is but the first of many such incidents.

At school, I'm in for even worse. The *Konyves Kalman Gymnasium* is an excellent school, and very selective. Andris and I are among a tiny minority of Jews who attend. Located on Istvan Street, the tile-roofed school occupies an entire block.

Despite our religion, Andris and I have many friends here. But one particular gang of boys in the fifth and sixth grades (these boys are 13 and 14 years old, and in the eighth and ninth grades by United States standards) hates us, demonstrably. So far, only nasty words have been tossed our way. As long as I have Andris around, they don't dare touch me; they're afraid of Andris because he's much bigger and stronger.

Because of the hostility directed our way, we study harder and receive better grades than the others. This, however, causes us other problems, like resentment among some of our peers.

One teacher, Mr. Szabo, tells me, "Pista, you're a good student, and I admire your maturity! You think like a man. Do you read a lot?"

"Yes, sir. I read lots of books on my own."

"Keep up the good work."

In the classroom, though, this often leads to jealousy among other students; it seems we're damned either way.

It's early afternoon, and I've just finished my Latin test. I approach the *Gymnasium's* botanical garden for a quick break before my next class. Lying down on the grass, I close my eyes and try collecting my thoughts, which are still racing from this morning's encounter with the anti-Semitic thugs.

Glancing up, I notice a particular sixth grade bully and two friends of his approaching me. He screams, "Get up, you stinking Jew!"

Quickly, I glance around for Andris. Of course, he's nowhere.

"Let's hang him on this tree!" suggests one of the others.

When those words register, I feel, suddenly, like a wounded bull in an arena full of vicious picadors. So I charge, knowing that taking them by surprise will give me my only chance. I knock over the smallest one, grab him by the feet, and spin him around like a human carousel, knocking the other two off balance at the same time.

The bell rings, ending my "rest period." The tough guys pick up their injured friend and limp away. I run back to class, my heart still pounding. Throughout history class, I feel numb, and every word the teacher says is mush to me. I'm lucky in one way, though: I'm not called on to recite today, thank God.

Every day, I remind myself to take the long view of all this. The current madness will have to end, eventually. I'll simply need to outlast it, rather than allowing it to weaken me.

Chapter Five
Unwanted Visitors, Leaving Arpad Street, and the Martinovits Factory

In 1944, when the Nazis first invaded Hungary, one of their first crimes was to confiscate businesses owned by Jews. Up until now, our jewelry store has not been seized. We don't know how much longer our luck will last. We're determined, though, to make the most of it.

After my father's death, Mother begins working there full-time, assuming Dad's former responsibilities. Ours is among the oldest, best known family-owned jewelry businesses around. As such, we've always had customers from every walk of life. Some of our clients' families have done business with us for generations; we're a Budapest institution. Lately, though, some of our newer, less cherished customers include members of Hitler's infamous SS. Our mother, often alone now in the shop, is scared to death of the Nazis, whenever they appear. If anyone can charm such people, Mother can. But the mere sight of them gives her heart palpitations, as even she admits.

One rumored incident involving Hitler's favorite army unit scares Mother, Andris, and me. Several neighborhood jewelry stores besides ours are Jewish-owned. One morning, a shop not far from our own fails to open at its usual time. Mysteriously, it remains closed for several days. Concerned relatives of the owner eventually come and investigate, and find the owner—an old man—lying dead in a pool of blood, having been shot through the head. The door to his office safe hangs open; the safe has been completely cleaned out. The local Ujpest police soon close the case, though, with only a sham investigation. Such atrocities are becoming common now. Often, regular citizens witness Hitler's SS men hurriedly leaving the scenes of such crimes. These uniformed criminals are never implicated, either by our press or by the local police.

Members of Hitler's SS are well built, fearless, and (as I've observed) without any apparent emotions: robots, capable of carrying out the most horrible crimes. Their sparkling uniforms, decorated with the SS marking and a skull, create fear in the hearts and minds of all who see them, myself included.

Listening to the BBC news (translated into Hungarian) each night gives Mother, Andris, and me our only source of badly needed hope. According to the BBC, which (unlike all other news sources around us) gives the *true* story, the Allies have recently forced the Nazis to retreat on most fronts. We must be extremely careful when and how we listen to the BBC, though, since it's now strictly forbidden to hear the British broadcast in our own language.

After tonight's BBC news, it's time to switch to the local Hungarian radio station. This provides our only source of warning of any upcoming air raids (these are most likely to occur at night, and the local radio station generally warns us 10 to 15 minutes in advance). Whenever an air raid is imminent, we all rush down to the bomb shelter located deep below our house.

Tonight, Mother, Andris, and I huddle together, listening to the Hungarian news for any warning of an air raid. Outside, it's pitch dark. We've experienced only two air raids this week, making it a relatively peaceful one by the standards we've gotten used to. Several businesses have been hit, although ours, fortunately, still stands. Each night, we sleep as if an air raid were imminent: warm sweatshirts and pants are always stationed near our beds. We're well aware that minutes, or even seconds, could in fact save our lives.

Soon, though, our one link to the outside world, our treasured radio, is confiscated. According to the latest Nazi decree, any Jew now caught with a radio will be turned over immediately to the Gestapo. Our world has become very small, and is shrinking still.

One evening, our own radio gone, I walk downstairs to a Christian couple's apartment to listen to their radio for air raid warnings. Mr. and Mrs. Gradi, who do all the housekeeping and maintenance work in our building, not being Jewish, have not had to relinquish their radio. We've heard they don't like Jews, but they've always been nice to Andris and me, maybe because we're just kids.

Tonight Mr. and Mrs. Gradi and I perch on the sofa inside their small living room, staring intently at the radio as we listen to the Hungarian news station. It's past 11 p.m. Suddenly, we hear a sharp knock at the front door. Mr. Gradi rises and opens up. Two nasty looking SS men have come calling. Clad in crisp, tailored uniforms, they loom ominously outside the doorway.

"On which floor do the jewelers live?" shouts the one nearer me. He has a long, ugly, reddish scar down his right cheek, as if a knife had slashed him there. "He was probably a street hoodlum before he joined up," I think to myself. That's just the kind Hitler likes.

Silence.

Then the unwanted pair sees the obligatory yellow star stitched onto my shirt.

"Who are you, Jew?" they scream at me, almost in unison.

"I am their son," I whisper, suddenly terrified beyond belief.

"WHOSE SON?" one of them bellows.

"I, I am. . . the-the j-jewelers' s-s-s-son."

Scarface then orders me to stand up. As soon as I obey, he shoves his Luger roughly against my rib cage.

"Please God, start an air raid! Drop a bomb. Anything at all would be better than this."

No air raid occurs. Instead, the unwelcome duo marches me upstairs to our living quarters on the 2nd floor. Scarface's gun is aimed squarely at my back. I try to take my time walking up, hoping, still, for some sort of miracle. Gruesome thoughts and images race through my confused mind: the murdered jeweler down the road; the gun at my back; Mother's and Andris's safety.

We arrive upstairs. My fingers trembling, I push the doorbell. Andris answers. Upon recognizing our uninvited company, his face turns white as edelweiss. Reluctantly, he admits us all into the hallway.

"Please, sirs, what do you want?" I now ask them in broken German, my voice quivering, as we near the end of the hallway leading to our living room, and our poor, unsuspecting mother.

Their only reply is for one of them to shove me, hard, onto the living room floor. There, I fall flat on my face at my terrified mother's feet.

Mother screams in fright and rushes at Scarface, who aims his Luger directly at her.

"No!" Andris and I scream together.

I cover my eyes, waiting for the dreadful sound of gunfire.

Seconds pass. I hear nothing.

I peek at the adults through my fingers just as the older, shorter SS grabs Scarface's gun, and not a second too soon. The older one declares that he recognizes Mother, who waited on him recently inside our store. He must have thought well of her service; he's decided not to kill us after all.

Mother's "savior" does grab a small white box of mine as he and the other thug depart, the one containing my most treasured stamps, collected over the years. I can only stand there, relieved to be alive, but still feeling violated beyond words.

Ever since the German occupation began, living conditions have only gotten worse and worse. Food is scarce. Long lines form each day at the grocery and dairy stores. Many times Andris and I wait for hours in them, only to learn, as we near the front, that all the supplies have just run out.

One day in April, our morning newspaper bears especially awful news: all

Jews must report to district offices; a Jewish ghetto is about to be established by the Hungarian government. We shall now be required to vacate the home we've lived in all our lives and abandon nearly all of our personal possessions.

Worse yet, we must find our own living quarters within the ghetto. Soon Mother, Andris, and I pound the pavement each day inside the restricted boundaries of what will soon be "our" ghetto, searching for a "home." Time is precious. The fascist government, with its Draconian rules, must be obeyed, or else. We knock on hundreds of doors, to no avail. Finally, on the third day, Mother ventures out alone and returns toward evening with "good" news.

"I've found a place for us with a nice family," she says. "I'd like to get started with the move, so I want you boys to help me pack."

"What about Anna?" Andris asks of our maid, who has lived in our house ever since I can remember, and seems almost like an older sister to us.

"Anna won't be able to come. She's not Jewish."

I feel numb as I do my share of the packing. Soon, our spacious flat is a mess, with suitcases and other items strewn everywhere. Our double front doors, one of which nearly always remains closed, are now both opened wide. Two husky movers carry our huge wicker baskets (those we've always used for summers at Lake Balaton) downstairs to their horse-drawn cart.

I gather up my precious books and toys. I really hate to leave anything behind.

"Pista, what on earth are you doing?" Mother inquires.

"Packing the things I need."

"Pistukam, you can't take everything. We'll have a one-room apartment, shared with another family."

"I'll leave my toys, then. But not my books."

One of Mother's hardest tasks is to say good-bye to Anna.

"Anna," Mother says, trying not to cry, as we make our final preparations to leave, "I wish we could take you along with us. Please take this suitcase I've packed for you, a small token of our gratitude. Come what may, we'll always consider you part of our family."

"My lady," Anna says, trying to fight back her own tears, without success.

By now, she's sobbing as she embraces Andris and me. "You're my family, and now we're being torn apart. Oh, Lord! This is cruel!"

We close the doors for the last time and go downstairs. The horse-drawn cart moves slowly down our beautiful, tree-lined, cobblestone street. The three of us walk solemnly beside our last remaining belongings, like grief-stricken pallbearers in a funeral procession.

Silently, I say goodbye to 42 Arpad Street, and, as it turns out, my youth. I wonder if I'll ever see this street again.

Our new home is on Karolyi Street.

Andris asks, "Mother, isn't this near the factory district?"

"Yes. The government put the ghetto beside the factories deliberately, hoping the Allies will spare the district and the factories from bombings. We're like hostages, in a way. Are you boys afraid of the raids?"

I nod. "They're frightening, Mother. But the Allies wouldn't hurt us on purpose."

"No, Pistukam. To us, each air raid is a promise. The raids say *'Hold on; don't give in, we're coming to free you!'*"

Our new home is cramped: one bedroom, a kitchen, a washroom, and an entryway. The latter doubles as an extra sleeping space. Not what we're used to.

Mother introduces us to Mrs. Swartz, with whose family we'll share our new quarters. "Andris is sixteen, and Pista almost thirteen," she tells her. I feel more like an old man already.

"Nice to have you all," says Mrs. Swartz. "Later, I'd like you to meet my family, too: my husband Jake, and our son Miska, who's fourteen. They're chopping firewood in the cellar, but they'll be back soon." Mother gestures toward us, and then says, "The three of us can just sleep here in the entry hall for a few days."

"Why? What do you mean for a few days, Mother?" asks Andris.

Mother frowns. "Sit down, boys," she says. "I need to talk to you." She pauses a moment, sighs deeply, and then continues: "It's only a matter of time before the Nazis ship us all to concentration camps. I've talked to an old friend of your father's, Mr. Martinovits. He's a Christian and owns a tool factory a couple of miles from here. He's willing to hire you both, and to pay you in food and board. You must understand: he's doing this to try save you, just possibly, from deportation with the rest of the ghetto. You must both live on his premises, and never leave his factory, since it's outside the ghetto."

"But what will happen to *you*, Mother?" Andris asks.

Mother sighs. "God is on our side. I'll stay here. Father is looking after all of us."

Three days later, Mother hands us a packed suitcase and a stamped permit she's obtained from the local police station. "This allows you to leave the ghetto for the Martinovits factory," she tells us.

She's sobbing hard before we ever depart.

Mr. Martinovits's war materials factory is a huge, single-story brick structure on Budapest's outskirts. In all, including the outside grounds where work materials are stored, it covers three acres. The building itself, surrounded by a sturdy wrought iron gate, is sixty feet long and eight feet high, and U-shaped. The main portion of the factory sits in the center of the "U." The huge double doors of the front gate let trucks carrying supplies in and out. The left wing of the building houses the area where Andris and I, and Mr. Szolosi, another Jewish refugee, will live; the right wing contains Mr. Martinovits's own office. The factory's underground air-raid shelter is a dark cellar reinforced by six concrete pillars. The door to this shelter lies flat on the ground. To enter it, you must pull the door straight up and then descend the ten underground steps in pitch-blackness, usually in a frantic hurry.

Even here at the factory, there's no guarantee of our long-term safety from deportation. Mr. Martinovits is an old friend, hopefully with enough influence to save some of us Jews. He's not hiding us, but merely sheltering us, along with his friend Mr. Szolosi. The Nazis know the whereabouts of all three of us, and could deport us at any time, should they so choose to do so.

Mr. Szolosi is fifty-five or so. Up to now, he's owned a thriving children's clothing business on our very own Arpad Street, right down the block. Andris and I have always liked him. He's about medium height, with thinning grayish hair and a gentle smile. When we were children, Mother often bought our clothes from him. Together, the three of us hope for exemption from being deported with the rest of the ghetto due to our "important" work making war products for the Nazis.

Everyone's labor here is hard and dirty. Andris and I are expected to perform like adults, although we're paid only in food, lodging, and the hope of survival.

Andris works in the casting department. I'm a buffer. As such, my days are spent roughing, grinding and buffing—eight to eleven hours at a stretch. Fortunately, our fellow workers regard us as friends, rather than as mere despicable Jews. Otherwise, life here would be unbearable. Mr. Feher, my foreman, is exacting but compassionate, and as far as I can tell, not an anti-Semite.

Today is a Saturday, a workday for Andris and me, like any other. Sunday is our day off, but even then, we dare not leave our "safe haven" for fear of being picked up. My brother and I have just finished our mid-afternoon meal in the factory's lunchroom.

Andris notices me picking at my food, rather than eating it with my usual gusto. "Meat loaf is your favorite lunch, Pista," he says. "What's wrong?"

"I'm not hungry."

"Don't you feel well?"

"I'm fine. I'm just worried."

"Are you worried about Mother again?"

"Yeah."

Andris wraps his big, muscular arm around my shoulder. "Cheer up, Pista. Mother's fine. You'll see. We'll hear something about her soon, I bet."

"I hope so," I reply, dully. "It's been a long time."

"Pista, why don't we continue our chess match. What's the score?"

"I've won thirty-five games. You've won twenty-eight,"

Andris grins. "Pista, take it easy. It's not nice to beat your older brother."

After our chess game (which I win) Andris and I return to our respective stations. The room where I work has a skylight through which the sun shines, revealing the beautiful April weather outside. This does nothing to elevate my mood; actually, it makes me feel even worse. I imagine thousands of things I'd rather be doing than working here: playing soccer; bicycling; attending Boy Scouts; even going to school.

Although I have no control over where I am or why I'm here, I feel like some sort of truant. This is the first year since I was five years old that I haven't attended school all year. This year, though, Andris and I had to quit in mid-March without taking our final exams, as soon as all Jews were forced to move into the ghetto. True, I've never loved studying for its own sake, as Andris does, but compared to living and working here, I'd rather be in my dreaded Latin class.

Mr. Feher interrupts my glum reverie by arriving at my station for his afternoon tour of inspection.

"Pista," he asks, "How many more stirrups do you have left to grind today?"

"Two more trays, sir."

"Good! Let me see a tray of your finished pieces."

"Yes sir." I fetch a heavy metal tray filled with my tedious handiwork.

Carefully, Mr. Feher examines several of my finished stirrups, one by one. "This one is good. . . so is this one. . . but this one here needs more grinding. Run your finger over it. See? Feel the roughness?"

"Yes."

"Go over this whole batch again. Don't let it happen twice."

"Yes, sir." I keep grinding, now more carefully. I'd never dreamed I'd be learning this particular trade.

As I grind away, I comfort myself with thoughts of an English writer we studied in school last year: Charles Dickens. The author was forced, at 13 (my age), to quit school and work in a bottle-blacking factory. Despite this setback, he went on to write great books. "If he could make it, so can I," I tell myself. But then, Dickens didn't have a bunch of Nazis after him.

Andris and I finish work each day around 6:00 P.M., sometimes later. Then we eat dinner with Mr. Szolosi in a utility room adjacent to our dormitory. Mr. and Mrs. Somogyi, the caretakers of the factory grounds whom Mr. Martinovits also now pays to cook our meals, have arranged for us to live here. Everyone but the five of us (the Somogyis, Mr. Szolosi, Andris, and me) gets to go home after work. When we finish dinner, Andris and I unwind for a few hours, usually with chess or crossword puzzles. Sometimes, all three of us will pass a long evening reminiscing about happier times. We all turn in, exhausted, around 10:00.

Mr. and Mrs. Somogyi share a separate living area, but Andris, Mr. Szolosi, and I all share a makeshift dormitory. It contains three folding beds with horsehair mattresses. Each of us has been provided two sheets, a pillow, and a blanket. We wash our own clothes in a laundry room adjoining our sleeping quarters. This is also where we get our drinking water and the water in which to "bathe" ourselves in a huge bucket. The toilet we share connects to the laundry room, on the opposite side.

Our day starts at 6:00 A.M., when we roll out of bed, wash and groom ourselves as best we can. Then we head next door to the utility room, where Mrs. Somogyi prepares us a light breakfast of coffee and toast with margarine and fruit jam. Occasionally, though rarely, there's a little chicken fat to eat, too, and some cheese. Such commodities are rare, however, with meat being the scarcest of all. For lunch or dinner, paprikas potato is a well-liked dish. On occasion, a small piece of pork sausage is added. Dessert will typically be an apple or a pear.

Mrs. Somogyi is very handy, however, with baked goods, for which ingredients are easier to come by. I'm always happy to eat these, especially since some of them remind me of things Mother used to make. One of

Mrs. Somogyi's specialties is *Szilvas Gomboc*, or plum dumplings. Her best confection, though, is one made from layered noodles, with jam and poppy seed filling.

In April, 1944, we finally receive roundabout news of Mother. She's still inside the ghetto. That same night, we hear the all too familiar wailing of sirens, warning us of an imminent air raid. Inside our dormitory, Andris and I sit near a long, narrow window, watching the air battle: searchlights, flares, bombs. Shrapnel peppers our factory's roof. By now, everyone but the two of us has disappeared down inside the underground shelter.

"Come on, Andris. Let's run to the shelter," I coax my brother.

We step outside, but quickly retreat. Fragments from anti-aircraft shells are landing all around us.

"We're safer if we stay here," replies Andris.

The shelter door lies 120 feet away from our dormitory: so close, yet so far. Just then, the sky lights up, bright as day. Directly overhead, a flare descends on a parachute. Our factory, with its tall chimney, is a huge sitting duck beneath the bright flare.

"Andris, I'm making a run for the shelter," I announce, my voice shaking.

"You're crazy," says my brother. But when I look over my shoulder, I see Andris right behind me. "Thank God he's come to his senses," I think.

I cannot see, hear, or feel the shrapnel fragments raining down on us; I'm simply running for my life, the fastest I've ever moved. I yank the rusty old door open and dive to safety. Then I feel Andris tumbling inside on top of me. Seconds later, a shattering explosion knocks us both around inside the shelter. Dust fills the air. I can hear Andris spitting out sand. I spit out a mouthful myself.

"You okay?" Andris asks me after most of the dust settles, brushing himself off.

"My elbow hurts a little. That's all."

After the air raid ends, we slowly and carefully climb back outside. The force of the blast has ripped the door of the shelter off its rusty hinges. Our dormitory, where Andris and I had sat watching the scary light show only minutes before, has now been leveled, as has much of the factory itself. All that remains where our dormitory had stood is a crater, twenty or so feet wide and fifteen feet deep, now filling slowly with water. We sit down on the edge of a concrete slab and view the ruins. The damage to the factory is immense.

We spend the rest of the day helping clean up the rubble. It will be months now, we agree, before any production can possibly start again. By midday, curious people mill around outside the factory's front gate. As the day wears on, the crowd grows even bigger. Obviously, word has been spread that the Martinovits factory took a direct hit last night.

Soon Andris and I are hard at work near the fence, helping clear away the mountains of debris. We're dirty, sweaty, worn out, and still unnerved. At one point, we sit down a few moments and take a short rest.

Suddenly, we hear the sweet sound of a familiar voice. "Andris! Pista! You're alive!"

We scan the crowd, and then we see her! "Mother!" we shout in unison. Our mother is hanging onto the wrought iron gate, dressed all in black, as if coming to a funeral. Tears of joy run down her hollow cheeks as she stares intently at us.

"My babies! Thank God! It's a miracle! God saved you both!"

We embrace her as best we can through the iron bars. It feels so wonderful to see our mother again, hear her voice, and embrace her, however briefly.

"Mother, where is your yellow star?" I ask her.

"*Shh!* I heard that this factory took a direct hit, and everyone was killed. I was so worried. I had to come see for myself, so I took off my star and came here," she whispers.

Now my heart beats fast, with a whole new worry. Mother is risking her life right this minute, just by being here, outside the ghetto.

"Mother, please go back. If you're caught outside the ghetto, they'll shoot you." I'm trembling now, visibly.

"All right, I'll go now, boys," she promises us. "Now that I know I still have something to live for, I promise you two I'll be careful."

We kiss her goodbye, and then gaze after her until she disappears from view.

The following days are spent working hard to help rebuild the ruined factory. The unnerving air raids come often now, but fortunately, we aren't hit again.

Around this time, Andris and I start hearing rumors from our factory co-workers, seemingly too awful to be true. People from the Jewish ghetto are being deported to Germany! We also hear incredible stories of gas chambers, ovens, and various other Nazi tortures.

Now I fear the worst. And so does Andris, I know.

Chapter Six
Deportation

One warm afternoon in May, 1944, Andris and I hear unusual sounds outside our dormitory, the sorts made by military transport trucks. We fear the worst.

Shortly thereafter, Mr. Martinovits calls us into his office.

The look of the office is a marked contrast to that of the rest of the factory—spacious, attractive, and well organized. A huge, highly polished desk reflects the image of a beautifully carved globe atop it. Drawing up two chairs Mr. Martinovits says, "Andris, Pista, please sit down."

We sit.

Mr. Martinovits is well past fifty, his gray hair parted in the center. Moving behind his desk for a moment, he produces from his waistcoat pocket a gold watch and then flips open its lid. A little tune, like a music box, tinkles merrily.

"I bought this in your store," he says, wistfully. "From your grandfather. You boys must have been too young to remember him. But he and I were friends."

We nod.

"You're both excellent workers, and you've done your jobs well." As he finishes his sentence, Mr. Martinovits removes his horn-rimmed glasses and wipes them with a tissue. "I knew your father, personally. He was a very fine gentleman. And your mother. . . so charming. . . here, boys, have a couple of chocolate bars." He offers them to us from a tin box, good Hungarian chocolate. We each choose one.

I finger my chocolate bar, glancing at Andris to see if he will eat his. He doesn't. Instead, his blue eyes fill with tears. Suddenly I realize what a handsome young man my brother has become these past months, tall and fair-skinned, with an athletic build and light brown hair. My heart fills with new sadness as I watch him cry. With difficulty, I fight back my own tears.

"Where was I?" asks Mr. Martinovits. He avoids our faces now. Quickly, he replaces his glasses, trying to conceal his emotions. But a teardrop escapes down his cheek.

Silence. Then Mr. Martinovits blurts out, with obvious difficulty, "I've just learned the whole ghetto will be deported."

"How do you know, sir?" Andris asks

"Because the German authorities notified me that. . . that they would soon come for you. And, and . . . those trucks you hear out there. . . have come now to take you boys from here. But please, boys. . . don't be afraid. There *must still* be a God, somewhere. I'll pray every day for your safe return."

Now he sits down, finally surrendering to his tears. When he pulls himself together again, he rises, looking intently at Andris and then at me through swollen red eyes, as if memorizing our faces.

"Andris, Pista, be brave," he calls after us as we make our way down the steps to the factory's front entrance and away from here, our knees shaking and our hearts pounding in our chests.

Then it's time for us to go.

Near the iron gate leading outside, a stern-faced, uniformed *Nyilas* (as the Hungarian Nazis are called) awaits us.

"Hey, Jew boys! Are you the Nasser brothers?"

"Yes," Andris replies for both of us.

"Into that truck!" He jerks his index finger toward a canvas-covered military vehicle waiting just outside the gate.

Andris and I move slowly toward the vehicle, hoping for a miracle.

"Move it!" the *Nyilas* yells, giving Andris a shove.

Andris stumbles, nearly falling. Now we speed up and walk out through the gate. Andris climbs onto the truck first.

"Grab my hand, Pista," he says. "I'll help you." He braces himself against the inside of the truck, then pulls me up beside him. When our eyes adjust to the near darkness inside the truck, we recognize our co-worker, Mr. Szolosi, sitting glumly beside us. A couple dozen or so others, their identities unknown to us (but probably workers, like ourselves, at other factories in the area) are already inside. But in the near darkness, we see only their silhouettes.

Standing, now, just outside the gate, the *Nyilas* continues bellowing at us: "Move right in! Sit on the benches! Those without seats, squat on the floor. No one is allowed to stand!" Minutes later, he hoists himself up into the truck and then stands just inside the canvas door, too close for comfort to the wooden bench on which I sit.

"Take it away, Geza," he shouts to the driver. Then he lights up a cigarette and blows the smoke directly into my face. I hate to satisfy him by coughing, but I can't help it.

At that, the *Nyilas* grins broadly. His left eye twitches as he purses his lips, and then deliberately funnels more smoke my way.

"Andris, where do you think they're taking us?"

"I wish I knew, Pistukam," Andris answers, letting out a long sigh.

"I hope we will meet Mother," I say a little louder.

"*Shh*…So do I. Pista, don't talk anymore now. That *Nyilas* is very unpredictable."

An hour or so later, the truck halts, abruptly. The *Nyilas* jumps off, and soon the canvas door of the truck is flipped open.

"Everyone out," screams the *Nyilas*. Twenty-five or so of us jump, stagger, or fall off the truck. When I survey our fellow travelers for the first time in broad daylight, I see we all wear the obligatory yellow star on our clothing.

"Line up, single file," barks the *Nyilas*, his eye twitching rapidly now. Then he hands us over to a German SS officer, dressed all in black. In his leather-gloved hands, the SS holds a riding crop. Bending the whip between his hands, he counts and re-counts us. Then he gives a loud, incomprehensible command in German. None of us move. Suddenly, the whip strikes the man standing nearest him full in the face. Now the SS screams, maniacally, at the top of his lungs and points at some barbed wire and wooden gates, still whipping away at everyone within striking distance. Like a herd of terrified cattle, we stampede toward the open gates, nearly trampling each other in our zest to avoid the madman's riding crop. Somewhere between here and inside the gate, Andris and I lose track of Mr. Szolosi, for good.

Once inside the gates, another member of our unfortunate entourage tells us we are at the Budafok Brick Factory, a huge open-air compound. The brick factory is filled, as it turns out, with thousands of other hapless deportees like ourselves, straight from the ghetto, no doubt. Crude barbed wire strips surrounding the perimeter of the compound separate us from the outside world.

Immediately Andris and I begin pushing and shoving our way through throngs of strangers, screaming, "Georgia Nasser! Mama! Georgia Nasser! Mama!" We shout ourselves hoarse, but we don't find her.

A couple hours later, night falls. It's already May, but the night air is still cold. We use Andris's overcoat for warmth, and mine as a blanket. Huddled together against the freezing ground, we sleep, surrounded by scores of strangers.

The next morning, we resume our search. By ten o'clock, Red Cross trucks arrive to distribute warm coffee and slices of bread. Before mid-afternoon we cover half the huge compound, still without any sign of Mother.

Around three that afternoon, we find Mother's sister, our Aunt Emma, and her husband, our Uncle Dezso. "*Uncle Dezso*!" Andris yells. Our aunt and uncle turn toward our voices, recognize us, and then smile broadly.

We run into their outstretched arms. They just about squeeze us to death.

"But boys, where is your mother?"

"We don't know. We can't find her."

"Let's not waste time, then," declares Uncle Dezso, immediately assuming leadership of our family search party.

Then, as if our aunt and uncle have brought us instant luck, we suddenly spot Mother and several other relatives, from both sides of our family.

"Mother, Mother! Over here!" Andris and I yell in unison. Not caring whom we push, Andris and I charge through the human sea toward Mother.

Then she sees *us*. "Andriskam! Pistukam! My darlings!" We all run to greet one another. When Andris and I reach Mother, we cling together in a tight three-way hug.

Mother looks as beautiful as ever, though careworn and tired. And there's sadness in her eyes like I've never before seen, not even after Father's death.

When I glance around, I see the rest. Among them are Aunt Bozsi (the wife of Father's youngest brother, Karoly, who was drafted last year as a Jewish forced laborer, into the Hungarian Army) and their five month-old baby, Peter; Grandmother Irma (on my father's side); Grandmother Roza (on my mother's side); and eighty-four year-old Uncle Mano. It's a family reunion of sorts, though not one any of us would have wished for.

That night, we're fed paprikas potato for dinner. Since we're all famished, the meal tastes good.

In the morning, frost covers the ground, turning the clayey reddish soil into a white crystal blanket. The sun makes the ice glitter, like thousands of tiny diamonds. *B-r-r-r!* I spend the night nestled between Mother and Andris, with the heat of both their bodies warming me. We've only two blankets to cover all three of us; Mother somehow managed to bring them along. A few feet away from us, Uncle Dezso snores peacefully.

An SS man patrolling our area stops now, for some unknown reason, right beside my sleeping uncle. Glancing at his watch, the German draws out his Luger, raises his arm, and points it toward the sky. Even with all the cruelties I've seen lately, I still can't believe my eyes. This idiot plans to wake people up by firing his gun! Then, apparently, he changes his mind. A devilish grin spreads over his face, and then he fires directly into the ground, just inches from my Uncle Dezso's forehead. The gunshot shatters the silence. People scream. Uncle Dezso jumps up, automatically, and charges the SS man.

The German fires another shot, straight at my uncle. I see Uncle Dezso double over, blood spurting from his mouth. Though injured, he lunges again. But the German kicks Uncle Dezso square in the stomach, and then watches him fall onto the icy ground.

Aunt Emma bends over her husband. "*Deszo! Dezso!* Darling, speak to me! Oh God! Someone help!"

Moments later my uncle dies. Several more SS appear from nowhere, and help my uncle's killer drag his body away. Aunt Emma, shaking and crying now, follows his body until an SS man forces her away.

"Get back, you Jew pig!" he yells. Aunt Emma has no choice but to obey. Then all of us watch, helplessly, as they continue dragging Uncle Dezso's body behind a kiln, leaving fresh, bloody heel marks on the ground.

After that, none of us feels hungry, but we know we must eat to remain alive. The warm coffee that is distributed somehow actually tastes good. This time, too, I'm luckier than I was at the previous "meal" here; I receive a *zsemle* (roll) instead of just a slice of bread.

After eating, we catch sight of a freight train backing into the siding of the brick factory, pulling thirty or so rust-colored boxcars. Obviously, it's meant to take us somewhere. Andris and I cling to one another, frightened anew out of our wits. A short while later, we're all ordered to board the boxcars in groups of eighty or so.

Various SS men with whips oversee the boarding process. Occasionally, we hear the whips crack viciously. Somewhere in the crowd, we've lost Mother. Before we can locate her again, Andris and I are shoved into one of the waiting boxcars. We find a place in the corner, under a small window covered with barbed wire, but without a glass pane. The car itself is about ten feet wide by thirty feet long, with sliding doors at the center, on both sides. One side is already locked; the other has just been slammed shut.

It takes several minutes for my eyes to adjust to the sudden darkness. Then I see several dozen strangers crammed inside with us. I've always loved trains. . . but not this one.

Next I spot two big metal buckets, one empty, the other with water inside it. These, I guess, must be for the eighty or so of us to relieve ourselves along the way to who knows where.

It's impossible for any of us to stretch without kicking someone else. I try to settle in, as comfortably as possible, for the journey. Then, with a sudden jerk, the train rolls out, its loud whistle instantly turning the nervous chatter among us all into a frightened hush.

The rhythmic click-clack of the train grows more frequent; we're gathering speed. A man sits partly on my right leg, which has now gone completely numb. Realizing I need to get some circulation back into it, I change positions, disturbing everyone around me.

Next, Andris introduces himself and me to the man who has been sitting on my leg.

The man replies, "I'm Elmer Kiss. I teach Algebra at the University of Nagyvarad."

"Algebra! Hmm. That takes logic," says Andris.

"Yes."

"You are a logical man, professor. Can you explain the logic behind our deportation?"

The man laughs, and then pauses to think. But before I can hear his answer, I nod off, even in my cramped position.

Ouch! Minutes later, I'm roused by a sudden jab in my ribs. A woman elbows me, trying to get comfortable.

"Sorry," she apologizes.

"It's okay. There's not much room in here."

Andris and the professor are still deciding the fate of the world, but I have more important things to do, like urinate.

"Andris," I say, interrupting the highly intellectual conversation, "I've really got to go."

"Just hold it," he replies, "until they pass you that damn stinking bucket." He wrinkles his nose involuntarily as he says this.

"I can't wait."

"Son," the professor says, echoing my brother, "just hold it a few more minutes."

Finally, the bucket, filled nearly to the brim with human waste, comes around to me. I relieve myself, which (despite the circumstances) makes me feel like I'm in Heaven.

For the time being, no one else needs the bucket, so it remains by my side, replete with its messy contents and nauseating odor. Its presence is still tolerable, though until several jerky movements of the train cause some of its contents to splash out onto the wooden floor and the clothing of some of us sitting nearby.

That's the last straw for the professor, who's just been hit with some of it. He picks up the bucket and passes it, insistently, to a stranger standing at the barbed wire open window, saying, "You *must* get rid of this! Many people still need to use it!"

Apparently deciding, from the professor's tone, that he has no choice, this man obediently lifts the bucket up to the window, and, turning it upside down, dumps its contents outside. So far, so good. But then, some of the content gets caught on the barbed wire, while some more of it is pushed back into the boxcar itself by the rushing air of the moving train. Anyone near the open window is splattered by the mess.

Fortunately, I'm now far enough away, (just barely) to be spared yet another "bath." But now, as I stand up again, trying to get more comfortable, I accidentally catch my pants on a sheet metal patch nailed to the floor. Suddenly an idea pops into my head. I find my pocketknife and, with the blade, pry off the metal patch. Beneath it is a hole in the floorboard about six inches by four inches. I can see the ground now, quickly disappearing beneath the speeding train. Ah! I've "uncovered" a solution to our agony. This is a perfect place from which to empty the bucket!

"I've just solved the problem of emptying the bucket," I announce to everyone around me.

Word of the opening in the floor soon spreads. Many begin lining up to make personal use of my "secret hole," foregoing the bucket altogether. Somewhere, we find a blanket to provide them a bit more privacy. But a distinct odor lingers in the air around my "secret hole."

Now the whistle blows as the train heads into a hard turn. It slows down, and we soon come to a complete stop. Outside, I hear the sounds of people rushing around, and of both German and Hungarian being spoken. This is a good sign, I tell myself. At least we're still in Hungary.

Door latches unlock from the outside, and one of our boxcar doors opens, suddenly, with a loud thud. Those sitting near the opening have the first chance to fill their lungs with cold, fresh Carpathian air. I can actually see the stale moist air steaming from our boxcar against the dimly starlit night. We're somewhere in the Carpathian foothills. A scent of pine hangs pleasantly in the air.

As I cautiously watch the guards taking up their positions, I realize how famished I feel, and how long I've gone without food since eating my scanty breakfast before boarding this awful train. About ten minutes later, a military truck pulls up beside the rails, and begins unloading huge kettles of steaming food. Until now, unpleasant thoughts of our unknown fate have fully occupied my imagination. But the sight of food makes my mouth water and my mind go blank.

The soldiers start distributing the food. They hand up to each "passenger" an individual tin can, filled with some sort of gluey, stew-like substance. I don't believe the recipe comes from any cookbook Mother would use; however, it's warm, and it actually tastes relatively good. We also receive a slice of bread about an inch thick, along with a portion of liverwurst about the thickness of an index finger.

Andris and I huddle together, devouring our rations.

"Do you have to make so much noise slurping?" Andris asked.

"I'm feeding my stomach, and letting my ears know."

That stops Andris's complaints. The rest of our "dinner" we spend quietly, except for my occasional slurping. My last drop gone, I next use my finger as a spatula, slowly circling the inner wall of the tin can, again and again. Then I suck each of my fingers clean of any leftover gravy. I could easily eat five times this amount.

Andris wrinkles his nose at me, clearly disgusted at my poor traveling manners. I look away for a moment. When I look back, though, he's licking his fingers, too.

Once we're underway again, the train's *clickety-clack* grows less frequent, meaning we're traveling more slowly. The whistle also blows more often as the train follows its winding uphill tracks. My ears are popping, now, from the change in altitude. From the spot where I'm crouched, I pull myself up to a standing position and touch my nose to the little boxcar window. I can see a picturesque white landscape beneath a full moon.

I've never before visited this part of Hungary, and can't help but find it breathtaking. After peace returns, I promise myself, I'll visit this area of the countryside again, but on my own terms. I can't help wondering what total peace and freedom would feel like. I can't even imagine it. How I wish the Americans would hurry up and beat the damned Germans!

I overhear a woman tell Andris about a place in southern Poland called

Auschwitz. Thousands of Jews are taken there by the Nazis, gassed to death, and their dead bodies burned in huge ovens. With shock and dismay, I realize I actually believe her. Twenty-four hours ago, I might not have believed her. That, however, was before I saw the Nazis murder Uncle Dezso in cold blood.

It's the next day already when we finally stop. Since it's now morning, hot coffee and bread, accompanied by a pat of hard honey, are distributed to everyone. It's not much, but it takes the edge off my hunger. Soon we're underway again.

After eating my scant breakfast, I locate a piece of paper and a pencil from somewhere and fashion a primitive checkerboard with some black and white paper "checkers." To pass the time, Andris and I play game after game.

"Hey, boys," pipes up a middle-aged man, sitting nearby with his son, "let's play with your checkers."

"Sure," I reply, "for a couple cookies and an apple."

The man doesn't like my offer, but since he and his son are very bored, he agrees to it. I cut the apple in half and share it with Andris. Then we devour the cookies.

"You're pretty sharp, Pista," Andris admits when even the smallest crumbs have vanished.

"It's called survival."

He nods, respectfully. His silent compliment warms me all over. At that wonderful fleeting moment, I feel, briefly, like a king in his castle instead of a hapless boy on his way to a concentration camp.

Now our train clickety-clacks along, again, at full speed. Elbowing my way over to the nearest window, I observe the faint line of the Carpathian Mountains far behind us. From this, I gather we've crossed into Poland.

Late that afternoon, we stop to eat. This time, though, the food isn't even warm. By now we're all feeling exhausted, impatient, and ill-tempered. To add to the misery inside our boxcar, the area around my "secret hole" has grown slippery from overuse, and its odor virtually unbearable. Right then and there, however, I make a decision: I'll bear whatever hardships or discomforts come my way, so long as they're not killing me. From now on, I won't waste energy on anything but making it through this nightmare alive.

"This damn boxcar and the people in it are driving me mad," Andris snaps.

"Relax, Andris. We can't do anything."

"How can *you* be so calm?" In the past I suppose, Andris hasn't thought of me, his doting younger brother, as being all that much different from himself.

Now, however, our distinctions of temperament are becoming more apparent to both of us.

"These last couple days I've done some serious thinking," I tell my brother. "I promise myself that I'll survive, one way or another, and this is how I'm putting it into practice. By staying calm."

He's quiet awhile, and then admits, "You're probably right." Then he falls silent again, withdrawing into his private world.

With the third day come similar trying routines: struggling to get up and down for exercise; squinting out through the small window; peeing through the increasingly rank and slippery hole in the floor; stopping for a bit of food; griping about what they feed us.

Early on the morning of the fourth day, the train slows as we pass through what seems a fairly large city. I see traffic on the streets and people moving about, en route to their jobs. Clearly life goes right on in places like this, as the world ignores our plight. Silently I curse the damn insane house painter, Hitler. . . the bloodthirsty hyena. For the first time since boarding the train, my pent-up anger gets the best of me. Then I recall the promise I've made myself earlier, and let the anger go.

Chapter Seven
Auschwitz

Our train chugs up to a formidable-looking compound. From our tiny boxcar window we see barbed wire fences all around, and turrets pointing high into the sky at strategically placed points. The area's circumference is massive. In the distance, huge chimneys belch murky, foul-smelling smoke. It swirls about, polluting the air with an awful stench.

A chill runs all through me. "Andris," I dare ask, "Are we. . . at . . .?"

My brother finishes my sentence. "Auschwitz."

When we finally stop, exiting our boxcar is a vexing, laborious process. The cars are opened, carefully, methodically, one by one, as if in slow motion. By the time Andris and I are sprung from our moving prison, at least two thousand other recent deportees mill around, each as frightened and confused as we are.

In a way, though, we're in luck. Just after we leave the train, Andris spots our Aunt Bozsi holding little Peter, only thirty yards or so from where we're standing. Excitedly, he points them out to me. "Pista, hold onto my coat, tight. Let's push our way over there."

"Okay." Gripping his coattail, I push.

Now we hear names being screamed in all different languages. To add to the cacophony, babies cry; children shriek with fear. Helpless elderly people, some barely walking, are shoved to and fro by the crowd. Some stumble and fall, only to be stepped on, again and again. Finally, we're within arm's length of Aunt Bozsi. And to our relief and delight Mother is standing right behind her.

"Andriskam! Pistakum!" Mother cries. "Thank God you found us!"

"Mother! Mother!" We wave and yell. In my haste to get to her, I accidentally step on a man's foot.

"Watch your step, punk!" I hear him shout, as I charge through a sudden opening.

"Mother!" I cry again.

Finally, I reach my mother, and she and I cling together in a tight hug.

Then Andris takes his turn hugging and kissing Mother. "When did you arrive?" he asks her and Aunt Bozsi, beginning to play with baby Peter.

Mother replies, "Just now."

"Thank God we're finally out of those cramped, smelly boxcars," adds Aunt Bozsi.

Suddenly, the roar of the crowd is overpowered by a bellowing, German-accented voice that blares from numerous loudspeakers. It commands the frightened people, again and again, in Hungarian: **"QUIET EVERYBODY! QUIET EVERYBODY!"**

Within minutes, the sounds of the crowd diminish to a murmur, and then a mere whisper. Next, the giant, disembodied voice continues:

"You have just arrived at the interning facility of Auschwitz. For the time being, men and women will be separated. Children will be taken care of at a separate compound. You will abandon all personal belongings and clothing before entering the disinfecting facilities and showers. Everyone's heads will be shaved to eliminate lice. After you have gone through the cleansing procedures, you will be furnished regulation prison uniforms. Anybody disregarding orders will be shot."

An eerie quiet settles over the crowd. Then the harsh voice of the invisible German continues:

"You Jews in the forward lines will now begin approaching the selection officers."

In an anxious tone, Aunt Bozsi insists, "I won't give them my baby. *I won't.*"

"Bozsi, darling," Mother coos, "Don't worry. I'm sure the separation doesn't include babies."

I'm less sure, but know my aunt well enough to stay silent. I just can't picture her voluntarily giving Peter up to the Nazis.

"Aunt Bozsi," I say a few minutes later, trying to fill the silence that has now set in among us, "let me hold Peter for awhile."

"Only for a minute," she replies, handing the child to me. I brush my cheek against my five-month old cousin's tiny face. He is so adorable. How could anyone not love him?

Then, all at once, the mob begins to stir.

"Pistukam," Aunt Bozsi soon says, "hand the baby back to me." Tenderly but purposefully, she lifts Peter from my arms.

Now the real commotion begins. First, we must relinquish everything: jewelry, family pictures, watches, food. From garments and various other hiding places, people in line begin producing prized foodstuffs, items they've hidden away for rainy days. Soon, everyone passes food around and eats: salamis, sardines, breads and rolls of all shapes, candy, pickles, cookies, and lots of canned food. The bizarre scene reminds me, in a strange sense, of a huge open-air *bar mitzvah*, with all the food flowing freely, but without the festive mood.

Despite my ever-mounting anxiety, I manage to enter into the strange spirit of things like everyone else; I eat until I'm so stuffed I can hardly move. Even then, I hold onto a favorite delicacy of mine, a stick of Hertz Hungarian salami. Initially I'm determined to eat it before anyone else can. But now my stomach simply refuses.

Looking back, I'm glad I've eaten well one last time; there shall be no more feasting for me here at Auschwitz.

Several hours later our weary, frightened party at last approaches the uniformed selection officer. As we wait, Mother tells Andris and me of her own experiences aboard the train.

"The worst problem was no washroom facilities. How did you boys manage?"

Andris chuckles, and then, to my embarrassment, tells Mother of my fortunate discovery and use of the "secret hole." I blush. Still, it feels good to share a laugh with Mother, almost like old times.

We all take turns holding Peter. Meanwhile, Aunt Bozsi's anxiety merely increases.

"Georgia," she asks my mother, again and again, "do you really think the Nazis won't take the baby?"

"Bozsi, dear, you worry about nothing. Even the Nazis wouldn't take a breast-feeding infant from its mother."

Something in my mother's tone makes me wonder if she's as convinced as she says. At any rate, I hope Aunt Bozsi believes her.

Then Mother adds, "Bozsi, you ought to feed the baby before we get to the front of the line."

Modestly, Aunt Bozsi unbuttons her white blouse and turns the baby to her breast. He immediately begins sucking his mother's milk, a vision of complete peaceful contentment.

Now the line moves faster. From our position near the front, we witness entire families being separated, to their silent horror. I observe healthy looking men and women, ranging from young to late middle-aged, being pushed to one side. The visibly sick, handicapped, and elderly, as well as the children, are pointed to the other side. As each person approaches the officer to be cursorily inspected, he gestures, lazily, left or right. It takes him a few seconds, at most, to decide on each one's fate.

Now it is our turn. Aunt Bozsi approaches the Nazi officer, with little Peter still sucking blissfully at her half-uncovered breast.

The Nazi motions to another SS, who marches over to Aunt Bozsi, and then rips the nursing Peter roughly from her breast.

Aunt Bozsi turns livid. "You damn bastard!" she screams. "Give me back my baby! I'll kill you!"

Then, before any of us can restrain her, Aunt Bozsi rushes toward the officer who has just snatched Peter, and sinks her fingernails hard into his face. Instantly, blood pours down his face, and spills onto the baby himself. Then a third officer, emerging from nowhere, swings the butt of his rifle at my aunt's skull with all his might. Aunt Bozsi collapses at his feet in a helpless, bloody heap.

Despite her injuries, my aunt manages to raise her head, slowly, as her eyes follow baby Peter. "My baby! Please let me have my baby back!"

Cursing like a madman, the bleeding SS, who is still holding Peter, tosses the baby high in the air and catches him, upside down, grabbing him roughly by his chubby pink ankles. Next, he raises the infant as high as he can over his own head, and slams little Peter down, head first, against the wheel of the nearest boxcar.

My infant cousin's skull explodes against the wheel with a dull pop. Blood and brain fragments instantly cover the rusty wheel itself, and paint the ground below it a bright, violent crimson. I pray that Aunt Bozsi has somehow been spared the whole scene.

Pandemonium ensues, even from this terrified crowd. The SS draw their guns to hold everyone back.

I vomit up everything, right on the spot. Somehow, I make it past the selecting officer when my own turn comes. The next time I look around, I'm past him. Andris walks beside me. We march very slowly, two men to a row, toward a group of barracks. The rest of our family is nowhere around.

"We've lost Mother again," says Andris. His voice sounds flat.

"I know."

A foul taste lingers in my mouth from vomiting. I spit on the ground several times, to no avail. Realizing the Hertz salami is still in my grip, I offer Andris my prized possession.

He shakes his head. Not wanting to waste the salami, but sensing it will soon be confiscated, I present it to a stranger behind me, who wolfs it down gratefully.

The line moves closer to a door, where the men ahead of us in line are disappearing into uncertainty. Fear of the unknown lurks in everyone's hearts and minds. The black smoke from the chimneys emits a nauseating odor as it spreads across the horizon, and then dissolves, ever so slowly, into the dusky sky.

Finally, we approach the barracks. Inside, we observe numerous mountain-sized heaps of abandoned clothing. Everyone is ordered: "Strip!" At this point, I'm still clasping my pocket- knife. I don't know how much longer I can hang onto it undetected, but so far so good. My brother and I undress completely, and then follow the line-up to another room.

In this room, barbers briskly cut each man's hair with double-zero hand clippers. Andris, who stands ahead of me, is first to be shorn.

Soon, our heavy-handed barber finishes with Andris.

Then it's my turn to be cropped. I feel the clipper working its way all over my head. The next man clips off all the hair between our legs. I wince, since he's none too gentle. Next, we raise our arms over our heads; our armpits are the last to be mowed by the clippers.

All this, and I still have my pocketknife in my left fist.

The next room we enter stinks of strong disinfectant. We must each step into a large metal container, forty by eighty inches or so, and ten inches high. We're ordered to rub the smelly stuff on our bodies, wherever the hair used to be. God, it stings!

In the shower room, we're instructed to wash every inch of ourselves, thoroughly, from top to toe. We halfway dry ourselves with damp rags, the only towels provided. Then we all shuffle, still dripping wet, into yet another room, where we're powdered, one by one, with some kind of flea-powder. Here, large brushes with very fine bristles are used on us. They brush the powdery stuff all over our heads, underarms, and loin areas.

The room to follow has yet another lineup. Inspection! Our mouths are searched for smuggled articles. Arms and legs are spread, fingers stretched—we all have to pass inspection. Quickly, I insert my pocketknife into my rectum, hoping for the best. An SS officer whose cruel stare gives me the creeps peers inside my mouth, checks quickly between my legs, and then waves me on. Ah, it's over! I've smuggled my beloved little knife through all this maniacal German efficiency.

Then we reach the final room inside the barracks. Here, great numbers of prisoners like us walk around in newly issued striped uniforms, clomping about in their ridiculous-looking canvas-covered wooden shoes.

Finally, we experience a ray of hope. During selection, we must have been sent to the correct side. So far, we've not been gassed or cremated.

"I wonder where Mother is," I worry.

"Don't worry, Pista. She was sent to our side."

"Are you sure?"

"I'm positive. I saw the officer gesture in our direction."

This makes me feel better. We receive our own prison garb and wooden shoes, as well as two charcoal gray blankets, but are issued no overcoats.

When we finally exit the barracks, night has arrived. It is, in fact, quite late. We're herded into a huge sleeping area, where we see the strangest sight yet. Thousands of Jewish men, of all ages and nationalities, each one a prisoner like ourselves, lie on their backs in long, even rows, either resting or sleeping. Each has his legs spread apart, with the next man in the same position between *his* legs, resting his head in the lap of the man behind him. My God! Sardines packed into a tin have it better! Having eighty people in one boxcar is a luxury compared to this.

Our massive sleeping area has cement floors, but no room dividers. The place looks like a hangar. Andris and I step over countless people, either lying down or perched in semi-sitting positions. Despite my exhaustion, I can't sleep a wink that night. It isn't the cold, the hard cement floor, or the proximity to others, though, that keeps me awake. Instead, whenever I close my eyes I see Aunt Bozsi's frantic expression, followed by an image of little Peter's smashed skull. Try as I might, I can't erase these pictures from my mind.

The next morning, Andris and I take time to rub some circulation back into each other's numb, cramped limbs. Neither of us has slept. We wander outside the barracks, where hundreds of other prisoners mill around aimlessly, some carrying enamel bowls.

Andris taps one such man on the shoulder. "Where did you get that bowl?" he asks him, politely.

Slowly, the man turns, and looks us both over carefully from head to toe. "You've just arrived?"

"Yesterday," replies Andris.

The man points a bony finger a few barracks down. "See those barracks over there? That's the *Magazine,* where they'll issue you each a canteen and a spoon." With that, he turns, mechanically, and walks away, seemingly more ghost than human being.

"Thank you, Sir!" Andris calls after him. But he just keeps going, as if he doesn't hear. This is but the first of many such encounters with the "living dead."

We walk down the main "street" for the first time, hoping to get an idea of the facility's size and layout. We discover that there are fifteen huge barracks, split down the middle by an alley between them. We also hear languages of all kinds being spoken: Polish, Russian, German, Rumanian, Czech, Hungarian, and others we can't identify. We see no women, though. I don't see anyone my own age; nearly every other inmate looks at least a few years older.

A man in late middle age approaches us, having perhaps identified us, from overhearing our conversation, as fellow Hungarians.

"This guy may know something," says Andris. "He looks like a seasoned inmate, poor fellow."

"Hello, Sir!" we call to him in Hungarian.

"Good morning!" the stranger replies.

We introduce ourselves.

"I'm Imre," he says.

"Imre, some of the people who arrived here with us yesterday are nowhere around. Do you know what could have happened to them?" Andris asks.

Imre points to the omni-present steadily rising columns of smoke in the distance. "You boys were spared because you looked fit for work. All the rest, old people, sick people, handicapped folks, children. . . they're. . . they're. . ."

"We understand," Andris replies.

"But Imre, our mother, for instance. . . she wouldn't be in that smoke if she was sent to the same side as us, would she?" I ask.

He looks us over again, carefully. "You're brothers?"

"Yes sir."

"Boys, your mother's probably alive, well, and worried about you, just like you're concerned about her. How old are you two, anyway?"

"I'm thirteen," I reply. "Andris is sixteen."

"You look older than 13, Pista. Both of you look strong, and healthy, and fit for hard work. That's probably why they spared you. There aren't many teenagers alive in Auschwitz today, especially as young as you, Pista. Follow me, and I'll show you boys around."

First, Imre shows us the washroom facilities. Then we stop by the magazine to collect our metal canteen cups and spoons.

The man distributing these appears so evil that he makes even the meanest SS look like a choirboy. A thick white band marked *CAPO* is wrapped around his upper arm.

His eyes scare me. They look wild and bestial, like those of a madman.

"When did you arrive here?" he barks abruptly at Andris.

"Just yesterday. My brother and I. . . "

The Capo reaches over the counter and grabs Andris by the collar. "When I want to know about your brother, I'll ask *him*, you ignorant Jew bastard!" he screams, shaking Andris like a piggy bank.

Fortunately, he doesn't ask me anything when my turn comes, but just shoves my supplies at me, a surly sneer on his face. Then we get out of there, fast.

Once we're outside again, Imre warns us: "The guys with bands around their arms are the Capos. Beware of them. They're hardened criminals, some of them political—like little Caesars. Take my advice and stay out of their way."

We nod. We won't need to be told this again.

As we stroll along, we approach a barbed wire fence.

"On the other side is a separate compound, with similar facilities."

"Why do the people over there look so thin and fragile?" I ask.

"They're women. They've had all their hair shaved off."

Andris and I glance at each other in dismay. Poor Mother! I can't bear to picture her without her beautiful, abundant light brown hair. I wonder how she's managing on her own over there, how she feels, all alone, without us or anyone else she knows. I would give anything to talk to her now! Drawn like a magnet toward the other side, wanting a closer look, I approach the fence.

"Stop!" Imre screams. "For God's sake, stop!" Freezing in my tracks, I back up, slowly.

"You stupid fool!" Imre explodes, his face blanching. "Another step, Pista, and you might very well have been blown to bits."

Perplexed, I glance around. "How?" I ask, innocently.

"Two yards within the fence is a mine field. The fence itself is electrified with high voltage. Don't ever do that again."

"I . . . I didn't see any sign," I blubber.

"They're everywhere." Imre grabs me around the shoulders with one arm, and with the other, points to a black and white sign, written in German.

"I see. Thanks for warning me."

Looking past the sign, I continue scrutinizing all the bald women, hoping to somehow spot Mother amongst them. Try as I might, though, it's hard to tell any of them apart, especially at such a distance. I could be looking straight at mother right now, without even knowing it.

Imre adds, "Son, if you want to live to be my age, I'd suggest you slow down around here, and remember to always look before you act."

"I will, Imre. Thank you for saving my life just now."

So. . . instead of going up in smoke I could have gone up in a blast.

I hear my stomach growling. Neither Andris nor I have had a morsel since yesterday's impromptu feast while awaiting selection.

"Imre, what kind of food do they give us here?" I ask.

Imre wrinkles his nose, as if he's just seen a disgusting insect.

"Well, boys, if you were old timers like me, you'd be used to it. But since you haven't tasted it yet, you'll probably spit it out the first time you taste it. It's horrible."

He clears his throat and continues, "But let me tell you, young fellows, it's the only nourishment you'll get here. Eat it, even if you think it will kill you. If you don't, the lack of it will."

Soon enough, Andris and I experience first-hand the awful menu of Auschwitz. At noon, long lines of prisoners begin forming for lunch. It doesn't take us long to each receive a portion of *"gemuse."* As bad as the name sounds, the stuff tastes even worse. I'd like to throw it away. But then I remember Imre's advice, and manage to force half of it down.

Andris doesn't do any better with his portion.

"At least we don't have to walk anywhere to give away the leftovers," Andris remarks. Our left over *gemuse* is taken by the first two prisoners we offer it to.

We do keep our "bread." Four by four inches, an inch thick, it's made from some unidentifiable dark substance. I wonder if it could have been made by a carpenter instead of a baker, since it seems to contain more sawdust than flour. Compared to the *gemuse,* though, it tastes heavenly.

The afternoon sun feels good, and Andris and I take advantage of it, basking in its warmth like a pair of zebras in our striped uniforms.

The following days pass relatively uneventfully, except for a couple instances of Capos beating prisoners with rawhide sticks. After awhile, though, even this seems routine. Like all prisoners here, we're becoming desensitized to our surroundings

And so it goes.

Chapter Eight
Escape

One morning after we've been at Auschwitz about a week, Andris and I wake early, a good night's sleep having eluded us again. We leave our crowded barracks and clomp aimlessly around outside in our canvas clodhoppers. We've yet to be assigned to a work detail, but, according to Imre, this will happen soon. As of yet, we've received no identification numbers; nor have we any tattoos on our forearms. We'll be getting these later, too, Imre promises. We also have no particular assigned places in the barracks. We eat and sleep where we can, two anonymous newcomers in a huge, involuntary army of sad, strange faces.

"You know, Andris," I remark, "if you and I disappeared into thin air right now, no one would even notice."

Andris laughs. "Okay, Houdini, let's do it. Abracadabra!"

"Yeah, right. I wish."

As we clomp along toward nowhere in particular, we spot a group of several hundred fellow prisoners lined up, two by two, inside a roped off area less than a hundred yards away. We wonder what they've done to be singled out thus. They appear young and healthy: not gas chamber material, as far as I can see.

I call to an older prisoner walking along a few feet ahead of us, "Hey, Sir, who are those guys?"

"Them?" he says, pointing. "That's a labor group waiting for transport."

"Huh?"

"They're a group of prisoners being transported to a labor camp somewhere outside here."

"Where is this camp outside here that they're going to?"

The man shrugs. "I don't know. There are lots."

We continue watching from a distance, our envy increasing, as the lucky assemblage is hastily counted down, and then left unguarded.

"Lucky guys!" says my brother. "They're leaving this God-awful place. I wish we were with them."

"Let's go ask them if they know where they're headed," I suggest. "Maybe we can find out how they got picked."

"Sure, why not?" Andris agrees. "We have nothing to lose."

As we approach the group, we see that the only divider between them and us is a rope stretching alongside the prisoners themselves. They stand around in double file.

"What labor camp are you guys going to from here?" I call in Hungarian, to whoever might understand.

A young man somewhere near the front of the line answers me, in Hungarian. "We're being shipped to a work camp in Bavaria." He's tall, hollow-cheeked, and hawk-nosed, with grayish eyes.

"Oh? Where exactly in Bavaria?" I've heard that southern Germany is nice at least in more normal circumstances.

"The guards didn't tell us. Just a camp somewhere in Bavaria. Where are you two guys from?"

"Budapest." I introduce Andris and myself.

"I'm Sandor. This is my cousin Zoltan." He gestures toward another young man about his age and size, but with a darker complexion. "Zoltan and I come from Maramoros, near the Polish border."

"You're both lucky to be able to leave here," Andris says.

"We really don't want to," Zoltan replies.

"What?"

"It's not because we *like* it here," Sandor interrupts. "But we have two brothers a few barracks down, and we don't want to leave them."

"Why don't you let us change places with you?" I offer, expecting everyone to laugh at the idea.

Instead, to my surprise the cousins look at us earnestly. "We *would* switch with you if we could," says Zoltan. "But if the Capos catch us, we'll all be beaten, to say the least."

"But if we *don't* switch, you'll never see your brothers again."

Zoltan and Sandor exchange glances, nod to each other, and, almost before we know it, slip outside the ropes. Quickly, Andris and I slip underneath, replacing them. Meanwhile, everyone around us pretends not to notice a thing.

We watch Sandor's and Zoltan's backs as the two disappear toward their brothers' barracks.

Before Andris and I can savor our miraculous feat, an SS officer marches down the main alley. "Look, Andris!" I say, with fear in my voice. What if this guy catches us, somehow? Ever since that night those two SS marched me upstairs to Mother and Andris with a gun at my back, the mere sight of an SS uniform sends chills through me.

"It looks like he's leading a detachment of *Wehrmacht*," Andris replies, calmly. "It's the regular German Army. *Pista, stop shaking!*"

Instantly, I relax. Not a second too soon, it turns out.

The SS stops in front of our group. *"Achtung!"* he commands. His voice is raspy, and his eyes a cold, cruel icy blue.

Each of us snaps to attention. *"Einz, Zwei, Drei,"* the S.S. counts us down in the typical self-assured, arrogant way of his elite unit.

"In Gleichschritt, Marsch!" he orders us.

The several hundred or so of us are marched through the gates, past the gas chambers and ovens, and through another gate to a waiting train.

The *Wehrmachts* then open the doors to all six boxcars.

"Pista, let's get into the first car," Andris suggests. "It looks fairly new." He climbs up and pulls himself inside. "Here, Pista. Grab my hand," he shouts down.

I do so. With his help and a little of my own effort, I pull myself up inside.

Our boxcar door remains open a few more minutes, allowing us one last look at the ghastly death factory we're about to leave. The sickening smoke still billows, sky high. My imagination plays nasty little games with the formations of the dark clouds. Then the door slams shut, at last.

The rhythm of the train, the fresh smell of straw on the floor of our boxcar, and the warm wool blankets we find inside give Andris and me comfort and our first decent sleep in well over a week. *Clickety-clack, clickety-clack.* . .the train speeds away from the worst place on earth, its destination unknown to its passengers.

A young man sitting near us asks, "Are you guys Hungarian?"

"Yes," replies Andris.

"Me, too. I'm Martin, from Sopron."

We introduce ourselves. "How long have you been at Auschwitz?" Andris asks him.

"Since 1942."

"That's two years!" says Andris. "That's a long time to endure a place like this! By the way, when did you get that tattoo on your arm?"

"Quite awhile ago. What? You don't have one?"

We both shake our heads. Then I explain, "You see, we just got deported here from Budapest about a week ago. When we saw a chance to leave here today with this group, we grabbed it."

"But, how did you two manage to get into this work detail so quickly? And without tattoos? Tattooed numbers on your lower arms are required for this work command."

"We didn't know that," I pipe up. "We just changed places with a couple other Hungarian guys who didn't want to leave their family."

Martin raises his eyebrows in disbelief. "My God! Do you know the risk you took? If that SS officer had seen your arms without tattoos, God knows what would have happened to you."

We fall silent. So! I'd been right all along to be so nervous when we were standing in line being counted. It's a good thing Andris calmed me down. If I'd acted as nervous as I felt, that SS might have indeed realized something was up.

"On the other hand, though," Martin continues, breaking the silence, "if you two had stayed in Auschwitz, you'd eventually have gone up in smoke. That's what happens to people in work details, as soon as they get too weak or sick. Right to the gas chamber, located on the premises for optimal convenience."

"How did *you* manage to avoid going up in smoke, since you've been at Auschwitz so long?" Andris asks.

"Just luck, I guess. I was strong and healthy when I arrived, and I've managed not to get sick. The key, I think, is to eat as well as you can. Never turn down any chance for extra food. Do anything you can to get enough to eat." Following that pronouncement, he rummages inside his pocket, producing a slice of dried bologna wrapped in paper. He then offers it to Andris and me. "Here, fellows, eat up," he says.

"Don't you want that for yourself?" Andris asks him.

"I've got more. This is your reward for being smart enough to escape. It's all you'll get. Believe me, there won't be a big welcoming banquet for you where we're going, wherever it is."

With my pocket knife, I divide the dried bologna in two, giving Andris half.

"That's right, Pista," says Martin. "You two eat it. Enjoy it."

"You're nice, Martin," I tell him, "We're strangers, and you're giving us your food. I wish we could think of something nice to do for you."

"Not necessary, Pista. Just pass the favor along if you get a chance."

Munching my bologna, I sit back and think. None of us have any idea of either our current whereabouts, or our destination, but I do sense we're moving west. Around noon, the train stops. We hear the familiar sounds of doors being unlatched, and then slid open. Then we hear *Wehrmacht* guards rushing around outside. Finally, our own boxcar door opens. I cover my eyes to protect them from the sudden burst of sunlight beaming into our darkened car.

Squinting hard, I peer outside. Several army trucks appear, and then pull up right beside our train. Then a military car also drives up. What is all this? I wonder. From the passenger side of the military vehicle, another SS steps out briskly.

His highly polished boots glare wickedly in the bright Bavarian sunshine. He pulls down on his jacket, and then waits impatiently for our train's commander, who approaches him at a fast clip. Their boots click to attention.

"*Heil Hitler*" they snap, exchanging the Nazi salute with outstretched right arms.

"The work convoy from Auschwitz is here," announces our commander.

"Assemble them on the platform," snaps the other SS.

Seconds later, we hear another soldier, this one a *Wehrmacht*, give the order, "*Alles herous!*"

Stretching our arms and legs, which are stiff and sore from hours of sitting, we climb off the high platform as quickly as possible. According to a sign I noticed earlier, we've arrived at the village of Muhldorf. From a geography class I had in school, I remember it's near the Inn River. Geography was one of my strongest subjects.

"*Achtung!*" shouts the *Wehrmacht*.

"*Einz, Zwei, Drei. . .*" he counts us down, row after row.

"Two hundred ninety two!" he announces a few minutes later.

"*Du dumkopf!* That's not the right number!" the SS upbraids the *Wehrmacht*, his face turning purple.

"*Abtreten!*" the SS orders the embarrassed *Wehrmacht*. Obediently, the soldier counts us all over again.

After the second count, which apparently satisfies the SS, we're instructed to board the waiting Army trucks.

Andris looks at me, shaking his head in disbelief. "These SS are *unbelievable,*" he says. "All that fuss over a counting mistake. You'd think the world just ended."

I start to say, "Just think if *that* guy would have caught us escaping," but think better of it. We still don't know exactly where we are, or who might be listening.

Now our convoy traverses the small village of Muhldorf. The fresh air feels and smells good as we ride along inside the open truck. Most houses we see are small, neat, single story, and whitewashed, with well-tended little gardens out front. Along the way, we also pass a cigar shop, a bakery, and various other small stores and businesses. The people walking these streets, as they go about their daily business, stare curiously at us and whisper. Children point. Our striped prison suits catch their interest. I wonder if these people even realize what the Nazis are up to. Even if they did, it would probably seem incredible to them. With Jewish prisoners routinely being driven through their town in army trucks, how could they *not* wonder what's going on? They're probably too scared to ask, though, I conclude. After all, look how that SS man back where we just came from browbeat his own *Wehrmacht*.

I inform Andris, "If my geography's right, Muhldorf is right along the Inn River, about fifty miles outside Munich."

"Thanks, whiz kid."

"I thought you'd want to know."

"All I want to know is when we're going to eat."

"Me, too. I'm starving." As I say this, I realize, though, that I'm getting used to being hungry.

After the village, we pass over a river. Then I see a sign informing us that this is in fact the Inn.

"Look over to the left, Andris," I say later, pointing to some lush green pine trees swaying lazily in the gentle breeze. To the right are wheat fields. Such beautiful scenery, despite our misery.

A few miles past the river, the trucks slow down and turn right. We approach several good-sized compounds of wooden barracks, surrounded, as always, by barbed wire fences. Wooden turrets, dominated by machine guns and searchlights, are placed at strategic corners, with ladders the only way up or down.

Andris cocks an ear. "Listen, Pista! I hear women's voices."

A group of women standing around behind the barbed wire fences wave to us and cheer. I stare at them, yearning to see one face in particular. But I don't.

"Andris, do you think Mother could be in there?"

"Don't count on it, Pistukam. By the way, you did a great thing this morning, figuring out how to get us away from Auschwitz." I realize he's changing the subject on purpose. "That took courage and imagination. I'm proud of you."

"But what will happen when she realizes we're no longer in the camp?" I ask.

"I don't know. But we had to get away from Auschwitz."

Thinking of Mother silences us both.

The truck halts, and we're all ordered to get off.

After we climb down, I nudge Andris and point to a uniformed figure coming toward us. "Look, Andris, isn't that the same *Wehrmacht* who just got bawled out by that nasty SS?"

"That's the guy," says Andris.

Coming closer, the *Wehrmacht* looks us over, and then fixes his gaze on me. "How old are you, son?" he asks.

"Eighteen, sir," I lie.

He smiles, clearly not believing me. But than he reaches over and strokes me gently on the cheek, as if to say, "I know you're not really 18, but that's okay." Once again, I realize the big difference between the uniformed Nazi storm troopers and the uniformed draftees; the SS carry out Hitler's cruel mission with genuine zeal. The *Wehrmacht's,* like us, would prefer to be somewhere else.

Next, the gates of one of the empty compounds are opened, and we're marched directly into our new quarters. No chimneys, smoke, ovens, or gas chambers! We're counted down again (we learn this procedure is called "Appel" here). Everyone must be accounted for at Appel, twice a day, morning and evening.

I smell steaming food, and then see a series of huge steel pots being carried out from one of the barracks. Apparently this barracks is the compound's kitchen area. Prisoners in striped uniforms like ours, carrying the steaming pots, set them down on a dozen or so wooden tables, placed just inside our new compound. Within seconds several lines of prisoners form before each table with its big pot. Finally, everyone in our famished group is fed lunch. The *gemuse* here has a bit more body to it than at Auschwitz, although it tastes the same.

After we eat, Appel is called again. A much longer wooden table is produced, and ten *Wehrmachts* take their seats behind it. We're then told to arrange ourselves in the lines alphabetically; each *Wehrmacht* will handle a particular group of names beginning with certain letters. Andris and I join the "N through R" line.

Night is falling. As our names are taken, we're assigned (alphabetically, again) a sleeping barracks within the compound.

The wooden barracks in which we sleep are about 150 by 30 feet. There is a door at each end, and several windows. In the center sits a wood-burning potbelly stove, its metal stovepipe winding up through the roof. Wooden bunks are lined up all the way down one side. The other side looks the same, except that a ten-foot area is left clear for the stove. This arrangement makes for a center aisle, door to door.

The barracks commander, a well-seasoned middle-aged Jewish prisoner, yells, "Everybody take a bunk."

I run to the first upper bunk and scramble up inside it.

"This is mine!" I cry, like a six-year old who's discovered a treasure. "Andris, I'm holding the top one right beside mine for you."

Andris, less enthusiastic, climbs into the bunk beside mine. "At least we have mattresses here," he says.

These "mattresses" are, in fact, sacks containing just enough straw to lessen slightly the misery of the cheap wooden planks from which our bunks are fashioned.

Soon we hear the whistle blow again, and must gather for yet another Appel. The count is correct, and we're dismissed. All this takes so long that it's already time to line up for dinner.

Dinner tonight proves an interesting experience. For every four prisoners, we're handed one loaf of sawdust bread. Each prisoner also receives his own tiny pat of margarine, a slice of liverwurst half an inch thick and two inches across, and another tiny pat of German "*honig*," or hard honey. Added to this is one cup of hot black coffee.

After receiving our rations, Andris and I return to our barracks to help our "group" divide our bread into four pieces. For this task, my trusty pocketknife comes in handy.

We four Hungarians sharing tonight's bread loaf wait for someone to make the first move to divide it. The oldest prisoner among us has gray hair, and looks honest. So I hand him my knife. He marks the loaf into four even sections, and then slices each section neatly. The three of us bend over him as he performs his careful surgery, eagerly scrutinizing his handiwork. We're all starved!

"You have to allow for the narrower ends," Andris reminds him. "Everyone should get the same amount."

Our appointed bread cutter nods, patiently.

Finally, the task is completed, but now everyone wants the two biggest slices.

"Let's mix up all four pieces under a blanket," I suggest, "and then we'll each choose one without looking at it."

"Good idea," the bread surgeon agrees.

But now, all of us want to be first to choose. So we decide to draw straws. Andris gets to choose first, but he selects an end slice, anyway. I choose third, but I get a big piece from the center of the loaf. I offer Andris some of my bread, but he refuses. "Eat it yourself, Pista. You need to keep your strength up."

"I'm going to save some of my bread for tomorrow, then."

"Good idea, Pista. But eat what you need now."

As we munch our meager victuals, we hear loud talk all around us.

"What on earth are they arguing about down there?"

"They're arguing about how to divide the bread," I reply. "We have a knife. They don't, remember?"

Andris laughs. "I've got to admit, you're a genius, little Brat."

His compliment fills me with warmth, once again. With Andris's support, I can make it through anything. I only hope my own support and love can do a little of the same for him.

"I'm so glad I have a brother like you," I tell him. "I wouldn't trade you for anyone." For the first time in months, we both feel happy, and even a little optimistic.

Chapter Nine
A Rude Awakening

The next morning, I wake at 6:00 to the sun's rays dancing outside the windows of our new barracks. It takes me a few seconds to remember where I am. Then, recalling yesterday's events, I grope beneath my thin straw mattress. Ah, yes! Last night's bread is still there. At that alone, I feel a bit of happiness: I've somewhere to call my own, even if it's just a hard wooden bunk covered by a dirty straw mattress.

Suddenly, I hear one of the doors to our barracks open with violent force. Squinting hard against the sunlight, I can just barely make out the frames of four burly-looking men. As they advance rapidly toward the bunks, I recognize their uniforms, if not their faces—two uniformed SS officers and their uniformed aides. The mere sight of these uniforms makes my palms sweat and my heart race.

"Achtung!" yells one of the brown shirts.

Everyone around me stirs, most of us having been awakened from a sound sleep by the newcomers' noisy arrival.

The bunk I selected yesterday happens to be first in our row, just left of the door through which our unwanted visitors have come. Suddenly, two uniformed SS officers stand right by my bed, their heads only inches from my bare feet, cursing in German at no one in particular. They've kicked up a lot of dust storming their way in here; I see it swirling in the air. One SS impatiently taps the side of his shiny black boot with a mean looking braided horsewhip.

I can't even imagine what any of us could have done to receive this torrent of angry words raining down on our sleepy heads. After all, we've only just arrived.

Now, some of the dust from the floor rises up and enters my nostrils. I suddenly have to sneeze. I try to suppress it; I'm already too close to these thugs for comfort, and don't want them noticing me further. But my efforts fail. My "**ah-aH-AH-AH-CHOO**!" sneaks out and echoes loudly all through the barracks.

The four scoundrels turn now to look at me. A big lump hops into my throat and sits there, as if cemented inside. My heart pounds against my chest like there's a drum inside. Terrified I sense that these sadists have found the random scapegoat they're apparently looking for—it's me!

I now understand the reason for their untimely visit. They've come to make a point: we prisoners may *sleep* in these barracks, but they're *not* our home! Therefore, we shouldn't get too comfortable here, or (heaven forbid!) try anything sneaky. They can do whatever they want to us, anyplace, anytime! Just watch!

Now, as if to physically demonstrate precisely that, one shirted aide steps over and dramatically rips the thin gray blanket off my upper bunk. Then he grabs me, roughly, by both ankles, and begins yanking me, feet first, from my bed. Quickly, I manage to roll onto my stomach. On my way down, I grab the kickboard near the foot of the bunk to prevent falling headfirst on the cement floor. Images of helpless baby Peter, his tiny head bashed against that rusty boxcar wheel at Auschwitz, run through my mind. Maybe I'm next. God, help me!

Now I'm suspended in midair, white-knuckled, holding onto the kickboard with all the strength my hands can muster. But I'm still being tugged away from my bunk, feet first, by the brown-shirt.

The rhythmic tap-tapping of the SS officer's braided whip suddenly stops. Oh, no!

"Lousy Jew!" the SS with the whip bellows in a hoarse, raspy voice. Meanwhile, the brown-shirt continues squeezing my bare ankles with a bone-crushing grip. I clutch the kickboard with all my might so I won't fall.

Now I brace myself for the worst, not knowing if I'll live or die.

The first hard stinging "snap" of the SS officer's vicious horsewhip lands on my back. Several strokes later, when Hitler's henchman finishes flaying my lightly clad back, he next attacks my shaven head, and finally, my outstretched arms. I grit my teeth and try not to cry out, but fail. As the whip cracks down on against my arms and hands, my fingers lose the strength to hang onto the kickboard anymore. Just as I've dreaded, I fall to the floor, hitting the cement headfirst. But the pain of the fall pales in comparison to the dozens of lashes I've received.

I lie on my back on the cement, a crumpled heap, bleeding and moaning. Before I pass out, the SS officer with the whip completes his assault on me with a couple swift kicks to my rib cage.

Appel is called a few minutes later, though I don't hear it. When I wake, it's to the sound of Andris's anxious voice. He's shouting in my right ear, and shaking me gently by the shoulder. "Pista, stand up! It's time for Appel!"

"Can't."

"You have to! Stand up, Pista, or the SS will come back for you!"

"I can't move!"

"You must! You have to go to Appel. You know everyone has to be there. Here, Pista, let me help you." There's real fear in my brother's voice.

"Okay, Andris. I'll try." Grabbing my brother's hand, I sit up, slowly, every bone and muscle in my body begging me to stop.

"Good boy, Pista, that's right," Andris coos. "Easy does it. Put your arm around me, as tight as you can, and hang on. I'll help you stand up."

I wrap my injured right arm around Andris's neck. Slowly, gently, he pulls me to my feet. "Ouch! Ow, Ow! Oh, God! Okay. . . I made it." Loudly, I exhale.

I'm on my feet now, but every step makes me wince. As we shuffle along, Andris bends down to compensate for my lesser height. As gently as he can, he guides me out the barracks door.

Somehow, I stand at attention for the solid hour of Appel. After that, the two of us stagger back to the barracks. I eat my breakfast (last night's bread and black coffee Andris brings me) seated on the lower bunk. Fortunately, its occupant is outside the barracks somewhere. The bread I saved last night comes in handy to ease my hunger, which is keen despite my pain.

After eating, I climb back up into my bunk, with Andris's help, and sleep restlessly for several hours. Toward evening, I wake, every inch of my battered body still screaming pain. Andris helps me hobble my way out to a water faucet by the outhouse. "I'll wash the blood off you," he says. "You've got it all over."

Indeed I do. Each stroke of the whip drew blood. The cold water on my broken skin both soothes and stings me. The lump on my head from where I fell this morning still oozes blood. I flex my muscles and fingers. None of my bones are broken, thank God. On our return to the barracks, I force myself to make it under my own power. Andris walks beside me, as watchful as a mother with her sick, toddling child.

"Andris, why did they beat me up?"

"Because they felt like it. That's all the reason they need."

We walk a bit further in silence. Then Andris asks me, "Remember that book we read in school, *Through The Looking* Glass?" The one where Alice falls through a rabbit hole, and nothing on the other side makes any sense?"

"Yes."

"Well, Pistukam, in a sense, we've fallen through a rabbit hole. And I don't know when we'll get back."

The rest of the day, I take it easy. I'm still hurting badly, though, when the shrill whistle announcing Appel sounds for evening. Everyone lines up, except for Andris and me. I limp, as slowly as a gouty old man, with my brother painstakingly helping me along.

Despite my efforts, I can't stand up straight. In my imagination, I resemble Quasimodo the Hunchback, and right now, I feel just as tormented, too. After Appel (which lasts as long as ever) Andris helps me walk back to our barracks for the night. When I'm safely installed in my upper bunk, he disappears to fetch us both our dinner. This, it turns out, is a repeat of yesterday's evening meal. After eating, I'm fast asleep again, hours before anyone else hears the Capo bark "lights out!"

At Appel the next morning (at which I arrive stiff as a board and even more sore than yesterday) we're introduced to a small band of new, non-Jewish, fierce-looking arrivals. The same SS who beat me senseless announces that these individuals will now be in charge of our compound. There's already been some whispering amongst us about a couple of them. Our compound's new *Lager Eldtester* (first in command) is apparently a convicted three-time murderer. Hard looking and tough talking, he's in his late thirties, and very thin, with a stern face and a sharp, jutting chin. His dirty blond hair is cut in a brisk style.

A younger fellow, a Croatian, is second in command. He's twenty-six or so, and extremely handsome. Through the grapevine, we've also heard he's homosexual. We've been warned, too, not to let his ready smile and seemingly friendly manner fool us: he's as brutal as they come.

These two wear civilian clothes with special markings. Several other tough-looking characters form up the rest of our privileged new group of overseers. These *Capos*, the political prisoners of the Third Reich, are still, whatever their crimes, considered better than us Jews. Their charge is to keep us continually terrified and thus unable to disobey or even question the order of things. These thugs wear prison suits like ours, but with special armbands denoting their status.

After Appel, we're dismissed for breakfast. Today, Andris and I sit on the steps of our barracks, devouring our meager meal. My brother has always hated the way I slurp my food and asks me to eat more quietly. I guess he thinks I'm feeling well enough to be chided again. I respond by slurping louder. Things are getting back to normal for us.

The *Capo* dishing out food yells just then that a limited number of second servings are available.

Andris jumps up, quick as a cricket, and runs to get in line. Slowly, I rise, too, and limp toward the food line, eating the remaining *gemuse* in my bowl as fast as possible along the way. My mouth is so full that some of the *gemuse* dribbles from one corner. By the time my slow-moving body reaches the front of the line, though, all the extra food is has been dished out to others.

I limp back to the steps and sit down again. Suddenly, Andris reappears, carrying enough of a "second helping" for us both. Bless his heart! We divide the food evenly. To show him my appreciation, I don't slurp my seconds.

We're filling our bellies contentedly when we hear another command shouted by a new Capo: "Everybody! Line up at the *Magazine* in rows of five!"

Like exhausted ants on the march, we all fall into a tired, crooked line and head to the *Magazine.*

"Ouch!" I yell, as a hurrying inmate trips me by accident and I fall and scrape an already injured elbow.

Andris glares at the guy and shakes his fist. "Damn clod!" he yells, helping me up. The man who tripped me then realizes I'm the "injured boy" (word of yesterday's beating has spread quickly through the compound) and apologizes. It's hard to be angry with him, though, or with anyone here. We're all in the same boat.

Meanwhile, a *Capo* kicks a couple of older, slower moving prisoners right in the seat of their pants, just to show his authority.

"You see, Andris," I point out, "these guys don't need a reason to mistreat us, only an opportunity."

We line up outside the *Magazine*, as instructed. Each of the five lines of prisoners is so long, though, that it's a full hour and a half before Andris and I get inside. Once there, we receive our official camp serial numbers (written in thick black letters on the right side of our prison jackets). We're also issued woolen caps, towels, and a pair of small triangular-shaped gray felt cloths to wear inside our canvas shoes, like socks.

The man in charge of issuing these articles is another Hungarian, whom, to our surprise, we know. Laszlo Brichta has been another Istvan Street businessman, like our own father. Mr. Brichta, owns (or used to own) a thriving shoe business. Although he's apparently been here at Muldorf awhile, he appears in better condition than the rest of us, less tired and better fed.

Andris and I wonder what his secret is.

When we finally reach the front of his line, Mr. Brichta studies us intently, trying to place us. Then he remembers and smiles at us.

"Andris and Pista Nasser! Hello, boys! How are you?"

"Hello, Mr. Brichta! We're about as well as possible," Andris replies, sounding tired. We tell him of our brief stay at Auschwitz before coming here. He asks about Mother, but of course, we don't know.

Then Mr. Brichta asks me, "Pista, is it true you were beaten in the barracks by the SS yesterday, for no reason?"

I nod. My, how word spreads!

Grimly, Mr. Brichta exchanges my blood-soaked prison jacket for a new one. "Thank you, sir," I say.

Andris says, "Pistukam, let me help you change your jacket." Carefully, he removes my blood-stained jacket, and hands it to Mr. Brichta. "Thank you, sir, for helping my brother."

"It's the least I can do, son. I'd do more if I could. You both remind me of your father, and I was fond of him."

After returning to our barracks, I sleep again, uneasily, until waking to the whistle announcing tonight's Appel.

I climb down from my bunk, more easily than before, and manage to trot, rather than limp, to Appel after the others. I still have aches and pains, but I'm on the mend.

After the countdown, Andris and I line up for dinner. Tonight, it's a square of bread for every four prisoners; plus bologna, and the usual pat of margarine. We carry our food back to the barracks and dig in. This time, the same four of us complete our bread-dividing ceremony without any trouble. Those who received the smaller pieces last night get the bigger ones tonight.

Other prisoners all around us are still arguing about the unevenness of their bread portions. When I climb back into my bunk, I carefully hide my pocketknife under my mattress, lest someone see it and try to steal it.

"Lights out" comes at 9 p.m. sharp. I don't need a lullaby to put me to sleep, I simply pass out from sheer exhaustion.

The next day, the shriek of the Appel whistle jars us from our sound sleep at 5:30 a.m. It's still dark outside when Andris and I descend from our bunks, dress hurriedly, and walk to Appel. The early morning air is cold and misty today.

Appel this morning is our longest yet. We stand at attention in the chilly

Bavarian air for over an hour as a new *Capo* takes the count with deliberate slowness. Meanwhile, several other *Capos* scream at us, randomly, and kick and punch various prisoners for minor "infractions," like not standing up straight enough or daring to make eye contact with one of them. When the count is finally done, the *Capo* in charge reports it to the *Lager Eldtester* waiting nearby. If it's wrong, it must be done again, meaning we must remain standing at attention, hoping our legs won't buckle under us. Once the count is right, the *Lager Eldtester* gives his own report to the SS commander, and we're finally dismissed. Today, the dampness of the morning dew penetrates right through our thin cotton uniforms. My teeth chatter as we wait for this morning's Appel to end.

"At ease," the *Capo* finally barks, after two complete counts.

Like a pair of helium balloons suddenly deflated, Andris and I relax, and then take turns rubbing each other's backs in order to warm one another up again.

At breakfast, we're served our usual morning coffee. It's nothing special, but it tastes delicious in today's cold weather.

Much sooner than usual, the whistle blows again for yet another Appel. I can hardly believe our bad luck. We force ourselves to our feet. This time, though, the Appel is conducted differently. A *Capo* begins calling each prisoner by number. In about half an hour, Andris's number, "87356" is shouted, followed by my own number: "87357." Our fears about not being tattooed turned out to be baseless. These numbers were sewn into our uniforms when we arrived at this camp.

We all fall into our appropriate lines and wait at attention. None of us dares to ask what on earth we're doing now.

When everyone's number is called, twenty rows of prisoners have been formed, four to a row. Two SS in front, two in the rear, and one on each side form our guards. Each of those officers has a gun slung over his shoulder.

The SS in command of our new formation bellows: "You'll be marching in regulation steps wherever terrain permits. Anyone not obeying instructions or left behind the marching detail will be shot. If you're ill, you have no place here, and must report to your *Capo*. This is strictly a work detail!"

He pauses a moment, but no one dares admit to feeling sick enough to report to a *Capo*. Instead, our group makes its way through *Appel Platz,* and turns right, past the barracks and the area where the *Lager Eldtester* and his aide live. We're heading out of the camp.

Chapter Ten
Working to Live

The commanding SS shouts, *"In Gleichschritt, Marsch!"*

"Links. . . Links. . . Links. . . und Rechts," sounds the rhythmic command.

As we march in step, our silly looking wooden shoes make lots of noise. I'm glad we've been outfitted with those flannel cloths, which at least make the shoes a bit more comfortable.

The barbed wire gates of our compound are next opened wide as we continue marching, now in place, on the gravel just inside the compound.

"Links und Rechts!" comes the command again as we leave camp and enter the main highway. Now, we're headed back in the direction of Muhldorf itself. But about a mile before the Inn River, we encounter a dirt road that leads to a lovely, majestic pine forest. By now the morning sun's golden face is rising above the horizon. I take a long, deep breath of the clear, pine-scented air.

"Andris," I exclaim. "Isn't this a beautiful spot?"

My brother puts a finger to his lips. . . *"Shh!"*

We form a narrow column, two to a row, in order to traverse the slender path cutting through the forest. We're not in regulation step now. The fallen pine needles cushion our footfalls. In my imagination, I'm back in the land of fairy tales, Hansel and Gretel's Black Forest. Occasionally, the sun's rays break through the parting branches, and I can see dewdrops glittering on their needles, like little diamonds. Gosh! How breathtaking!

"Pista, watch your step!" Andris's voice interrupts my reverie as I narrowly miss running into a tree stump.

By the time the first clearing in the forest appears we've marched for over an hour. Meanwhile, the landscape has changed drastically, right before our eyes. Inside the huge clearing, construction is going on in all directions

We halt. Andris points leftward in amazement. "The SS wasn't kidding when he said this is a work detail. Look at all that equipment. . . those narrow gauge trains, the tractors, the work huts. . .!"

"There's even more stuff on the right," I tell him. Fallen trees, tree stumps, and roots are *everywhere*.

Our commander greets an Army engineer, to whom our detail is then released. Our other SS guards spread themselves around, finding comfortable spots from which to observe us working. Using their tent-like raincoats as blankets, they produce thick, meaty-looking sandwiches from their pockets, pour themselves steaming hot drinks from their thermos bottles, and eat and drink their luncheon fare with gusto. Just watching them makes my mouth water.

Next, our group is divided and taken, in smaller numbers, to a huge wooden chest full of picks and shovels. Andris and I both receive picks for tools.

"My God!" I exclaim. "This thing weighs a ton."

"Give it to me, then," Andris says. He takes my pick and compares its weight with his own.

"Take mine," he says, handing me his lighter one.

Our job for now is to dig around the many tree stumps and free some of the main roots. A heavy chain is then secured to the root, and a tractor pulls it, along with the attached tree stump, up from the ground.

Swinging as high as possible with our picks, we begin breaking virgin earth. The ground is fairly soft, with some occasional pebbles. Once in a while, though, the pick strikes a big stone. Then, little pieces of rock fly upward, and my arms hurt from the unexpected jolt.

As we work, the weather warms up. Soon, the hot sun and the swinging of the pickaxe overheat me. I remove my jacket. Perspiration runs down my bare chest. The physical workout actually feels good, at least for now. Whenever we discover any main roots, we get to rest, since it takes awhile to secure the chain around the exposed roots and hook them up to the tractor. During these interludes, we lean on our picks and sweat a lot.

Noon comes, and I'm starved. A canteen truck pulls in. We each receive a big portion of *gemuse* and a slice of bread. It tastes better than usual, because I'm really hungry from all the exercise. Everyone even gets an unexpected second helping today!

After lunch, Andris and I are sent to a far side of the clearing, near some trains. Here, Andris receives a giant wedge-shaped lever, made of solid wood and reinforced with strong metal. His job is to insert the lever underneath the rail, and then, with a block of wood placed beneath the lever itself, exert a lot of power in order to raise a section of the rail about a foot off the ground. Although my brother is tall, strong, and in good physical shape, the effort makes him groan. Once Andris manages to raise a small section of the rail, my job is then to shovel ten inches of gravel beneath that uplifted section.

We've been at it awhile. "Pista, put a couple more inches of gravel under this section," he says. I do so, as fast as I can.

Then I tell him. "I've got enough gravel under there. You can let go."

Andris eases the pressure on his lever. Ah! That section of the rail is successfully raised.

And so it goes, hour after hour in the hot afternoon sun.

It takes two weeks to clear out all the stumps and roots. We then begin cutting into the forest. For tools, we receive big axes and tandem lumber saws. Every now and then Andris and I switch off, since the swinging of the axe is especially tiresome. After chopping into a tree and removing a chunk of it, slice by slice, we saw into the trunk from the opposite end, and finally make it fall by pushing it over with a long pole.

"Timber!" we then shout.

The giant pines hit with a thud, crushing all the branches underneath.

By noon, we typically have a couple dozen trees lying around, like helpless fallen giants. Next, we haul away the trees. To do so, I first step over the trunk of one and hack its branches off with a smaller axe. This operation is not nearly as hard as felling the trees themselves. Some branches come off easily, while others cling stubbornly to the trunk.

One afternoon, when hard at work on our tree-clearing task, Andris and I hear a faraway drone. Dozens of white streaks appear high in the air, plowing through the cloudless sky.

Somebody yells, *"Look! Planes. . . the Allies!"*

At this, the SS guard fires a warning shot. Quietly, our group resumes clearing away branches. But we all have sudden new hope and energy. Everyone thinks the same thing: perhaps the Allies are near; our captivity could end soon.

The weeks drag by. The hard work, long hours, minimal food and rest, and frequent beatings begin taking their toll on even the strongest amongst us. Back at the camp, one barracks is set aside for those too ill to work, although no medical facilities of any kind are kept there. Basically, "Sick Bay," as they call it, is a place to be warehoused until you die. There are only two ways out of that particular barracks: the front door, which means immediate resumption of work, or the back door, through which the dead bodies are removed. Few ever leave through the front.

Should one be so unfortunate as to enter Sick Bay, he will immediately find his food portions drastically cut, leading soon to total malnutrition and finally, starvation. This will eventually kill him, even if the sickness or injury that brought him here does not. The worst cases are sent not to Sick Bay, but a separate "Dying Room" at the extreme end of our compound, guarded by the SS.

One morning after Appel, two *Wehrmacht* come by and select fifteen of us younger prisoners for a special work detail. Andris and I are both chosen.

"Pista, this is a good sign," Andris observes. We've been assigned *Wehrmacht* guards instead of the SS."

An open Army truck pulls up. Our group is in an especially good mood since we don't have to march to work.

I jump up into the truck with the others, with Andris right behind me. Craning my neck, I study the road ahead. It's familiar; we pass this area on our daily marches to and from work. Today we drive past the Inn River and the main street of Muhldorf's village. Soon we're in picturesque farm country. The dirt road ahead curves into a meadow. Beyond some green thickets, a large whitewashed farmhouse comes into view. As I glance back, I can see clouds of gray dust swirling in the wake of our vehicle. Our truck comes to an abrupt stop, its brakes squealing, and we're unloaded near a barn.

I point toward the big farmhouse, from where a man, a woman, and four children of various ages emerge. They stare at our bedraggled party in open bewilderment. "That's probably the farmer and his family," says Andris. "What a sight we must be to them!"

The farmer wears simple work clothes. His face, tanned by the elements, is kind looking and deeply lined. He surveys us, one by one, with a concerned look on his face.

"So you're the fellows they've sent to help us? *Mein Gott*! You boys all look starved!"

I almost reply, "Yes, sir, we are!" but think better of it.

"Sit down over there in the hay, fellows! Let's get some food into you before you start work!" He tells his family to bring us out some food right away.

The food his wife, son, and two daughters soon bring us tastes wonderful. There is fresh milk, white bread, cheese, ham, and genuine butter and honey. We can hardly believe our luck!

Andris gets right to work devouring his portions. With every bite, he closes his eyes, savoring the taste. "Best ham I ever had!" he declares.

After we finish eating, our two *Wehrmacht* guards have the farmer sign some sort of paper. Then we follow the farmer to his tool shed, where he distributes shovels and baskets, and next leads us into his potato field to help harvest his crop.

Soon we're hard at work, but feeling strong and happy from our breakfast. "Hey Andris, let's take some potatoes back to the barracks tonight," I whisper to my brother, who digs beside me. He's sitting on the ground, hunched over on one knee. "Good idea, Pista," he says, "but let's be careful."

"Sure." The morning sun sits just above the horizon, bright and shiny, and promises a good day ahead.

By midmorning, we've gathered lots of potatoes, but haven't yet to made a real dent in the huge field. Meanwhile, our *Wehrmacht* guards relax, enjoying themselves, soaking up the sunshine.

As I observe them lying around in the sunshine, the scene reminds me, somehow, of our family vacations at Lake Balaton. Just two years ago, Mother, Father, Andris and I sunbathed and swam there, without a care in the world. Now the whole world has changed, right beneath our feet. What I wouldn't give to know where Mother is now, what she's doing, and that she's all right.

"What are you thinking about, Pista?" asks Andris, taking a break from his toil.

"Oh, nothing."

"Come on, Pista. You're never quiet this long. *Something*'s bothering you."

"I'm just thinking about Mother."

"I thought so. If I know Mother, Pista, she's fine, and thinking about us, too, right this minute."

"You mean like mental telegraphy?"

"The word is *telepathy.* Anyway, Mother's fine, Pista. She's just missing us, the same way we miss her."

"I hope you're right, Andris."

I can't help wondering if Andris actually believes this, or if he's just talking this way for my sake. He's always so protective of *my* feelings, so keen to reassure me. I can't help wondering what actually crosses his mind about Mother, though, when he's all alone.

We resume work for a couple more hours.

When I next glance up, the sun is straight above my head. "Look Andris, it must be noon already. And there's the farmer, waving at us!"

In a loud voice, the farmer calls to our group in the field, "Everybody! Wash up for lunch!" Without removing the long-stemmed pipe from his mouth, he adds, in the same voice, "You've one hour to eat and relax in the hay."

At lunch, we're given all kinds of delicious food, including a German stew with big chunks of meat in it. We consume our lunch greedily. We even get pears and watermelon for dessert. When I finish, I'm too full to move for a while.

Once our lunches digest, we waddle back to the potato field for more digging and gathering. At the end of our day, the farmer, pleased with our productivity, gives us each a thick slice of homemade white bread. By now I have my jacket tucked into my pants, and stick my bread inside my jacket alongside the potatoes I've put there. I smile at Andris, who sports a similar little bulge around his middle.

On the way back, our truck passes the rest of our detachment (which has had to form a lumber detail today) trudging home. By the time it arrives, Andris and I have already gone back to the barracks and hidden our prized potatoes inside our mattresses.

After Appel that evening, we're served our dinner—the usual portions. For the first time I'm not hungry, so I save this food for later.

After dinner, Andris and I undress and climb into our bunks, covering ourselves with our blankets, heads and all, to take inventory. I have twenty-three potatoes; Andris has twenty-five.

"Today was like a birthday," Andris says.

"Speaking of birthdays, what month are we in, anyway?" I ask. He doesn't know, but we agree that most of the summer has passed.

When the whistle blows for Appel the next morning, the sun is already up. During today's countdown I sense something different about the mood of the SS. After we've been counted, our two SS guards are smiling, joking, and clapping each other on the shoulders.

"No work today!" one of them announces.

At first, no one moves. Did we hear him correctly?

"There will be no work today!" the SS repeats, louder this time, as if we all were deaf.

What's up? I wonder. Soon, brooms and rakes are issued to us instead, and we're ordered to thoroughly clean the grounds and barracks, inside and out.

After lunch, we're given orders to gather the blankets from our bunks and report to the Magazine. Here, we're given two much thicker blankets in exchange, and warmer uniforms to boot. Even our shoes, which are in the most miserable shape of all, are replaced for most of us. For the first time, we're even issued shirts, but no underpants.

By mid afternoon we have the barracks clean, and even the outhouse disinfected with special chemicals. For the rest of the day, Andris and I just sit around trying to figure out what is happening.

Jancsi, another Hungarian prisoner a little older than Andris, who before the war had trained to be an opera singer, leans against the barracks wall right beside us. "The Americans are getting closer," he says. "Maybe we can expect them any day." Could that be what all this sudden cleaning is about—the Third Reich trying to paint a pretty face on our miserable camp in case the enemy shows up? I wonder.

"But if they're so near, why don't we hear the shelling of the guns?"

I pipe up, "Maybe its because the Germans surrendered and the war is over."

In truth, none of us have any idea what's going on, but our speculations help us pass the time.

The next morning, hot coffee is served to us, along with a roll with margarine instead of sawdust bread, another first. By noon, when the *gemuse* smells different, and contains potatoes (instead of the usual peels) and chunks of meat, we know *something* is up!

Andris and I, with Jancsi and two others, sit on the barracks steps and try to sort it out.

One of Jancsi's friends insists, "The war *must* be over."

Jancsi's eyes sparkle. "If he's right, we'll be free soon!"

Andris comments, "*Something* is happening, but it might be a bit early to celebrate. If this war were over, why would the SS guys be so happy?"

We argue back and forth some more, without reaching any conclusion.

Then we all hear sounds of Army vehicles approaching. Jumping up, we see Army trucks passing through the compound gates, with bright red crosses marked on their sides.

All the SS officers, immaculate in their uniforms, stride up to the trucks in orderly fashion, followed by their *Wehrmacht* counterparts.

"Everybody into their barracks!" one of the *Capos* barks. We see military personnel, wearing uniforms we do not recognize, being welcomed by the SS.

As ordered by the *Capo*, we all line up in front of our respective bunks for inspection. It takes some time, though, before our barracks commander orders us to stand at attention.

The doors open. Nicely dressed military men in the strange uniforms we saw earlier enter. Maybe the war *is* over I think, hopefully. But the language I'm hearing these people speak is unfamiliar. Two high-ranking SS officers follow the strangers around inside our barracks.

"At ease!" another SS shouts at us, and we all relax our rigid posture.

Mercifully, this inspection is short. For an hour afterward, though, we're confined to our barracks. Then the whistle blows for Appel, and we rush outside. The trucks are gone by then, as are the mysterious strangers. The only evidence of their visit is a huge stack of cardboard boxes marked with red crosses. Before our eyes, these are quickly carted over to the compound housing the SS and the *Wehrmacht*.

Andris and I are so curious about the whole affair that we summon the nerve to approach our feared *Lager Eldtester* and ask him about the strangers.

"Sir," Andris asks bravely, "could you tell us who those foreign officers were?"

He doesn't say anything, but just stares at us with cruel blue eyes.

"So," the *Lager Eldtester* says, finally, "you want to know who they were, eh?"

"Yes, sir, if we may," Andris replies, haltingly, with deliberate diffidence.

"The strangers were Swedish and Swiss—they represent the International Red Cross." After that, the word spreads through the barracks like wildfire.

After the countdown, we see no SS or *Wehrmacht* anywhere around, which is unusual, although the *Capos* appear.

"Everybody!" one *Capo* commands, "Report to the Magazine with your new blankets."

By now it's clear—the big change of heart was not because the war is over, but just a farce to show foreign Red Cross officials that we prisoners are well treated, fed nourishing food, and provided warm blankets.

All lies, of course.

At the *Magazine* that evening we lose the thick blankets given us earlier, and never receive the parcels of food intended for us by the visiting Red Cross. But we have gotten two days off work, new uniforms, and better shoes.

And, with our hundreds of intended food parcels, the SS and *Wehrmacht* feast, courtesy of the Red Cross, for several weeks.

Chapter Eleven
A New Project

From today's vantage point at the opposite end of the big clearing, we've a bird's eye view of the colossal scope of the project on which we're being forced to work. Below us yawns a man-made canyon of gigantic proportions, at least two hundred feet deep and half a mile wide. I can't estimate its length, since it's already solidly built in, with only the roof still under construction. From here, what's already been built resembles a giant web of steel. The unfinished section of the roof alone is five hundred feet long. As for the rest of it, who knows? It stretches 'way under the forest. Trains already run into the structure on two different elevations. It looks like the entrance itself is three stories high, and the roof easily adds another fifty feet. Over this steel maze bridges span across, wide enough to carry narrow gauge industrial trains with their cargo of ready-mixed cement.

The next afternoon, we also meet a group of new prisoners from another concentration camp in the forest, called Wald Lager, a few miles away. This group is assigned to various other sections of the huge project.

The march home takes place without incident. About a mile from the barracks, Andris calls to me that he's spotted a semi-squashed dill pickle near the soft shoulder of the road. Quickly, he grabs it without the guard's seeing him. Just a few yards from there, I pick up a dried chicken bone. As always, we share our findings. Crunching away on the bone and sucking out the marrow, we enjoy every bit of it. Then we attack our respective portions of the pickle.

Back in camp, Appel takes longer than usual, as if to make up for the brevity of this morning's roll call. The *Capos* go over the count, again and again. Barracks are searched. All this goes on while we're still standing at attention, wondering what's up.

Then the SS commander steps forward. "One man is missing," he announces "In five minutes sharp, I want information on his whereabouts. If not, you Jew bastards will be sorry!"

Andris and I glance at each other fearfully. The minutes pass quickly.

The SS glances down at his watch. "Two minutes to go," he roars. Then he speaks again. "Anyone who comes up with information will not be harmed." He takes another hasty look at his watch. "Only one minute to go. . . thirty seconds. . . *You Jew bastards just ran out of luck!*"

Next, he rushes over to the first row of us, starting to count rapidly as he walks. *"Einz, Zwei,. . . nine, zen! Heraus do swine."* He grabs the tenth one of us by the collar and jerks him from the line-up.

The poor man just stands there, petrified. *"Einz, Zwei,. . . nine, zen! Heraus!"* With that, the SS officer pulls another terrified prisoner from line. By now, he's getting too close for comfort to where Andris and I stand. Will he make a third selection of, perhaps, one of us?

Whew, it appears not! Instead, the SS turns away from the line and barks a quick, raspy series of orders to two *Capos*, who then rush to produce, from a shed nearby, a long wooden table and a nasty looking whip. This instrument of torture sports a short handle and has dozens of leather strips attached.

Next, the Capos seize and manhandle the two selected prisoners, stripping them of their shirts and jackets and yanking their trousers down around their ankles. They then bend each man over the table, tying his fists and ankles tightly together underneath it, thus immobilizing him. The taller, burlier Capo next spits on his hand, seizes the whip, and begins furiously striking one man, then the other, with fast, vicious blows. Soon, each prisoner screams in agony. Blood drops spatter onto the table and then the ground beneath it. One prisoner's already passed out. The other moans loudly. By the time the twenty-fifth blow is struck, both have lost consciousness and lie still and helpless atop the red-specked table, like huge slabs of bloody meat.

I think I may be sick. But then I swallow hard and force down whatever wants to come up; I can't afford to draw attention to myself now because the SS in charge has begun his fierce tantrum again. "I want information!" he screams. "Step forward."

Everyone remains in place, silent.

"You have one minute." Dramatically, he checks his watch.

No one says or does a thing.

Our one minute elapses.

"I warned you bastards!" the SS screams wildly, his face now as red as a lobster's. With firm steps, he returns to the place in line just to the left of Andris and me, where he had ended with his previous count. Please, God, don't let Andris or me. . . *"Einz, zwei. . . "*

Andris is nine, and I'm, I'm number **TEN!** I gulp with horror. My whole body goes numb all at once. I can't believe my horrible luck.

I pray for God's help. But it doesn't come.

The *Capos* seize me, rip my clothes away, and hog-tie me naked beside the others. Soon after my beating begins, I lose count of the blows. Before passing out, I manage to look up and see Andris. He's standing at attention as best he can, with tears streaming down his cheeks.

I come to when a splash of cold water hits my face. I have no idea how much time has passed. I'm untied now, but still lying on the table as if cemented there. I'm afraid to move. The pain is indescribable. Andris gently cleans my wounds with a canteen of water he's fetched from the faucet near the outhouse.

"Are you badly hurt?" Andris asks through his tears. His eyes appear swollen, bloodshot, and bright blue from crying.

"I don't know." He finishes cleansing my injuries. A few minutes later, I gather all my strength and slowly stand up. As with my last beating, Andris must help me to stand. I walk, with difficulty, my gait slow and waddling. As we shuffle toward the barracks, each step brings me new agony.

Back inside the barracks, it takes me several minutes to maneuver myself into my bunk. Once up inside, I lie on my stomach. Andris tries to comfort me.

Despite my throbbing body, I'm actually hungry. Today's ditch digging was exhausting in itself, even without this later ordeal. As always, I've had little to eat, and today even less than usual.

Andris slices a boiled potato for me, and then adds a little margarine and a sprinkling of salt. He then fetches me a slice of bread from our secret stash beneath his mattress.

"Thank you," I mumble, and try turning sideways. I struggle to discover a way to lie down that will cause minimal discomfort. Try as I might, there's no way to get comfortable. They've really worked me over this time. With difficulty, I finish my dinner and switch positions again, and again, and again. Nothing helps. Whenever I move to a previously unexplored position, it hurts in new places, and in all the old ones, too. I don't want to tell Andris, but I'm very badly beaten, much worse than before.

"Do you know who was missing at Appel?" I ask him.

"Yes. While you were lying on the table passed out, one of the guards discovered a Polish prisoner in the outhouse. He was hanging from the rafters, hidden from view. A suicide."

So, as it turns out, I've been beaten half to death for nothing at all.

I don't tell Andris, but the pain from my beating feels so bad right now that I'd change places with the poor fellow, given the chance. Instead I say, "Those guards sure know how to spread the misery around, don't they?"

I don't know if Andris replies. Exhausted, I fall right to sleep, despite my agony, but it's the worst night of my life. I wake numerous times to try to get more comfortable, but always to no avail.

Chapter Twelve
Of Potatoes, Wood, and Bread

The next morning the whistle signals Appel. It's a slow, painful process climbing down from my bunk and walking to the *Appel Platz,* but I make it. Today, I'm selected to work in a farm detail, again to pick potatoes for a local farmer (a different one this time). Andris isn't chosen to accompany me. Instead, he must go with our usual lumber detail. I vow to bring him back some food from the farmer's kitchen though, and of course some souvenir potatoes.

The farmer for whom we work today is less pleasant than the previous one. And this time, before leading us to the potato field, our *Wehrmacht* guard announces:

"Anyone caught stealing potatoes will be severely punished."

Now I can't risk taking any potatoes back to Andris, and just when our stock is running low, too.

It's tough for me to bend down and work, due to my fresh wounds. The day passes, however, without incident. The food the farmer gives us is better than camp rations, but not as good as at the previous farm. I'm lucky, though, that I don't have to march to and from work today, or (heaven forbid) swing a pick.

This time, our farm detail returns to the camp later than the lumber detail does. We slide off the open Army truck to the sound of Appel being announced. I look for Andris, but don't see him. Just as I'm starting to worry, I spot him on Appel Platz. We embrace like long lost friends.

"Ouch!" I yell.

"Sorry. I was so happy to see you I forgot. How was potato picking?"

"The food was good, but I couldn't chance bringing back any souvenirs. They forbade us to."

"I'm glad you didn't. Apparently, in another potato detail a couple days ago, some guy was caught with potatoes on him and beaten to a pulp. He's in Sick Bay with internal bleeding and broken ribs."

Several days later, after lunch, I hear the sounds of airplane motors in the sky. I stretch out beneath the afternoon sun, near the electrified fence, and watch the German planes land. Beside my feet, I noticed a piece of broken clay brick. Picking it up, I'm about to toss it over the fence when an idea strikes me. I open the small blade of my pocketknife and begin chipping away at the clay brick. In about an hour, a tiger's head begins taking shape, complete with a mouth and fangs. Grabbing my new treasure, I run inside the barracks to find Andris.

He's lying on his bunk resting. For the first time I noticed how much weight he's lost and how hollow his cheeks have become.

"Andris, look what I've made!"

He sits up and looks at it. "Did you really?"

"Yeah, with my knife."

"Looks good, Pistukam. But what will you do with it? You can't eat it."

"Oh yes we can. I'll trade it with the guards for food. Wait till tomorrow. You'll see."

"You look tired, Pista. Why not lie down and rest?"

"Resting will not get us any extra food. But my carvings *will*!"

With that, I leave the barracks and scour the grounds for more carving materials. I find several pieces of clay and shove them all in my pockets. Walking by Sick Bay, I notice that one more barracks has been added. Hard daily labor and near starvation are cutting down our numbers, day by day. I have to find a way to get more food for Andris and me. I don't want either of us ever going to Sick Bay.

The next morning, as I march to work in the lumber detail, I find it noticeably harder to lift my feet. Either the distance is becoming longer or I'm getting weaker, fast.

Andris also drags his feet. "Does the march to work feel harder than before?" I ask him.

"To tell you the truth, yes," Andris admits. "My shoes feel like a diver's leaded boots." He points to some other marching prisoners. "Look at those fellows! They're in even worse shape."

I glance over at them. It's true; every one of us has lost considerable weight and strength, some much more than others.

"Andris, as long as I have my hands, my knife, and bricks to carve from, we'll have enough to eat. I just know I'll be able to trade my carvings for food."

"Okay, Runt. If you say so."

At the clearing, Andris and I are assigned, again, to dig ditches. Our *Wehrmacht* guard today looks friendly. He's graying, with a long droopy mustache and round, rosy cheeks. He sits on a boulder, his long legs stretched out before him, surveying our detail of twenty prisoners starting work.

I approach him. "Uhh. . . Herr *Wehrmacht*?" I begin, haltingly.

"Yes, son?"

I glance at Andris for moral support, but my brother looks worried about the conversation I've initiated.

"Go on son," coaxes the *Wehrmacht*. "Don't be afraid. What's on your mind?"

I swallow hard, summon up all my nerve, reach into my pocket, and produce my tiger carving. With an unsteady hand, I hold it out for the *Wehrmacht*'s perusal.

He inspects it, with admiration. "Beautiful!" he declares. "Where did you get. . . Hey, you. . ." he calls out to Andris and a couple other prisoners watching us. "Start digging those ditches!"

He turns back to me. "Where did you get this statue, son?" He takes a closer look.

"I carved it, sir," I say proudly. "Would you buy it from me?" I hold my breath.

"How much do you want?"

"Just some food, sir."

"All right. Let's see what we have here." He reaches inside his knapsack and produces half a loaf of bread. "Will this do?"

"Yes, sir!" I reach for the bread.

"Son, can you carve me a horse's head?"

"Sure! I'll have it finished for you tomorrow."

"Then I'll have some more food for you. In fact, I'll buy all the carvings you can produce. How's that?"

"That's wonderful. Thank you, sir."

I turn to go back to work.

"By the way," he adds, "we'll keep this a secret, won't we?"

"Of course, sir!" I remove my jacket, wrap my treasure inside, and then walk back to my shovel. Andris's glance catches mine as I resume digging. He smiles at me and winks.

At our lunch break, I give Andris half my "payment." He can't believe his eyes. "You're amazing, Pistukam. You never give up, do you? You're going to make it out of this hell, I know."

"We both will."

"Pista, when I see you doing all these amazing things, like getting us bread today, I know you have what it takes. If anything happens to me, promise me you'll always be brave. Carry on for both of us, and Father and Mother, too. All right?"

I can't hold back my tears. "Andris, what are you talking about?"

"Pistukam, I don't feel well. I haven't for awhile."

"You'll be all right, Andris. You just need to eat more. That's why I'm doing the car. . . car. . ." Now I'm crying and can't finish my sentence.

"Stop your tears, Pista, and pull yourself together. Our lunch break is almost over. Besides," he teases me, "you don't want your new sculpting patron to see you crying, do you?"

After lunch, I return to my ditch digging, shoveling the earth with a new vengeance. I try to dig and shovel my sadness away, but it just won't go. Andris has now admitted what I already know, but haven't wanted to voice, even to myself. I can't let the thought get hold of me. I can't give up on Andris, ever, no matter how bad he looks or feels. I'll carve wood or clay every minute for food. I'll destroy my whole headboard, and my kickboard, too, if that's what it takes. I'll keep my brother alive, damn it! See if I won't!

Before "lights out" tonight, I finish the horse's head, and even have fun doing it. Working on my carvings helps me keep my unpleasant thoughts at bay. After I finish, I begin sculpting a tiny Statue of Liberty. Doing this one makes me think of the United States, that magical land of the free, where *everything* is possible! How I'd love to see it someday!

Next, I think about all the thirteen-year-olds like me, all over the world, going to school, taking tests, learning Algebra and Latin. . . going home to a mother and a father, keeping their rooms clean, running errands—all the chores I used to detest. This kind of life now seems more like a fairy tale than a reality I once shared with other kids my age. What I wouldn't give to have my old life back!

In the morning, I deliver my horse's head to the *Wehrmacht* and show him the Statue of Liberty in progress. He wants to purchase both, so I promise him I'll finish the Statue of Liberty as soon as possible. For the horse's head I receive some German salami and some honey. Andris and I have a feast at lunch! While we eat, Andris's eyes shine with pride at my latest accomplishment. "Pista, you amaze me."

"Just wait, Andris. The best carvings, and maybe the best food, are yet to come!" I know somehow I've got to keep my brother's spirits up.

That afternoon, Andris and I resume our work on the ditches. Rain begins to fall. Our guards don raincoats and take shelter beneath the big trees, but our own work must continue. Soon our thin cotton prison jackets are soaked clear through. The brown clay we've been shoveling turns to mud; every shovel-full weighs a ton. My wooden shoes begin to feel like impossibly heavy leaded diver's boots.

Our work does not progress, but we must still go through the motions, rain or shine, instead of doing something sensible (like returning early to the barracks). According to those who run our camp and the superiors from whom they take orders, if a hundred of us die, new replacements can simply be brought in. But first, every ounce of work must be squeezed from us, even if it kills us. Literally.

The march back is rough in today's weather. As we trudge through the forest, chilled and shivering, our sopping wet prison jackets hang heavily on our backs. Stumbling along as best we can in our cumbersome prison shoes, we slip, slide, and occasionally fall in the mud.

Marching back to the barracks in these conditions makes me wonder how many in our detail, most already weak and starving, will likely end up in Sick Bay sometime soon. After Appel that night (during which we stand outside at attention, still freezing, for another full hour) the downpour finally eases a bit. We all receive our wet food; then rush to the barracks, where we clean the mud from our shoes as best we can and then rinse the shoes with our canteen water. We wring our clothes out and hang them all over our bunks. By now, my teeth chatter uncontrollably. I climb into the bunk beside Andris. Tonight, he and I use all four of our thin blankets to try to keep warm.

At Appel the next morning, many from our work detail are absent. Rumor has it that over in Sick Bay they've begun squeezing two "patients" into one bed, it's so crowded. With so many of us ill and unable to work, it's virtually certain that new replacements will soon arrive.

After Appel and breakfast, Andris and I march doggedly through the gates to work. Instead of actually marching, though, most of us drag our exhausted bodies (still wrapped in wet garments from yesterday's downpour) reluctantly along. By the time we reach the forest path, our advance has slowed noticeably. Midway through the forest, the SS officer stops the command and calls for a five-minute rest period.

Our eyes scan the whole muddy area, searching for dry patches of earth on which to sit. Unable to locate any, though, we turn our metal canteens upside down and perch precariously on those.

The SS, meanwhile, make themselves comfortable on the trunk of a fallen tree.

Seated on my canteen, I observe a tall slim Nazi taking a swig from a container. Then, from his knapsack, he produces a hunk of bread and a lump of smoked bacon. Whenever we had smoked bacon at home, Mother used to save the bacon rind, one of my favorites, and cook it in paprikas potato. I drool at the mere memory.

The Nazi cuts off the bacon and eats it, slowly, along with his bread. After a few mouthfuls, he carefully removes the overhanging rind and tosses it in the mud, four feet from where I sit, already salivating like one of Pavlov's dogs. I can actually smell the bacon from here. Or am I just imagining I can? I really don't know. Either way, I'm suddenly craving the taste of that bacon!

"Andris, did you see that bacon rind?"

"Yes."

"I'm going to grab it."

"Don't! It's a trap! That SS threw it there just to tease us. Look at that smile. He's just waiting for someone to make a move, like a lion stalking his prey."

"Alles abtreten!" the commanding officer shouts.

Ignoring my brother's warning, I lunge, right then, for the bacon rind with my right hand, and grasp it quickly in my palm. It's mine! I can practically taste it. . .

Sudden needles of pain all over the back and side of my hand. . . blood and skin and. . . oh no, what happened? I glance up, realizing, just then, that the same SS who threw the bacon rind in the mud has stepped straight down on my hand with his nail-studded Army boot, just as I grabbed for it. My hand hurts fiercely. But I refuse to cry out. I won't give the bastard that sort of satisfaction.

The sadist moves on without batting an eyelash, leaving my hand a bloody mess. Loose skin is ripped off in sections. I lick my wounded hand, and spit muddy blood back onto the ground. Animals lick their wounds; so can I.

"Stubborn brat! Look what that monster did to you!" I refuse to cry, but now Andris is crying for me.

I try to calm him down, to no avail. "Honestly, Andris, I'm all right. . . it doesn't hurt," I lie. "Here, have some fresh bacon rind."

"I hate bacon, especially now! Look at your hand! I'd kill that bastard with my bare hands if I could." His blue eyes blaze with hate.

Now the Nazi grins back at the two of us, me with my wounded hand, and my brother with his tears. I can't stop Andris from crying, but I won't let the son of a bitch know he's hurt me. I simply refuse.

I chew on the bacon rind while we march, telling myself the delicious tidbit almost compensates for my crushed hand. In my heart, though, I'm not so sure. I wonder how I'll manage to work today, or to do anymore wood carvings for my *Wehrmacht* benefactor.

Today, the *Wehrmacht* guard, now my friend and "fan," awaits me at the ditch-digging site. I present him his finished Statue of Liberty.

"Son," he tells me with hushed but genuine respect, "*this* is a work of art. You are very talented!" He thoroughly inspects the tiny statue, running his fingers gently along its fine details. "Let me shake your hand for a job well done!" he declares. With that, he reaches for my right hand.

"Sorry, sir, but I'll have to shake with my left hand today."

"My God! What happened to your hand?"

I tell him the story of the bacon rind and the nasty SS.

"Animals, beasts," the *Wehrmacht* mutters, and sends me off to clean my wounds as best I can.

He must have really taken a liking to me, I realize. Besides trading me more salami and real bread for the Statue of Liberty, at lunchtime he even brings me a portion of soldier's rations.

"Isn't this salami delicious?" I ask Andris

He doesn't answer, but just stares at my hand. "Does it hurt bad?"

"Just a little," I lie. "How is the *gemuse* the *Wehrmacht* gave us?"

"You can tell it was made for the soldiers, not us. It's delicious, with real chunks of meat in it. Pista, keep that wound clean, so it won't get infected, please."

"I will," I sigh. "Please, Andris, stop worrying about me and just enjoy our Statue of Liberty Lunch."

"I'd enjoy it more if I weren't worrying about what stupid thing you might do next."

When the Nazi with the bacon rind crushed my hand, my career as a carver ended abruptly. In fact, it's even hard for me to grab the shovel, now, and for a long time to come. What hurts most, though, is losing a way to "earn" the extra food that we, and Andris in particular, need so much.

Chapter Thirteen
Berry Bushes and Dog Food

After work today the SS guards march us back to camp via a different route, a less muddy one. Marching back is easier. By now our wrinkled clothes are dry; the late autumn sun has been on our side today. I estimate it must be late September or early October. If I'm right, Father has been dead a year already. We've not seen Mother in five months, and have no idea where she is. Is she being beaten? Going hungry? These thoughts make my heart ache as time drags on and on. How much more of this will we have to endure?

On our alternate route back to camp this afternoon, Andris and I march through a small meadow in the forest. Suddenly, some of the prisoners in front of us come across a strange-looking berry bush. The SS keep us moving, but everyone within reach grabs for a few handfuls of purple berries while marching past. By the time Andris and I reach the bush, no berries remain.

"Just our luck," I splutter. "God won't allow us even a few lousy berries."

"Calm down, Pistukam."

On we march; I watch a prisoner near me hungrily devour a berry.

"How does it taste?" I ask.

"A little sour. But delicious."

Back at camp, I try trading bread for some berries, but none remain.

After Appel and dinner Andris and I both lie down, exhausted. We realize we're getting weaker by the day. There's no hiding it from ourselves, or each other, anymore.

"Andris, do you remember that little place in Budapest opposite the Railroad terminal, where we bought French fries steaming hot, with salt on them?"

"You bet. Real hot fries."

"And how about the hot dogs with mustard and horseradish we bought in Angol Park?"

"Yeah. Yum. Those were the days."

"How about the Palatinus pool on Margaret Island? That water, and the artificial waves. Remember the hot thermal pool?"

"Boy, if we could just lie in that pool for five minutes!"

"And how about when we sat on the terrace overlooking the pool, and ordered some fresh Hungarian pastries and cakes?"

"Don't forget the hot perked coffee with whipped cream," Andris adds.

We both sigh, turn over on our empty stomachs, and fall asleep, visions of happier times filling our heads as we drift off.

The whistle blows for Appel. Quickly, we get up and prepare to head outside.

On our way out Andris points to a man in our work detail, doubled up in his lower bunk, groaning in misery. "I wonder what's wrong with him? He was fine yesterday."

"What's wrong with your buddy?" I ask the prisoner climbing out from the bunk beside the sufferer's.

"It's those berries from yesterday. Some of the men who ate them have died already, and others are dying. They were poisonous."

At this news, I stiffen. "Thank God, there were none left for us," I tell Andris. Then to myself, I continue, *"Thank you, God, for sparing Andris and me from that poisoned bush."* I keep my thoughts going, as if talking to God. "In the future, dear Father, I will not ask for your help when I'm in trouble. But when I've solved my problems, I will thank you for the strength and wisdom you have given me. Is that all right with you?"

I receive no answer, but the earth doesn't swallow me up, either. Right then and there, I settle my differences with the Almighty.

Today even more prisoners are missing from the count. We wait in anguish to see if we'll be punished for the absent ones. Fortunately, though, Appel comes and goes without incident. The absentees are in Sick Bay, apparently. Daily our peers are dropping like flies.

Marching to work this morning, there's a sharp bite of cold in the air; we must keep moving to stay warm. Frost blankets the meadow. Clearly, winter is around the corner.

Replacements soon arrive to maintain the total work force. The cycle continues. New people arrive, and then rapidly waste down to our own sorry condition or worse. When they can't hang on any longer, they're sent to Sick Bay. From there, nobody knows what becomes of them.

One cold morning, gentle snowflakes melt against my hot breath as we march to work. I can see my breath in the frosty air. The pine trees are dressed in white. Our clumsy wooden shoes leave big imprints in the freshly fallen snow.

When Andris and I arrive at work, we're assigned to the roofing operations with about eighty others. The steel webbing is now completed, arching over a big ditch. The cement trains must have been busy for some time, dumping their slippery cargo onto the steel webbings. Only about twenty feet remains to be filled in. I'm given a long round pole with a craterlike metal sleeve at the bottom. This pole must be moved up and down in the cement to remove any air bubbles.

It's a real job to climb down inside the metal webbing, five feet above the level of the mushy concrete. I try to be sure-footed, not wanting to become a permanent part of the roof by falling, feet first, into the cement quicksand. I stand at about a fifteen-degree angle to conform to the arched steel structure. In half an hour, though, I'm sick to my stomach. Standing on an inch-thick bar, at a slant, suspended in midair, and pumping continually on a pole make me feel extremely dizzy. My feet are ice cold, too, and my thin clothing gives me little protection against the icy wind. My fingers have grown completely numb. The cement below actually looks inviting: a quick solution to end my suffering. I reject the thought, though with effort, and keep working, stamping my feet and blowing warm breath onto my fingers. By now, my exposed ears are almost ready to fall off. Why do we have to have so many body parts to make us miserable at times like this?

When lunchtime finally comes around, it's a challenge to climb back to ground level through the giant maze. My frosty fingers don't want to bend normally, and my legs don't wish to move at all. But I make it back, slowly and carefully, to collect my portion of hot *gemuse*.

Beside the shed, where the cement sacks are stored, lie a lot of empty sacks. Andris and I dig into them. Then, with help from my knife, we fashion two sweaters, first cutting off the corners for armholes, and then cutting "V" shapes for the head openings. Then we wrap our legs, up to the knee, and tie on our new "leggings" with strings we unravel from the seams of the cement sacks. Next, we design hoods for our new "jackets" by cutting open one of the long seams. After that, we place our new "jackets" over these hoods to keep them secured to our bodies, thus protecting our heads, ears, and backs. After lunch, we climb back into our frosty maze, still feeling the cold, but now much better protected against it.

The result is amazing! The cement sacks retain our body heat and make the weather far more bearable. My dizzy, nauseous feeling returns, though, as soon as I resume my slanted position agitating cement.

Meanwhile, the cement trains keep coming over the bridge, continually dumping their loads. After a couple more hours of agitating cement, I must now climb higher, since the cement level itself has risen nearly a foot. Together, the trains and the cement mixers make an almost deafening racket.

Snow starts falling again this afternoon, making Andris and me especially grateful for our new "jackets" and "hoods."

A couple hundred feet from where we work, some kind of excitement is happening.

The falling snow obscures much of our view, but from here it looks like someone has fallen into the cement. I motion to Andris, since he's working too far away for us to actually talk. He, too, is busy trying to figure out what's causing all the commotion.

The afternoon passes slowly. By the time I finally emerge from the maze for good today, I really feel sick.

"Hey, fellas!" calls a prisoner still working near the cement mixer, as Andris and I both waddle past him on our rubbery legs.

"I wonder what he wants," Andris remarks, brushing lots of snow off his eyebrows (one of the areas our makeshift hoods and jackets don't protect).

We approach the half-frozen prisoner who's just called to us. When we draw close, I notice his fingers are blue from cold as he shovels spilled cement into a wheelbarrow.

"Hi. Did you call us?" I ask him.

"Yes. Were you two on that roof detail, agitating cement this afternoon?"

"We were," Andris answers, stomping his feet and blowing on his numb fingers to prevent frostbite.

"Did you see my brother Tamas fall into the cement?" the man asks, leaning on his shovel as he bursts into loud sobs.

"We saw something going on, but. . . "

"There were five of us brothers," he interrupts. The poor fellow is shaking now, with a combination of cold and grief . "They're all dead now but me. Tamas was the last of them to go."

Andris and I try to comfort him as best we can, knowing there's nothing, really, that we can say to ease his suffering. To be all alone, especially in a God-awful place like this, must feel unbearable to him! Silently, I thank God, once again, for my one and only brother. "God, don't let anything happen to Andris. I don't know what I'd do without him."

After work, marching back to the barracks is harder than ever. Many prisoners slip and fall along the way, from sheer exhaustion. Others must be helped along, especially for the last mile. Soon after getting back to camp, we notice a lot of strange new faces. These are replacements, we glean, for numerous others who have either died or become too ill to work.

After our usual dinner, Andris and I take inventory of all our hidden supplies. We have two extra portions of sawdust bread and salt. We also have an extra spoon, one pencil, my knife, and our newly fashioned cement sack winter "wardrobes." I hide my portion of surplus bread under my mattress, just below my head, and shut my eyes.

Closing my eyes always helps me enter a private sanctuary of thoughts. Tonight, I use this time to review the situation Andris and I find ourselves in, and to try and make some survival plans for the future. Hunger is my Number One enemy, followed by weakness, cold, and the unexpected beatings.

I'll need to save as much bread as I can for those days when we'll need extra energy. Still, I *must* find a way to get more food, if Andris and I are to make it through all this. I think hard for a solution, but tonight nothing comes to me.

The bad weather soon, in fact, proves to be a major killer of our already sick and weakened work force. Colds develop into pneumonia and other respiratory miseries. Now my feet begin giving me trouble with increased regularity, too. I develop sores on both ankles from my endless tramping around in ill-fitting shoes and inadequate socks. The sore on my left ankle has opened up, and pus now oozes out regularly. I use a strong saltwater solution to minimize the infection, but still, it won't disappear. Sometimes it heals a little, only to break open again.

I cut pieces from the paper cement bags that have now piled up under our mattresses and make a pattern to fit inside my shoe. This will keep my frostbitten feet warmer, I hope. If I cut the cement papers into small sheets, I can even start my own diary. I'll pierce the pages with a nail, and then connect them all with wire. A few sketches added to the various pages will give the diary a colorful touch. Art was always a favorite subject of mine in school, so why not put my talent to use? At the same time, I can while away some of the long evening hours.

A dog's sudden bark interrupts my thoughts. I must have been lying there with my eyes closed for quite awhile. The lights in the barracks are out already, and everyone's asleep. I climb down from my bunk to visit the outhouse. Outside, the night is dark and windy, with the snow flurries zigzagging around in crazy patterns. The lights outside the barracks tint the bright white snow a golden hue.

No one is allowed outside the barracks between "lights out" and Appel. Going to the outhouse is the only exception. This regulation is clear and strictly enforced. From barracks door to outhouse, the shortest path must be taken. We've been ordered to walk close to the barracks walls, where it is well lit, and observe a ten-foot wide imaginary corridor to and from the outhouse. The guards manning the turrets have strict orders to shoot any prisoner stepping out of this corridor during the curfew.

The cold wind blows snowflakes in my face as I step outside the barracks door into the freezing night. Across the corridor sits a small barracks occupied by the *Lager Eldtester* and his aide. Outside their door, a doghouse shelters a well-fed German shepherd, chained most of the time. His bark must have been what woke me earlier. Only the tip of his tail protrudes from his doghouse opening. I'm thirty feet from him when I pass, but he doesn't move. He can't be hungry, since he still had his bowl of food, mounding high with snow. The outhouse, as always since the weather turned cold, is engulfed in rising manure steam. I take a deep breath, and then quickly let myself inside. My stay outlasts my breath. Involuntarily, my lungs suck in some more air before I can finish. *Phew!* Then I wait inside the doorway, thrusting my nose out often for fresh air as I begin to scheme. The searchlight from the far-end turret barely sweeps by. I leave the outhouse and step into the well-lit corridor. Instead of heading back to my barracks, though, I quickly move out of the bright lights and enter into the forbidden side. I walk softly in the fresh snow toward the doghouse, realizing, with a sick feeling, that I'm taking a chance of being discovered and shot for snatching some dog food.

I can still change my mind. But I don't. The image etched in my mind of Andris's hollow face makes me risk it. The wind is in my favor, blowing from the direction of the doghouse. Hunched over, and with butterflies turning summersalts inside my stomach, I reach toward the dog's bowl, keeping my eyes glued to the tip of his tail. My fingers grab the food but I can't lift it out! Apparently, the dog's food is frozen to the bowl. With my arm stretched all the way out like this, I simply don't have enough power to lift it up. That damned SS who stepped on my hand! It's still impossible for me to move it normally.

Uh oh! Now I see the dog's tail move, just slightly. I freeze in my strained position, like a human icicle. Minutes pass, long ones. My knees and legs ache from supporting my chilled body in this awkward posture. Now the searchlight comes around again. I mustn't panic. The light hits me! I hold my breath. The light stops, about six feet past me, and then slowly continues. I must make my move; it's now or never. I'm twenty inches from the sleeping dog. If I use both hands, I can remove the frozen food from the bowl. Quickly, I grab the food, pry it from the bowl, and hurriedly conceal the icy pack beneath my jacket. Cautiously, I make my way back to the corridor and my bunk. I place the dog food in my own *gemuse* bowl, and hide it beneath my mattress. Bow-wow! What a feast for tomorrow!

And what a night it's been!

Appel comes, very quickly.

Andris shakes me. "Pista, get up!"

"I've hardly slept," I say, sitting up and rubbing my eyes. "But look what I have for us." With a flourish, I lift the mattress, exposing the dog food.

"Where did you get that?"

"Let's get to Appel and then I'll tell you the whole story."

After Appel, the warm coffee we receive helps us get circulation back into our bodies, which are numb from standing at attention in the freezing cold. I then share the dog food, and my adventure, with Andris.

He hugs me. "Pista, you're *terrific*. I don't know what that dog had to eat, but *our* food is delicious."

Mostly new faces meet us when we assemble for today's work detail. These prisoners appear in better shape than Andris and me, at least for now.

Chapter Fourteen
Toil and Trouble

This morning, the march to work through the cold muddy forest is tougher than ever. Andris falls often in the mud. With increasing difficulty, I help him up, usually slipping and sliding myself in the process. We both look like muddy messes by the time we get to work, and we feel the way we look.

Today we're assigned to the cement detail, same as yesterday. Before we start work, I find a few more empty cement sacks with which to fashion us some new "hoods" and "jackets" against today's bad weather. I plan to use the left over cement paper to supplement the diary I'm writing.

This morning we work beside a huge wooden structure, two stories high. A long ramp extends from the first story to the second at a forty-five degree angle. Filled cement bags (each weighing seventy-five pounds) must be carried up the ramp on our shoulders. At the top of the ramp, two fellows wait to remove the cement bags from our shoulders, open them, and dump their contents into a large funnel, which then feeds the cement to a giant mixer. Twenty-five feet away, on the same platform, sits a mound of sand mixed with pebbles.

Beside this mountain of dirt is another funnel, about six feet by six feet. This funnel is five feet deep, with a cylinder-like rotor, its steel blades stretching across the bottom to crush the pebbles and mix them with the sand. On the other side of the structure sit all the other various heavy pieces of mixing equipment.

Right below where we toil, trains move continually back and forth, their special tiltable cars filled with cement. One after another, they cross the bridges to dump their cargo onto the massive roof structure, webbed under by the steel maze. This whole operation ticks along like clockwork.

Today, Andris and I are put right to work carrying cement sacks up the ramp. At the bottom, other prisoners place the heavy sacks across our shoulders, halfway up to our heads. We must grab the corners of the bags above our shoulders, and in a stooped position, carry bag after bag up the ramp. We then go back down for more.

In almost no time, the strain of toting the sacks overwhelms me. After just a few trips, my legs give out, as if made from straw. Weak as a scarecrow, I tumble down the ramp, bursting the cement sack I've been carrying along the way. Dazed and breathless, I glance up from my sprawled position only to see the same SS who crushed my hand advancing menacingly toward me. His eyes look crazy with rage. Looming above me like the monster he is, he kicks me in the ribs, screaming, "Get up, you lazy Jew bastard!" I'm almost halfway up when he kicks me again. "On your feet quickly, you louse!"

He orders me back to bottom of the ramp to get more bags. Now my legs feel like thin rubber sticks, ready to collapse beneath me any minute. Tears of exhaustion and despair stream down my cheeks. From the corner of my eye I see Andris's tortured look as he watches my predicament, unable to help me.

I'm halfway up the ramp when my legs fail me again. But this time, the Army engineer in charge of this operation stops the SS from further abusing me.

"This operation is my responsibility," the engineer tells the sadistic SS. "Can't you see that this boy is too weak for this work?"

The SS glares at me, and curses me under his breath, but returns to his post.

"Come with me," the engineer says. My wobbly legs move as fast as they can to follow him back up the ramp.

Somehow, I make it to the platform, where he then hands me a shovel. "See this sand?" he says. "Shovel the sand into this funnel. Make sure to pick out the big stones and throw them down there." He points to the ground, where a circle is marked to contain the stones.

"Yes, sir."

"One word of caution, son: *Don't slip into that funnel.* See those steel blades? They ground up a guy few weeks ago! Nothing left of him! He's now part of the ready-mixed cement!"

"What a horrible way to die," I think, recalling yesterday's accident that killed the brother of that guy we met late in the day. But I say, simply, "I'll be careful. And thank you, sir, for your kindness. You've really helped me out."

He smiles reassuringly at me before departing. It takes me half an hour, though, to overcome my nausea from being kicked, and to catch my breath from the strain of lifting and carrying all those sacks. My new job is painless. But now I fret about Andris, who's been working doggedly all this time, in his own poor condition, at the sack-lifting job I can't handle. I stop to glance at him whenever he nears my platform toting more sacks. With each trip up the ramp, he appears more pale, more stooped, and closer to collapsing.

"Please, God," I pray, "I know I told you I'd never ask you for favors for myself. But I'm not asking for myself. I'm asking for Andris. *Please* help him! He can't take this punishment much longer!"

In about fifteen minutes, the same engineer who saved me earlier relieves Andris, and switches him to the much easier task of removing the cement sacks from the shoulders of others.

"Thank you, God!" I begin weeping again. But this time it's from relief.

Today, though, instead of marching back to camp at our usual time, we're given extra hot food and ordered to keep working into the night. The cement machines just can't be stopped at this stage. We're given an hour's rest at dinner, which is served in shifts so that some of us prisoners are always working.

Andris and I have separate dinner breaks tonight. We've both been up since before five-thirty this morning, and it's now 7:00 p.m. The dinner break over, I'm quickly back shoveling sand and throwing big stones down into the circle. Andris looks a little better, though, having rested and eaten. Maybe the worst is over.

A few minutes later, however, my shovel hits an unusually large stone. I must use both hands to lift it, but when I do, it's too heavy for me to throw into the designated circle. Deciding I'll deal with it later, I set the big rock down and resume my shoveling. When I glance up at the sound of heavy footsteps, I recognize my nemesis, the hand-crushing SS who also kicked my ribs today.

Rushing over to where I stand shoveling, he jabs his finger at the marked circle. "*That's* where the stones go, you stupid ass!"

"Sir, I tried, but that stone is just too hea. . . ," I attempt to finish my sentence, but before I know what's coming, he knocks me to the ground with a solid fist, right to my nose. Blood runs down my throat. I swallow it and catch my breath, just barely. I'm lying on the ground, right beside the giant grinding funnel. He kicks me hard in the ribs again, several times. I manage to grab his foot, just above my face! I see those steel nails coming down on me, and God knows, I've felt them before. I can't allow this beast to mangle my face like he did my hand. Infuriated further by my resistance, the monster grabs my shovel and begins beating me with its handle. I curl myself into a ball. Finally, I manage, somehow, to grab the shovel. This makes him just about foam at the mouth, like a rabid cur.

Next, he yanks the shovel from my hands and aims its blade straight at my head. This is a fight for survival!

I deflect the blade by swinging my arm sideways. He misses. I grab for the handle and wrestle the shovel away from him, tossing it into the funnel. Soon I hear the loud crunch of steel and wood against the grinder as it quickly and greedily devours the SS monster's lethal weapon. But then, my enemy lifts me up by the waist, prepared to toss me alive into those hungry steel blades. And then. . . blackness!

When I come to, Andris's pale, frowning face hovers over me. He tries gently to lift my head, but he cannot. The blood that has dripped from my head as I have lain there unconscious has actually become frozen to the cement sack I lie on! From somewhere, someone brings enough hot water to thaw the frozen blood from my face. Finally, I'm able to lift up my head from off the sack.

Andris helps me to my feet. I'm determined to walk on my own, and I do, but shakily.

I move my hand about my face, feature by feature, making sure everything's still attached. Nothing is missing, but my nose and lips are badly swollen, and both hands are cut, scratched, and bloodied.

"Andris, what happened to me?" I ask.

"What's the last thing you remember?"

"That last things I saw were the blades of the grinder. Before that, the SS had lifted me up and was going to throw me in. I don't remember anything after that."

Andris says, "I was unloading cement bags at the top of the ramp with my partner when I heard screaming. I looked over and saw the danger you were in, and I yelled for help. The engineer came charging up the ramp. When the SS lifted you up to throw you into the funnel, the engineer ordered him to stop and yanked you out of the SS arms. He's the one who laid you down on the cement sack, too. Later, he went and got the hot water to thaw your blood from the sack."

I turn to the engineer, my savior, who still hovers nearby, watching me stagger around trying to get my bearings. *"Danke schoen,"* I tell him softly, through my swollen lips. "Thank you so much, sir, for saving my life, and for everything else you've done for my brother and me today."

He just looks at me, offering no reply but a nod. The mere look in his eyes seems to say it all, though, *"I'm ashamed of the German army, the SS, and the whole so-called human race."*

Andris and I turn to descend the ramp, slowly, and thus begin our long march back to camp. Halfway down, I glance up at the engineer again to wave good-bye. He's facing away now, with only his profile visible. He's stooped over, his head in his hands. It looks like he's weeping.

On our way back to camp, I need a lot of help just to keep moving. Poor Andris tries to hold me up, but he needs assistance himself. Somehow, though, we both make it back

It seems the whistle signaling Appel the next morning comes around in record time. I struggle to wake up and get going, even more than usual. Before getting out of bed, I feel the pulse in my wrist. I've developed a fever overnight. From his bunk, Andris leans over me, carefully examining my wounds.

"Your face looks awfully swollen, Pista, and your nose and lips look like they're running into each other. Can you make it to Appel?"

"If I don't, they'll send me to Sick Bay." We both know, without saying it, that going to Sick Bay would simply put me one step closer to death.

"Let me help you down, then," says Andris. With Andris guiding me, I make to the floor from my bunk. From there, each step is a separate struggle. I'm stiff and sore, from head to toe. I don't know what hurts most: my rib cage; my head; my hands and wrists; my back and shoulders; my legs; my hips; or some other part of my body. I must admit, Hitler and his cohorts have weakened me, physically. Mentally, though, they never will!

After this morning's Appel, the SS sends a fresh unit of prisoners to the cement detail, thank God. Andris, and I, and all of others who worked late yesterday are assigned easier jobs around the camp. I'm selected as a kitchen helper. Andris is sent outside the fence to the SS barracks for duties.

The kitchen (the same one from which I once stole potatoes) is a long barracks with two doors: one in the front, the other in back. I'm taken through the back door where the German chef, a big man with sandy hair, assumes custody of me.

Upon first seeing me, he's horrified at how I look. "What on earth has happened to you?" he asks.

I explain.

"Sit down, son," he says when I finish.

I sit. He disappears, soon returning with a first-aid kit. "Take off all your clothes," he says. I do as I'm told. Then, taking a few step backward, he surveys my naked body, a shocked expression on his face. "*Oh my God!* Did one man cause all these wounds?" Without waiting for my reply, he begins feverishly applying a disinfectant all over my body with fresh cotton swabs.

"Some are old sores from previous beatings," I tell him. I wince whenever he cleans an open wound. He works on me for half an hour, cleansing and dressing all my wounds.

When finished, the chef disappears again, this time bringing back a cheese sandwich with butter on it, and a cup of hot coffee with sugar. His kindness makes me feel guilty about having once stolen potatoes from him. I sense, though, that he'd understand.

After I eat, I actually feel pretty good, considering the rotten shape I'm in. My wounds have been treated, my stomach is full, and the kindly chef's kitchen is warm and cozy. I feel almost human again.

My new job in the SS kitchen is to peel potatoes. These peels must be thin. I'm given two buckets, one with clean water, into which I must drop the peeled and quartered potatoes, and another empty one, where the peelings are to be disposed of, later to make up part of the prisoners' *gemuse* diet. It takes me a while to get my fingers working, but the chef is patient. I try to keep moving around as much as possible as I work, so my aching body won't stiffen up even more.

Lunchtime arrives, and to my surprise I receive regular SS rations. This food is excellent; there is meat, potatoes, and real bread with butter. If I can keep this job, I'll survive, I realize.

Around 2:00 P.M., I'm dragging out the garbage through the back door of the kitchen when I glance up, suddenly, in the direction of a loud whining sound. Sirens! Soon, the whining noises mix with other sounds of explosions and machine gun fire. Instantly, I hit the dirt.

Then, as if from nowhere, American planes appear in the heavily overcast sky. The military airport nearby is under major attack! From where I lie, I can see German pilots scramble for their planes, many of these men falling to the ground as they go, beneath showers of bullets. Some of the Messerschmidts attempt to take off, but none make it above treetop level—they're blasted out of the smoke-filled sky and then crash and burn on the ground.

After the surprise attack ends, the airstrip is ruined: it's now filled with craters, burning fuel, damaged trucks, and other useless equipment. The surrounding buildings are shattered.

Now I hear a fighter plane right near the kitchen barracks make a final low sweep, blasting away with a machine gun. The ground right beside me is ripped apart, leaving a dusty trail, swirling rapidly toward where I lie. Just in time, I roll over and switch positions. The trail of bullets misses me by only a couple of feet. I wait until the gunshots and other noises sound like they're coming from further away, and then walk back into the kitchen to resume my work. The whole ordeal lasts less than fifteen minutes, but seems much longer. Thank God for the Americans, I think, even though they nearly killed me just now!

After calming down, I return to work, just as if nothing at all had happened. I certainly can't share with my bosses in the kitchen my joy about the closeness of the Americans, or all the damage they've inflicted.

Just about now, another man enters the kitchen through the same back door. He looks to be a tough character. He turns out to be the second chef in charge, but he obviously lacks any of his boss's friendliness or kindness. He struts around self-importantly in the kitchen, supervising various workers and activities. When he arrives at my work station, he appraises my battered face.

"Got a beating, eh?" he says sarcastically. "You probably deserved it. You'd better do your job and follow orders, or the beating you got before will be nothing compared to the one I'll give you."

I say nothing.

He continues, "Here in this kitchen, you prisoners get exceptionally good food. Don't ever take any of it from here! Eat what you're given and leave the rest. Understand?"

"Yes, sir," I reply, in a tone I hope sounds humble enough.

During Appel that evening, I search for Andris, wondering how his day spent in the SS barracks has gone. But during the count he's nowhere in sight. Standing at attention, I don't have a clear view of everyone, I realize; I'm probably just overlooking him. When we all line up for dinner, though, I still can't find him. Now I'm worried.

Quickly, I return to the barracks; maybe he's there for some reason. But when I reach our bunks, Andris's mattress is folded over, a sure sign of an abandoned space. A lump forms in my throat. I swallow hard. When I see our barracks commander standing around nearby, I rush over and ask him, "Sir, have you seen Andris?" By now, I'm already half crying.

"Your brother was taken to Sick Bay early this afternoon," he reports. "He was too weak to perform his duties."

Instantly, I'm filled with dread.

Next, I rush over to the Sick Bay barracks. Here, I'm told by the *Wehrmacht* on duty, "No visitors allowed." Frantically, I ask him, "But have you seen Andris? Have you seen my brother? A tall, light-haired Hungarian fellow. . ."

"There are many new people here. I don't know."

"May I go in and look?"

"I am sorry. No visitors are allowed inside."

Tonight I can't sleep. I toss and turn, worried and scared. This is the first night Andris and I have spent apart since this whole ordeal began.

By morning, my swollen eyes match the rest of my misshapen face. I still have my kitchen job to do, though. Today I must be extra careful; the nasty second chef is the one in charge of the kitchen and all the workers.

Andris is probably all right, I tell myself. He's just having a much needed rest for a change, which will do him good. I'll figure out a way to smuggle him some food.

At lunch, the meal tastes good, but the portions are smaller than yesterday's. I wish the other chef were here. After eating, I write in my diary. As I work, I feel someone's eyes on me. Looking up, I see another prisoner. He's skinny and pale, like the rest of us, with a long face. His lower lip hangs to one side. His unwanted attention annoys me; I wonder to myself if he's as stupid as he looks.

"What are you writing?" he inquires.

"A letter of complaint to Hitler."

"Really? That might be a good idea. Do you think it could help us?"

I don't bother answering. My anxiety over Andris's condition has put me into the worst mood I've been in since I came here.

That night, I discover Andris's bed had been assigned to someone else, a Greek Jew. He looks like a nice enough guy, but we can't communicate.

A week passes, but still no word of Andris!

Pista (the author) as a baby.

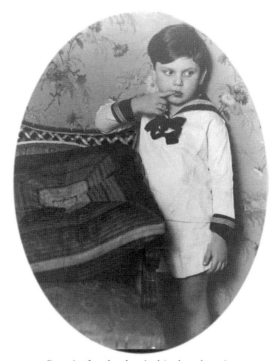

Portrait of my brother Andris, then about 8.

Brother Andris and I in front of our apartment. I was about 11 and he about 14.

Passport photo taken when I left for Canada, 1948.

My family and friends when I was 4. My mother, Georgie, is holding her hand on my shoulder; Aunt Manci is at the right.

My girlfriend Vera took this photo of me as I left Budapest at 17.

My Boy Scout troop in front of our high school in Budapest. I am the boy with white socks in the center.

Family photo about 1907. From left, Aunt Manci Szentmiklosi, Grandmother Rosa Marmorstein, Uncle Pali Marmorstein, Grandfather Ignac Marmorstein, Aunt Emma Veres. In front, my mother about 3 yars old, about 1907.

Passport photo of my father, Dezso, about 1942, about age 42.

Andris and I fishing at Lake Balaton.

Clockwise from top, Charles Nasser, my mother Georgie, my father's cousin Klara Rosenberg, and Bozsi Nasser, about 1943.

Peter is held by his mother, Bozsi Nasser.

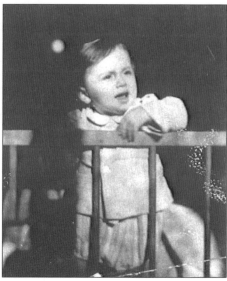

Peter Nasser, the boy who was murdered in the train station at *Auschwitz*.

Pista, Georgie, and Andris, about 1939.

Family portrait about 1942. Clockwise from upper
left, Aunt Manci Szentmiklosi, my father Dezso, my
mother Eugenia or Georgie, family friend Vicky,
Aunt Emma Veres, Uncle Dezso Veres, Grandmother
Roza Marmorstein, Andris, and me, Pista.

Four generations: Clockwise from upper left are Peter's grandmother Bohm, his great-grandmother, Peter's mother, Bozsi Nasser, and little Peter Nasser himself.

Charles and Bozsi.

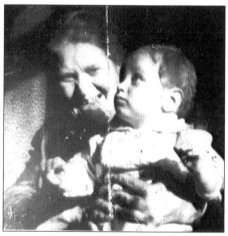

Grandmother Irma Nasser with Peter Nasser, about 1943.

The streetcar was blown into the Danube, with its passengers, in the 1940s. When the Communist regime rebuilt the bridge, it restored the streetcar and made it the first to cross the bridge.

The Nasser Jewelry Store about the mid 1930s. The family lived on the third floor (which is called the second in European terminology.) They rented out the apartments between their floor and the ground floor.

License for my Grandfather's jewelry store, established 1872.

The building where Americans hospitalized me in Seehaupt, Germany.

The caption published with this news photo, of American liberation of a Holocaust death
train in 1945 at Seehaupt, said in this boxcar alone 64 were dead. But I believe one was alive.
From the position in which I was lying when I passed out, and other evidence, I am 99
percent sure I am the person lying with his head closest to the door.

The artist who used broken metal to fashion the memorial sculpture "Never Again," posed with his work and myself at Seeshaupt.

After the war, back in Budapest.

Uncle Charles (or Karoly) Nasser in Budapest about 1990.

In 1995, under the cement roof of a munitions factory, where I had seen five people buried alive.

The cement roof structure that claimed the lives of many prisoners at Muhldorf. It was still standing when I visited in 1995. (I did not take this picture but it looked just like this.)

With my spouse, Francoise, in 2001.

Chapter Fifteen
"Resting Up" in Sick Bay

My days and nights are dominated by worries about Andris. If I only knew which of the two Sick Bay barracks he was in, I could probably sneak in at night.

The tasty food in the kitchen and my sheltering surroundings here help heal the wounds from my last beating. I have to keep this job; it's a matter of life or death.

After work and Appel, I sit on the edge of my upper bunk, eating my *gemuse*. I think about Andris and Mother. I'm equally worried about both now, and very lonely, too.

The barracks door near my bunk opens slightly, and a prisoner peeks inside. "Is there a Pista Nasser here?" he asks softly.

"Yes," I call down to the stranger from atop my bunk. "That's me."

The prisoner comes inside. He looks to be in his early twenties. He's small in stature, dark-haired, and half-starved, like all the rest of us. "So, *you're* Pista," he says, smiling, as if meeting someone well known. "My name is Geza. I have word from your brother!"

Immediately, I slide down from my bunk, grab the fragile man by his shoulders, and bombard him with questions. "Is Andris alive? If so, how is he? Where in Sick Bay is his bed? How does he feel?"

"Please, Pista, one question at a time. First, your brother *is* still alive. He speaks of you often. Unfortunately, though, he's getting weaker. He's in Sick Bay Barracks Number One. I was there with him until this afternoon. I'm lucky; I was discharged."

Geza pauses and takes a deep breath to gather his strength. Then he continues, "Andris wants me to tell you not to take any unnecessary chances; you should maintain your good attitude. If you do both, you'll survive."

My eyes fill with tears. I bury my head in my hands. "No," I say to myself, trying to stop the tears. "It can't be."

"Pista, I'm. . . I'm sorry. But I promised Andris I'd relay his whole message to you."

"Yes, Geza. Please go on." I wish I were dead. Why is God so cruel?

"Andris said to tell you that after he's gone, he and your father will always watch over you. You're not to make them miserable with your sorrow. They want to see you smiling; they want to be proud of you. Andris knows you'll make it!"

"Thank you very much, Geza, for finding me." We shake hands, and he departs.

Even with such bad news, I refuse to admit defeat. Today, I'll steal some food from the kitchen for Andris!

It's late afternoon already, when the ill-tempered second chef makes his rounds. The smell of fresh meat loaf wafting all through the kitchen is mouth-watering! I asked the mean spirited fellow for permission to go to the outhouse. He nods curtly toward the door, and then disappears to another area of the kitchen.

Then, without actually leaving the kitchen, I first open the door and then shut it, as if I've really gone out. Quickly, I get on my hands and knees, and crawl, catlike, behind the long kitchen counter. I'm hidden from view. It's hard to keep my wooden shoes from scraping the floor, but I manage. I figure I've got five minutes to complete my mission to steal some food for Andris before returning from the outhouse. I inch my way toward the meat loaf, where a junior chef cuts it into slices. Every time his knife comes down with a click, I move forward a bit. I have about twelve more moves to go. *Click. . . stick. Only ten more.* Already, I've passed a few pairs of feet. Finally, I reach the shoes of the person whose hands are busy slicing up the meat loaf. Anxious moments pass as I await my opportunity. If I can't get Andris some food pretty soon now, I'll have to turn back empty-handed. Now the clicking stops, but the feet don't move. Their owner turns around and takes half a step. Then he changes his mind, and (. . . *click*) continues cutting. My time is all but running out when I hear the voice of the second chef. "Give us a hand with the boiled potatoes!"

The clicking stops abruptly, and I watch a parade of feet marching toward the front of the kitchen, where the potatoes are boiling away in their huge pots.

Slowly, carefully, I stand up behind the counter and peek over it. What a beautiful sight! Before me, for the grabbing, sit slices and slices of unattended meat loaf! I grab four of the plumpest and then stuff them quickly inside my jacket.

I then walk back in the direction from which I came, still hunched behind the counter. The sounds of my own wooden shoes go unnoticed now, since at the other end of the kitchen, everyone is busy carrying heavy containers of potatoes.

Quietly, I open the back door, and then slam it shut as if I've just come in from the outhouse. Then I return to my work area, where I calmly sit down and continue peeling potatoes like before.

"Where've *you* been so long?" the second chef inquires of me, sneering. "I see you've managed to avoid carrying any of the heavy potato containers."

"I'm sorry, sir, but I had the runs."

"Hell with you!" he shouts in my face. Clearly he either doesn't believe me or doesn't care. "The next time you go to the outhouse, you'd better be back in here in half the time, or else. This is a work area, Jew boy, not a *bar mitzvah* party!"

"Yes, sir," I reply.

His face is red as a swastika flag. I'm relieved when he finally walks away.

Meanwhile, the temperature of the damned meat loaf right next to my skin is burning me, and its juices are fast soaking into my jacket. Oh well, I'll can stand it awhile longer, I tell myself. I'm almost finished with work for today, anyway. After all, my mission itself has been accomplished. I now have plenty of nutritious, strength-building food to smuggle into Sick Bay for Andris. After Appel but before "lights out," I'll sneak the meat loaf in to him. Already, I visualize my brother's face lighting up when he sees the rare delicacy I've brought him!

Finally, work ends for the day. I'm on my way out the back door when the second chef hollers, "Hey, you! Come back here!"

My heart starts pumping rapidly as I walk back into the kitchen where he still stands, scowling, with his legs sprawled far apart and his arms folded across his chest.

"Yes, sir?"

"Tomorrow," he says, "you come in half an hour earlier to make up for all that time you wasted today in the shithouse."

"Yes, sir." I turn again to leave.

"Not so fast, Jew boy. You stay right there!"

"Yes sir?" Now I'm panic-stricken.

"Why do you smell so much like meat loaf? Did you snitch some extra meat loaf and eat it?"

"Oh, no, sir. I wouldn't eat meat loaf that's not mine." This is true, actually.

"What's that in your jacket, then?"

Realizing I'm caught red-handed, I decide to explain Andris's dire situation and hope, somehow, for mercy from this monster. I stammer, "It's for my brother, sir. . .you see, he's in Sick Bay dying, and I. . ."

Before I can finish, the fiend picks up a rubber hose and begins striking me all over with it repeatedly, using all his force.

"You thieving Jew son-of-a-bitch! So you *do* want something for nothing!" he roars maniacally. His wild eyes look like they could truly spew fire. Dozens of blows rain down all over every inch of my body. The thuds of the rubber hose and my irrepressible screams fill the entire kitchen. I try running for cover, but he grabs me again and continues beating me, all the while cursing like a madman.

Before passing out, I entertain scattered, nonsensical thoughts: hot juices in my jacket, bad pain, meat loaf, awful pain, Mother, Father, Andris, pain, meat loaf, Andris, meat loaf, Andris, meat. . .

When I come to, I've arrived in Sick Bay, but not as the concerned relative of a patient, as I'd planned before. Rather, I'm now a patient myself. I'm in one of the lower bunks with someone else. It takes me awhile to review, in my confused mind, the series of events that has led to my now being here.

To my enormous surprise, I can see no blood anywhere on my body. The second chef's rubber hose must have done all its damage internally, since I'm covered head to toe with brand new purple bruises. My hands are already turning black and blue. I must have used them to protect my face, I realize.

Painfully, I reach inside the jacket I'm still wearing, where I'd hid Andris's meat loaf. Only a few stray crumbs remain, and it takes effort to grab hold of them and place any of them between my own sore, swollen lips. I must have dropped the rest, or maybe that monster second chef removed most of Andris's delicious dinner from my jacket, even after beating me unconscious. However it happened, there's nothing left of my ill-gotten meat loaf to sneak to Andris, even if I could get out of bed.

My bunk partner, a weak, emaciated old man, sits up with effort and leans over me. "Hello, young man. I'm Bernard Fuchs, from Budapest. Call me Bernie," he says in

Hungarian. At least we can communicate.

"Hello, Bernie, sir. I'm Pista Nasser," I manage to mumble through my inflated lips.

"Which barracks are we in, Bernie?" I ask him.

"We're in Sick Bay Number Two."

I recall Geza's telling me that Andris's bunk is in Number One. Right now, though, I'm in no shape to go anywhere, even if Andris was somehow only two bunks away.

"When was I first brought in here?" I ask Bernie.

"Last night. I overheard that the main chef came into the kitchen when the second chef was apparently beating you, and the main chef stopped him. Then the main chef carried you in here. You were completely unconscious when they put you into this bunk with me."

"How long was I out?"

"All night and all morning. You just came to right now, in fact. It's almost lunchtime. But please, take it easy awhile longer, son. Hand me your bowl, and I'll get your lunch for you."

This kindly old gentleman is in terrible condition himself. If anything, I should be assisting *him*. But since fetching my own lunch is out of the question, I allow him to do it for me.

Poor Bernie strains to slide out of our cramped bunk before shuffling off to collect both our lunches. Having two of us in one space, despite our skinniness, doesn't allow for much room.

In a few minutes, my ancient bunk mate returns. I'm still lying down, trying to gather enough strength to sit up and eat. Bernie places my bowl near my left hand, where I have the best chance of reaching it. Then he sits at the end of our bunk, slowly spooning extra-watery *gemuse* into his mouth.

"Thank you for getting my lunch, sir," I tell him as I shift slightly and reach for my bowl. *Gemuse*, Sick Bay style, is more water than anything else. The portions here are especially tiny, barely enough to keep a two year-old alive.

I share my observations about the "hospital" food with Bernie.

"Of course. They're starving us," he replies with an ironic smile. "That's the whole idea." With that, he squeezes back into the bunk beside me.

"Ouch!" I wince as he brushes against my aching body.

"I'm sorry. You must be awfully sore, Pista. Just look at all the welts and bruises all over you! You need a lot of rest."

"Bernie, I'd like to say I look worse than I feel, but that wouldn't be true."

"I can't think of anything a boy like you could have done to be beaten like that."

"You don't need to do anything in particular to be beaten like this. In this case, though, I did do something. I'd say the second chef overreacted to it, though."

"What did you do?"

I tell him about my aborted attempt to steal meat loaf for Andris. Next, I describe the beating I got from the SS the morning I arrived here, and the more recent one I received during Appel when the prisoner who killed himself was mysteriously missing at the evening countdown.

Bernie shakes his head. "You poor lad. By the way, didn't your parents have a jewelry store in Ujpest?"

"Yes."

"I remember it. It was a beautiful shop. And your father was a nice man."

"Thank you. All that seems a lifetime ago."

"Didn't you have an older brother who plays soccer? A big, fair-haired boy?"

"That's Andris. He's in here somewhere, too. He's even worse off than me."

"What a shame. Such handsome lads, both of you," Bernie mumbles, drifting off. I close my eyes, too, but know I must avoid the temptation to fall asleep; it would only delay my plans to see Andris!

Andris has already been here several days, I remind myself. He must be weak and starving, even more so now than when he first arrived. I resolve to save him all the food I can. To do so, though, I must conserve my own energy. I'll need to visit him with extra food numerous times, until he's strong enough to leave Sick Bay. I'll succeed with my plan, I'm convinced, because I *have* to. I can't let my brother die! I simply cannot let it happen! My thoughts drift next to Mother. She *has* to be well and alive. She just *has* to be. Andris and I will find her, right after the liberation. My thoughts begin to blur, and then fade. My own exhaustion and weakness are gaining the upper hand. I can't fight the urge to sleep any longer.

The third day I'm in Sick Bay, my aches and pains lessen—or perhaps I'm just growing used to them. I can walk around now, even though it hurts a lot. I'm also well enough to notice the sordidness of our conditions. The stale atmosphere of the teeming barracks is dominated by a strong urine odor. Many of us keep rusty cans under our mattresses to save ourselves the energy required for trips to the outhouse. Doctors, nurses, and medicines are all unavailable. The sole purpose of Sick Bay is to warehouse the ill and dying until they can either recover or be disposed of. Very few Sick Bay patients ever recover.

Consequently, the count in our barracks changes quickly. On average, five to ten people die each day. Their bodies are then removed through the back door. Other nearly dead bodies are dumped into the bunks to fill these vacant spaces, even before the beds of the newly dead are quite cold.

There is, however, one positive aspect to my being in Sick Bay. When we hear the dreaded early morning whistle summoning everyone to Appel, we don't have to go. Instead, our barracks commander takes count of us twice a day, and then reports his numbers to an Appel clerk.

Our barracks receives its food daily according to the morning count. I'm saving most of my food so I can sneak it into Sick Bay Barracks Number One and give it to Andris.

I'll go and visit Andris right after dinner, I tell myself. I have enough food saved up now.

But, when the time comes, I don't go. I just can't make it physically. I decide to go tomorrow instead.

I wake several times during the night. It's hard to turn over, or even to move at all, without waking Bernie. He moans loudly each time I disturb him.

In the morning, the Appel whistle stirs me from my usual unquiet slumber. I feel a slight weight on top of my blanket, like someone giving me a gentle touch. When I turn over and look, I find Bernie's arm resting against my leg.

I sit up. Bernie lies still, sprawled on his back, his mouth and eyes wide open, as if in shock. I've seen this look before on the faces of other deceased prisoners around here who've died from overwork and malnutrition.

Suspecting the worst, I take his wrist in my hand and feel for a pulse. There is none. His hand feels icy cold. I place my ear over his chest. No heartbeat. The poor man's suffering has finally ended.

I close his eyelids and mouth. A chill like none I've ever felt before runs up and down my spine.

Somehow, I know I must see Andris tonight.

Next, I search Bernie's dead body for any extra food, but find nothing.

Breakfast arrives. I report Bernie's overnight death to the barracks commander as I collect my own food.

He replies, "We might as well just leave him in the bunk with you for three more days. The extra food we collect for him, you and I will share. Is that all right with you?" It's more a command than a question, since he's in charge here, not me.

"As you say, sir," I agree. I'm not thrilled about sleeping beside a corpse for three more nights, but at least it's the corpse of a nice person. And if sleeping alongside a dead body helps me collect more food for Andris, it's worth it.

Returning to "our" bed, I tie Bernie's right hand to his body with some cement sack string I find lying around, since it has now stiffened in an outward position. Clearly, *rigor mortis* has begun setting in.

For the rest of today, I plan my visit to Andris. By nightfall, I'm ready. When the time comes, getting out of my own Sick Bay barracks through the back door is surprisingly easy. I have no problem, either, moving unnoticed between the two Sick Bay barracks.

Now to find the bunk where Andris lies, amongst all these others.

Chapter Sixteen
Good Night, Sweet Prince

Slowly, stealthily, I open the door to Sick Bay Number One. The same familiar smell of urine, decay, and death hits me in the face as soon as I enter. Clearly, I've come to the right place.

Moving as quietly as possible from bunk to bunk, I call, softly, "Andris. . . Andris. . . Andris." My throat feels dry; I can barely swallow.

No reply. Starting back down the other side, I'm all the more determined. He's *got* to be in here, somewhere.

"Andris. . . Andris. . ." As I pass a bunk, I think it sounds like someone has just answered me. I stop and bend over the lower bunk, where two prisoners share the narrow space. It's dim, and the odor is nauseating.

"Andris?"

The two prisoners occupying this bunk huddle beneath a single blanket. I can't make out their faces.

"Which Andris are you looking for?" asks one of them weakly.

I describe my brother. With a bony finger, he points back to the side from which I've just come. "Try your luck over in that one," he suggests in almost a whisper, indicating a particular bunk.

"Thank you." Crossing my fingers for good luck, I approach the bunk indicated. Bending over the kickboard, I see two prisoners lying side by side. They look back at me with dazed expressions, scarcely alive.

"Andris?" I whisper, tenderly.

The blanket moves and a skinny arm reaches toward me. I swallow hard. My eyes brim instantly with fresh tears as I recognize my brother, looking more like a skeleton than a human being. I swallow again and again, clearing my throat. Then I remember what he told me a while ago. "Pista, be brave!"

Gently, I hold the bony fingers that just one year earlier had had the strength of steel. This breathing collection of bones is all that remains of "Potyi," the well-liked, handsome soccer star, the brilliant scholar and physician to be, my own beloved Andris. The Nazis have succeeded in destroying all that he was and could have been. Damn them! Damn the whole world!

"Andris," I whisper, still refusing to give up on him. "I've got some food for you. Eat it and you'll feel much better."

His lips move in an effort to speak.

I motion to his bunkmate. "Would you mind letting me slide in beside my brother for a few minutes?" I ask him.

He obliges me, even though he's in sorry condition himself. I thank him.

"Andriskam," I begin, bending over him and kissing his hot feverish forehead, "you've got to eat." I prepare to feed him my painfully saved dinner portions. His lips open, and he whispers a barely audible "Nice. . . to. . . see. . . you. . . lit. . . tle. . . brat."

As long as he's still alive, there's hope! "Here, Andris, I'll break this sawdust bread up for you into tiny bites." I do so, and try placing a piece of it inside his mouth.

But Andris shuts his lips stubbornly and instead whispers: "Un. . . der . . . my. . . blan. . . ket. . . some. . . bread."

I reach under his blanket and, to my amazement, discover five untouched portions of sawdust bread.

"You haven't been eating, Andris!" I scold him gently. "No wonder you're so weak!"

He tries to answer, but can't force even a whisper from his mouth.

Meanwhile, Andris's bunkmate sits on the bed near our feet, clinging to the bedpost for support. He tells me, "Your brother is starving and very ill. His stomach can't hold any food. You came here just in time."

His words hit me hard! Then I hear Andris's own voice again, inside my head: *"Pista, Dad and I want to be proud of you and to see you smile again. That will make us happy."*

I swallow my tears. I can't act like a crybaby during my brother's last minutes. I want to see him smile again.

Holding his hand, I say, "Remember, Andris, how we used to go to Angol Park, and all the fun we had there?" He makes an effort to squeeze my hand, and a faint smile appears on his face.

"And, how about your last birthday party?" I sputter on. "Do you remember that delicious *Dobos Torta* we had? Remember how I ate myself sick, and had to put my fingers down my throat so I could eat some more?"

Andris is still smiling; but now his eyes are closed.

"After liberation," I continue, trying not to choke up, "you and I will find Mother, and we'll celebrate again with a cake just like that! Maybe we'll even have one with marzipan filling."

Andris's hand goes limp now, but his smile remains. He dies with that smile on his face.

I cover him with my body; I blow into his mouth to try to revive him. I cry; I swear; I beg—none of it makes a difference. Andris has now joined Father.

I feel as hollow as an empty sack, like a body with no soul. The sudden grief sweeping over me is so deep it's unfathomable. I'd give everything to bring him back. But I can't. I can't. I can't.

I lie in the bunk next to him awhile longer, holding him close, soaking both of us with my tears. I know he's gone, but it still feels good to cling to him. *"Oh, God, I don't want to let him go."* Eventually, my tears are spent, all but an occasional sharp sob.

I lie in his bunk with him awhile longer, silent now, just holding him in my arms. Than I feel his bunkmate tapping me on the shoulder.

"You had better go," he suggests gently.

"I know," I reply. "Thank you for your kindness."

"You're welcome. I'm sorry."

Gathering the five uneaten portions of bread, my brother's last gift to me, I clasp his cold hand in mine once more.

"Andris," I tell him silently, *"I will get out of this hellhole alive, for your sake. I'll do it in your memory. Just let them try to stop me now!"*

Before turning to go, I gaze down at him one last time. He's still smiling.

"Andris, I promise you I'll take that beautiful smile of yours from this God-awful place with me, and when this madness ends, I'll use it. I'll use your smile to help make this a happier world, somehow."

In shock I make my way back to my own Sick Bay barracks and crawl into my bunk. The next morning, Bernie's dead body still lies beside me. I never receive the extra food I've been promised in exchange for "baby-sitting" his corpse. The barracks commander must be keeping it all for himself, I figure. I find, though, that I really don't care. Andris is still taking care of me with those extra portions of bread he saved me at the very end. And, I find, I need only close my eyes and think of him, and there is Andris, always smiling down at me, helping me go on.

The third morning after his death, the smell of Bernie's decaying body inside my bunk is getting hard to bear. Finally, it is removed from the barracks. When he's carried out, I see that his baggy, ill-fitting prison pants are full of discharge.

The days pass, and I begin feeling better. Andris's additional bread portions and the bed rest itself help me recover. I'm determined to keep Andris's smile alive, somehow. To do so, though, I must get out of Sick Bay and rejoin the work detail.

Chapter Seventeen
Back to Work

Today at lunch I sit on my bunk eating my watery Sick Bay *gemuse*, as usual. Suddenly I hear the ear-splitting wails of sirens, followed by explosions of bombs not far away. It's a lengthy air raid this time, lasting well over half an hour. There's no doubt in my mind; the Americans have attacked Muhldorf itself this time, and hit it hard!

After dinner, a Capo enters our barracks and announces, "I need volunteers for an air raid detail. Muhldorf Rail Station must be repaired tonight. Volunteers will receive a special dinner!"

"There must be lots of damage if they're even asking Sick Bay for volunteers," I say to myself. Whatever the reason, here's my chance to be sprung from Sick Bay and rejoin the living! In all, three of us from this Sick Bay barracks feel strong enough to volunteer for the emergency air raid detail.

It's night, and very dark and cool outside when we board the open trucks for Muhldorf Rail Station. The rest of our emergency work crew has already put in a full day's work on that murderous, never-ending cement project that almost killed me. That's one thing I sure haven't missed! These poor, exhausted fellows have been ordered to report directly from the cement detail to tonight's air raid detail, with no rest whatsoever.

Just as I've imagined, Muhldorf Station is in shambles. Torn-up rails point at the sky, like sharp, twisted fingers. Bomb craters yawn out of the ground everywhere. Boxcars and their remnants have been tossed around during the air raid like discarded toys in a messy child's room. As we jump down from the trucks and prepare to begin work, powerful searchlights cut into the moonless dark night. Brand new rails and railroad ties, brought in on huge trucks, await us. We're divided up into small groups under the command of both the SS and the *Wehrmacht*.

I'm given a shovel and told to start filling in a small bomb crater. The crew beside me works removing the pretzel-like rail, part of which hangs over my crater. In an hour and a half, I finish my part. New ties and rails quickly replace the twisted wreckage.

I'm tiring quickly though, not having worked this hard in quite awhile. Still, I take my shovel and move along to the next crater to be filled in. But my motions are slowing down, and I must now put my full weight (probably less than 100 pounds at this point) on my shovel by stepping with both feet onto its metal edge. Then I have a hard time keeping my balance, and occasionally I slip off the shovel entirely.

I'm wearing out fast, and our middle of the night "dinner" is still several hours away. Soon I slip off my shovel again, but I'm too tired to do anything this time but just let myself fall to the ground. I hit the earth, collapsing from exhaustion like a man made of sticks. Soon my limp body is rolling, tumbleweed-like, down the grading.

I don't have to wait long before a guard appears. Fortunately, this one is a *Wehrmacht*, not an SS. With his foot, he rolls me onto my back, slapping my face gently a couple of times.

"Hey you, get up!" he says, bending down to listen to my heartbeat.

Next, I hear brisk footsteps, followed by the sound of another, louder, voice. "What's going on here?" that voice asks, from somewhere above me. From the corner of one eye, I look up and recognize an SS uniform. I shiver involuntarily.

"He fell over. . . he's out cold," the *Wehrmacht* explains.

"We'll see about *that*," declares the SS.

Seconds later, the SS officer's surprise kick to my ribs just about breaks them, but I manage not to move, cry out, or respond to the kick in any way. "I guess he *is* out," says the SS to the *Wehrmacht*. "We'll just leave him here awhile, then." I hear the two men's footsteps as they clomp off elsewhere. I smile to myself. Andris and Dad must have somehow given me strength to withstand that awful kick.

Having tricked my captors into letting me "sleep" awhile, I now nod off in earnest. When I wake a couple hours later, refreshed, I hear the sounds of running feet, and I smell delicious food.

My convenient "blackout" having served its purpose, I get up quickly, dust off my prison uniform, and walk toward the smell of the food, fully prepared to devour my "rightfully earned" dinner portion. We're served roasted pork with real potatoes (not skins) and vegetables (not peelings), as well as genuine (non-sawdust) bread. I've never been fed so well courtesy of the Nazis, not even during the short time I worked in the kitchen barracks.

After tonight's detail, I'm permanently reassigned to a working barracks. Those of us who participated in this air raid detail, though, have the next day off. Physically, all things considered, I feel pretty good for a poorly nourished 13 or 14 year-old. Having lost track of the days and months, I don't even know my age anymore. But deep in my heart, I feel lonely and empty beyond description. I've never been so sad, or so incapable of shaking my sadness even for a moment. It's nearly unbearable at times. I've never known life without my brother Andris. He's been my helper, guide, and best friend, right from the start. Now, I must learn to live without him, and under the worst possible conditions.

I know Andris and Father are watching over me, but I also know I'll never hear their voices again, or feel them hug me. I miss them both so much! Who will ever again call me a "little brat" with so much tenderness? Who else will be proud of me with such unconditional devotion?

But their love lives on inside me. When I need them, I close my eyes and see them smiling. I know that the love my father and brother had for me can never die, as long as I'm determined to keep it alive.

Exhausted from my nightlong foray into work straight from my sick bed, I sleep all morning and wake up around noon. My blanket is soaked with tears, but somehow, something inside me feels better now. I'm even more determined to survive this hell—now for the sake of those I've loved so much and lost.

After lunch, we prisoners must all line up at the Magazine for haircuts. Nearly a dozen haircutters await us. These are in fact our fellow prisoners, who (with no great skill) act today as barbers. When we first see how one of them, using a double-zero clipper, cuts an inch and a half wide path right through the center of the first man's head, from the forehead to the neck, we all laugh. These are unique haircuts, obviously designed for easy identification in case of an escape attempt. By the time my turn comes, we've nicknamed the new style "The Lice Path Look."

The next morning, I'm back marching through the forest with my old cement detail, although by now almost all of the old familiar faces have been replaced by those of strangers. Despite my improved mental outlook, I can't avoid realizing how very weak I still am. Even walking to work is a challenge, and I'm already exhausted before we begin.

Today I'm assigned to fill new cement sacks from a large wooden crate of broken bags of cement. The job is dirty and dusty; I can actually feel the gray cement powder settling in my nose and throat. Earlier, I would have found this job a snap. But now it takes all my energy not to fall over.

Marching back to the barracks that afternoon, I slip and fall several times.

Thanks to various other prisoners, most of them strangers, I'm not left behind in the forest. I make it back to camp in one piece, but, for the first time ever, not under my own power.

Tonight I fall asleep very early, and slumber like a rock until the whistle shrieks for Appel.

The next morning after Appel, I'm sipping my coffee when a cold rain starts to fall. By the time our work group reaches the forest, the morning rain has turned into slushy wet snow. The new cement-bag garments I made myself yesterday give me some protection against the weather as I work. But I'm unable to clear my throat of the pesky cement powder. By mid morning, the constant irritation in my throat grows into a full-fledged cough. My body feels feverish, too. I dread the thought that I'm getting sick again, just three days after leaving Sick Bay.

As soon as possible, I calculate my pulse. It's 120! And my cough's growing rapidly worse. My chest aches, too, from the continuous coughing. Whenever the guards aren't looking, I stand around and rest, leaning against my shovel, the same sort that SS tried to kill me with, as if it's a stalwart old friend.

After lunch, I continue my diary. It has increased, now, to many pages. If. . . no, *when* I get out of here, I'll see about publishing it, so the world will know what these Nazis were really up to! It's hard to sustain the energy now, though, even to sit and write in my diary. As the afternoon drags on, I feel worse and worse. My lips are cracked and bleeding, with a layer of cement dust caked on them. I probably look like some sort of ghoul, dusted gray from head to toe, and clad in my weird-looking cement sack garments. Now I'm breaking out in a cold sweat, too My face must be a real sight, with dozens of perspiration beads cascading down my dusty gray forehead.

Finally, work is over! Now to just make it back to the camp and through Appel. After that, I'll go right to sleep. On the long march back to the barracks, I concentrate on Andris's smile, which gives me strength to put one foot in front of the other on what seems like the longest march ever. Today it feels as if some fiendish force keeps stretching the never-ending road.

When I finally see the outline of the barracks, I suddenly realize that I'm not walking under my own power. Two of my marching partners are propping me up on either side. Without them, I could not have made it back to camp today.

We're standing at Appel. It seems as if days pass as we wait for the count to finish. I'm alternately hot and cold, I cough, and I sweat profusely. My eyes play tricks on me, and the barracks start to move around. Then, suddenly, my knees fold, like well-oiled hinges. I hit the ground with a sudden dull thud.

My buddies around me try dragging me to an upright position. I want to get up for Andris's sake, but my willpower can't command my helpless muscles anymore. I'm just too weak.

An SS officer stands beside the *Capos*, supervising the Appel. "Get up, you *Swinehund!*" he yells.

Now I know the feeling of being a knocked-out boxer who can't get up for the count, not even if it means defeat. I can hardly raise my head, and my body won't move at all. I'm lying at the feet of the SS officer, who's now ranting like a lunatic.

"If you don't stand up by yourself at the count of ten, you must be half dead!" he yells again. *"Einz. . . zwei. . . nine, zen. . . Take him to the Dying Room!"*

Two *Capos* drag me to the far side of the camp, where I'm put into an isolated room.

"This is the Dying Room!" I say to myself, as if in a dream. I know it well by reputation, although I've never seen it before. This much I know, however: no one ever leaves here alive!

Inside the dying room, I'm stripped naked, tossed onto a lower bunk, and given a blanket. When I open my eyes, the beds are swinging and the walls are moving like crazy. I must be delirious. The next thing I remember is a uniform bending over me. Now a hand forces coffee down me, spilling it all over my face.

When I open my eyes again, the room has stopped spinning. I even manage to keep my lids open for a few minutes.

I wake up when a *Wehrmacht* guard comes in to ask if anyone wants to eat.

"Yes, please," I reply weakly.

He doesn't hear me. With all my energy, I try again.

"Yes, please!"

He turns and comes toward my bunk.

"Oh, you're conscious now!" His voice is gentle. "Can you eat some *gemuse*?"

I nod. He brings me a bowlful, saying, "This is your third day here; you haven't eaten anything but that little bit of coffee I just forced down you."

The door opens and I recognize the uniform of an SS officer. "When is the next opening?" he asks the *Wehrmacht*.

The *Wehrmacht* points toward my bunk. "This boy might last through the day," he says of me, "but it'll be a miracle if he's still alive tomorrow. He has typhus and pneumonia!"

Even in my extremely debilitated state, these remarks hit me like an electrical current. So they're all set to bury me already! *"Not so fast!"* I want to shout. Now I feel my anger building up, and even giving my weak body a shock of adrenalin.

As soon as the door slams shut again, I roll out of my bunk and pull myself up, slowly, using the bedpost for support. My legs look like fragile spindles, and they feel extremely wobbly, indeed. But at least I'm standing up. In my semi-delirium, I bite into the post and chew the wood, thinking that somehow it's something to eat! This isn't too smart. . . the wood makes my gums bleed.

I take my first step. *"Oh, God, give me strength!"* Amazingly, I don't even fall down. Slowly, I make my way around the bunk. Every step is a separate agony as I grab onto the bunk to steady myself. I feel very faint.

I look around me. There are five bunks with ten spaces. All are occupied with dying prisoners. I'm the only one moving a muscle. Death fills every nook and cranny of this room, except the spot where I stand. But I won't give in to it. I simply will not!

Now I grow more daring, even taking a step without holding onto anything. I'd better sit down now and finish my *gemuse*, I tell myself. Enough is enough for now.

The food feels good in my empty stomach. I look around for something else to eat. The bedpost is definitely out! I try the straw from the mattress, but it's impossible to chew. When I grab a handful, I find some kind of grain mixed in with the straw. I search the whole mattress and find a good supply of grain. I don't know if it's supposed to be edible, but I eat it anyway.

I lie down to rest again and count my pulse beats. . . seventy. At last, my fever has broken. I still feel very weak, but my mental outlook is growing stronger again. I feel Andris at my side. *"Those Nazis, I'll show them. I'll walk back out through those doors and rejoin the living! Nobody will carry me out of here feet first!"*

For the remainder of today I just rest and eat the small portion of food they give me, supplementing it with additional sustenance from my hidden grain supply.

After dinner, I take a walk, unassisted! *"Thank you, God!"* Now I glance more carefully into every bunk. One dying man offers me the rest of his food.

He just can't eat it. I take it.

In the morning, four bodies are carried out by two of the *Wehrmacht* guards. Within an hour the bunks are refilled.

One *Wehrmacht* guard comes over to my bunk and asks me with sincere curiosity, "Son, what powers do you possess? It's a miracle the way you've recovered. Do you have any explanation for it?"

"It's hard to explain in words," I say. "It's a deep love my brother left me. It gives me a lot of strength, I guess, just thinking about him. My brother's love is just stronger than all this hatred around here."

I don't know if he understands what I'm saying. Words can never explain the bond that existed, and that I know still exists, somewhere, between Andris and me.

The *Wehrmacht* just stands there, a puzzled look crossing his face. I don't think he's afraid of me, but perhaps he regards me as somehow unearthly. His hand shakes when he hands me my lunch portion. It's a large serving too, much bigger than anyone else's. He must realize I'm not about to waste it.

"Thank you, sir," I tell him. "You're very kind."

I'm getting stronger rapidly now. I can feel it in my bones. My chest still hurts, especially when I cough, but it's nothing like the past few days. I count fourteen open wounds all over my body. I try to shut thoughts of them out of my mind. I'm too busy gathering the strength to leave this death hole!

Late this afternoon, three more bodies are removed from the Dying Room. I peer through the window near my bunk and see them being carted away.

Tonight I sleep in relative comfort, coughing only occasionally.

After my morning coffee, I eat some more grain and walk around without support. What a wonderful feeling! It's almost as if I've risen from the dead!

The sixth day of my stay here, an SS officer enters and grabs me by the arm. *"Herous!"* he shouts. Confused, I stand up, still naked.

"Take your blanket and report to the *Magazine* for clothing! There is no place here for a person who refuses to die!" With these words, he kicks me out, bodily, through the door.

Chapter Eighteen
Hanging On

I'm now outside that ghoulish building, most recently my home, still half-wrapped in my bunk blanket and nothing else. I pull myself to my feet and readjust my only current possession. It's cool and windy out, and I'm unstable on my bare feet—both from weakness and from the crushed stones underfoot. I've no idea what happened to my prison uniform once I entered the "Dying Room," but chances are it has been issued to someone in better condition than I. If I wish to be re-outfitted, now, I'll have to make it somehow over to the *Magazine*, about 100 yards from here. If I'm in luck, Mr. Brichta, the shoe store owner and friend of my father's from Istvan Street, will be on duty.

Picking my way slowly, carefully, across the rough gravel underfoot, I eventually arrive at the *Magazine*, dizzy and breathless. I enter through the front door, which squeaks on its hinges and feels very heavy to me. I'm in luck: Mr. Brichta is there, stacking something on shelves near the back door. Silently, like a little ghost, I pad across the length of the *Magazine,* about half that of an ordinary barracks, before Mr. Brichta first catches sight of me.

When he finally does, it takes him several seconds to realize who I am. Then his eyes bulge with disbelief and his mouth drops to his chin, as if he *has* seen a ghost!

"Pista Nasser!" he gasps. "Is that *really* you? I saw you being dragged off to the Dying Room a few days ago. I was afraid you, you. . ."

"Yes, sir. I came close, actually. But I'm better now, and out of danger. They've just now released me, and I need some clothes."

He shakes his head in amazement. "You're a remarkable boy, Pista. I thought no one ever left the Dying Room. Not until they were dead, that is."

"I thought so, too. But I guess they kick you out after a week or so if you refuse to die."

This draws chuckle from my father's friend, who then turns and begins rummaging through a big box behind him. In a moment, he turns back around, a zebra-striped prison suit in his hands, and says, "Here is an outfit, my friend. This should be all right for you, better than that blanket, at least."

"Thank you. Would you have an extra pair of shoes?"

The former shoe store mogul shakes his head, sadly. "I haven't a single pair left. But. . ." he brightens a bit, "I can give you some rags to wrap around your feet. Do you have any cement bags?"

"No sir."

"Well, here, I'll give you a couple of cement bags and some string."

"Thank you, sir. You've really helped me just now, and I appreciate it," I reply. Poor Mr. Brichta's ego must be bruised from being unable to do any better by me. A shoe salesman with no shoes. My expression of gratitude makes him smile, just a bit. But I can't help thinking how different he and I have both become, in our distinct ways, from being here so long. And not for the better.

"Oh, Pista, by the way, I've got something else for you here. At least I *think* it's yours."

"Oh?" Maybe he's found my old shoes, somehow That would be nice Instead, though, he produces my abandoned diary!

"Does this belong to you, Pista?" he asks me. Another prisoner from your old barracks brought it here after you were taken to the Dying Room. He said he'd found it near your empty bunk, and thought it might be yours."

"Yes, it is! Thank you so much, Mr. Brichta!"

He hands me the diary, which weighs a lot. But I somehow find the strength to grasp it in both hands and take it with me.

Next I survey the Magazine area for a semi-private place to dress and fashion myself some "shoes." Retreating to a dark corner, I begin dressing, never taking my eyes from my diary. Thank God it was found! I resolve never to lose it again.

Soon I'm back to my same old routine, except that I'm assigned to a new barracks. Once here I look around, trying to get my bearings. So many prisoners are missing. I see lots of empty bunks, and even inside the occupied ones, many new faces.

I settle myself into my new bunk for the night, asking the prisoner on my right, "Are you asleep?"

"No." He sits up, supporting himself on one elbow. His gaunt face and weary eyes make me think he's been here awhile, perhaps even longer than I.

"I'm Pista, originally from Budapest," I tell him. I've just been kicked out of the Dying Room. I was there seven or eight days. I haven't ever been in this barracks before. Why's it so empty in here?"

"I'm glad to meet a survivor of the Dying Room. I didn't think there were any."

Then the dark-haired fellow sighs deeply, pulling his knees up under his chin. "I'm Joska, also from Budapest. You're wondering why it's so empty in here? It's because a few days ago, several hundred prisoners were shipped out. There's a rumor that the Allies are finally closing in, and I think it might actually be true this time."

I sit up. "Why would it suddenly be true *this* time?" I ask. "For over a year I've been hearing these rumors, too. Nothing but stories and lies!"

"I understand what you're saying, Pista. But they've never actually evacuated people from this camp before until just now. You noticed all the empty bunks first thing, remember?"

"True," I concede. "I guess I'm just afraid to get my hopes up again."

"I don't blame you. But we can't give up."

"Sometimes it's hard to remember that, though. Like when your brother, the only one you ever had, just died in your arms of starvation and typhus."

"I'm sorry, Pista. You're just a kid, and you've been through too much. How old are you, anyway?"

"Thirteen or fourteen. I don't know for sure," I reply, bitterly, starting suddenly to cry. "I, I c–couldn't tell you what month, day, or year it is. I just feel so trapped, so c–cut off from anything civilized or normal, j–just s-stuck here in this h–hole." The tears keep coming, despite my efforts to stop them.

"I think it's going to be over soon, kid. Hang on just a little bit longer."

"Thanks for listening to me Joska," I say, forcing myself to snap out of it. "I guess I shouldn't tell you all my problems. You must have plenty of your own, like everyone else around here."

"I don't mind, Pista. That's what they used to pay me for."

"Huh?"

"I'm a psychologist by profession. I was just starting to build up a nice private practice, plus teach part time at the University of Budapest, when. . . Well, you know the rest."

"Yeah. I bet you're a good psychologist, Joska. Something about you makes me comfortable telling you personal things. I don't usually talk to people this way."

He smiles. "I'll take that as a compliment."

"Joska," I continue. "You look so young to be a psychologist already. How old are *you,* may I ask?"

"I'm twenty-six or twenty-seven. I think."

We both laugh at his dark humor.

Then he says, "Get some rest, now, kiddo. You may be home again before you know it. You don't want to be out of sorts when you first see that pretty blue Danube."

His words make me smile. I'm lucky to have him to talk to, I realize, drifting off. He's so nice, so intelligent. He makes me feel less alone, too His life, like mine, has been brutally interrupted by the Nazis and their schemes. So many plans, wishes, hopes, and dreams of so many people, squashed down, postponed indefinitely, or wiped out altogether.

The next morning, our *Wehrmacht* guards seem more relaxed than ever before. In fact, I don't even see any SS around. Maybe they've all run from the advancing Allies. Maybe, just maybe . . . this will finally all be over soon.

Today, the march through the forest with my old cement detail is even slower than usual. Our relatively relaxed pace helps me manage to walk on my own and not stumble around so much. I still cough, though, and this morning's damp coldness penetrates clear to the marrow of my bones.

I'm put to work in that same wooden structure with the ramp going up from which I tumbled, like a scarecrow, the last time I worked here.

"You prisoners will carry the sacks up this ramp," the engineer commands. I recognize him at once: he's the same man who saved me awhile ago from the hand stomping, rib-kicking, demonic SS!

Apparently, he remembers me, too, because when it's my turn to carry the cement bags on my shoulders, he calls a halt to the whole operation.

"This boy belongs in a hospital!" he shouts, "not carrying cement! Follow me, son," he tells me briskly, striding up the ramp and onto the same platform where I'd been beaten so badly not long ago.

He leads me into a sheltered room and then points to some broken sacks.

"Just put these in order," he says as he walks away.

This work is easy, even for me. I shake and flatten the empty cement bags. The only problem is the cement dust rising up all around me. By noon, my cough is worse, and the pain in my chest more severe. Soon my bronchial cavities are full of thick mucus, causing me severe discomfort whenever I cough.

Despite the easiness of the work itself, my afternoon still passes with agonizing slowness. The constant cough, irritated by the abundant cement dust, soon wears me out. By the end of the day, even with my army engineer savior's continued kindness, I'm in worse shape than before.

I survived the day, somehow, but the march back to the barracks is one of my toughest yet.

The *Wehrmacht* guards, being far more humane then their SS counterparts, march right along beside us. Even so, each step is a struggle. I hope my new bunkmate Joska is right about the Allies getting closer. I wish we had a radio, or a newspaper, or anything at all to give us news of the outside world.

So vividly do I daydream of liberation on the march back that I don't even realize my legs are failing me again. "Watch out!" the *Wehrmacht* beside me yells, just as I fall. He gives me a hand getting up again. "Take it easy, son. We're almost at the barracks." The rest of the way back he holds me up by placing his own arms beneath my armpits, so that I may remain on my feet.

With our barracks half-empty, the Appel countdown goes very quickly. Most of the remaining prisoners then immediately busy themselves scrounging around, scavenger-like, for food left behind by those who've departed. They search empty bunks, mattresses, the areas beneath and between bunks— everywhere they can think of. I try searching for food a bit myself, but my strength is just too limited. My stomach wants to eat, but the rest of my body prefers to sleep. The rest of my body easily wins out.

I lie down on my bunk and fall asleep immediately. Even my wet, nagging, cough can't wake me tonight.

In the morning, I wake up feeling even worse. In fact, I barely make it to Appel. Once there, my legs have a nearly impossible time just keeping me upright. But they manage to do so, somehow.

The whistle blows, signaling, finally, that the count is over. Relieved, I sit on the barracks steps, waiting to be assigned to my usual work detail. But today, to my astonishment, we're simply dismissed. I'm not sure what to think. No work, no announcements, and no SS around anywhere, for days on end now! I like it this way. I only wish I knew what was coming next.

With nothing else to do, I drag myself back to my bunk and lie down. Joska is already in his bunk, resting. He smiles broadly when he first sees me.

"Hey Pista! I just heard the Americans are advancing fast, no kidding! All the SS took off out of here a few days ago. And one of the *Wehrmacht* just told me Hitler's dead!"

"Do you believe him?"

"I do. See, Pista, it's almost over, just like I told you."

"That bastard Hitler actually dead? Hooray!" If I weren't feeling so weak right now, I'd jump for joy, dance on top of my bed, and do a string of cartwheels in the aisle betwen the rows of bunks. Instead, I must settle to just wave my arms around, grinning like a Cheshire cat.

"Pista, in a couple days we'll all be free. But right now, get some rest. You need lots."

I close my eyes and smile to myself, thinking how far I've come, but also how dearly Hitler's folly has cost my family, myself, and so many others, including Joska. Come what may, my life will never be the same again. I've aged decades in a year, and experienced the worst—and best—of humanity as few boys my age ever do, or will. My thirteenth year has come and gone inside the barbed wire confines of this camp. No one here has marked my coming of age with a *bar mitzvah* ceremony. Yet I know I've become a man.

No one need tell me I'm a man now; I know it myself, deep down. I know it when I force myself from bed for Appel once more when I'm sure I can't. I know it when I think of Andris and want to die, yet will not let myself. I know it, too, when, despite all I've lost, I feel hope, optimism, and love still burning—brighter than ever—within me.

Tonight in my dream, I'm playing soccer in a huge stadium, filled with thousands of fans. I'm on Andris's team. He's Captain. The other team's just tied the score. But now Andris has the ball. He's dribbling it quickly, skillfully, toward the goal posts. We all know we're about to win! The fans are on their feet now, clapping, cheering: Andris, Andris, Andris! I glance over, and there are Mother and Dad in the stands, smiling broadly, beautifully dressed, surrounded by friends, and oh so proud!

Then suddenly Andris slips and falls, tumbling to the ground. He can't get up! *"Andris, Andris, are you all right?"* I run toward him on the field, but he yells at me, with uncharacteristic roughness in his voice, ***"Get the ball, runt. Don't waste time!"***

I'm after the ball now, just as he's told me to do, running faster than I thought I could, kicking the ball, to my surprise, right out from under my opponent's feet, reversing, dribbling like a champ. When the time comes, I set up my shot, kick the ball squarely, and there it goes, right between the goal posts.

I look up into the stands for Mother and Dad. How proud of me they'll be! But. . . but they're gone. The spot where they stood is empty, as if they were never there. Next I run to Andris. Maybe he still needs my help! But when I arrive at the spot where he has fallen, he's gone, too, into thin air. *"Andris, I saved the game for us, just like you said I should! Andris, we won! Andris. . ."*

The shrill whistle for Appel jars me awake. My pillow is drenched with my own tears, and I'm still calling, though now fully awake, "Andris, Andris, Andris!"

Joska, who is sitting up in his bed, his legs crossed in front of him like a Buddha, looks over at me with concern. "Bad dream?"

"Yeah." My whole body is drenched with sweat.

Outside, we all line up for Appel, as usual, but to our astonishment, no countdown follows. Instead, we're simply herded, the entire several hundred of us still remaining in the camp, to a nearby railroad siding just outside the camp.

It's a warm spring day. The far-stretching railroad tracks shimmer in the bright sunshine. I see a row of boxcars just past the puffing steam engine, which emits gray smoke and white steam into the cloudless sky.

The *Wehrmacht* guards scurry around, helping us feeble prisoners board the train. Joska jumps up into one of the beaten-up old boxcars. He bends down and reaches for my hand. "Let me help you up, Pista."

I grab his hand and hoist myself up beside him. "Where do you think they're taking us?"

"Back to Budapest, I hope," he replies. It's about time." We're sitting near the door, our backs against the wall of the train.

"I agree with you, Joska, but I doubt they're taking us there."

"I heard from a *Wehrmacht* that the Americans have seized Muhldorf, and that the SS had wanted us to evacuate the camp by train. The train engineer was given strict orders to take us up to the Bavarian Alps for execution."

"All this we've gone through, just to be executed now?" I interrupt him.

Joska puts up his hand for silence. "Pista, Pista, don't worry. The *Wehrmacht* also told me that his own commander just gave the train engineer another order: delay the train and hand us over to the advancing Allies!"

"Oh, thank God." I let out a huge sigh of relief.

"See, Pista. What did I tell you? You're going home. Or away from here, at least."

On the verge of leaving this place for good, I look around and see the place differently for the first time, not as a prison camp of many horrors, but as a beautiful, serene, out-of-the-way spot in the Bavarian countryside. Farm fields stretch for miles, bordered by majestic snow-capped mountains. Right outside our train, rows of lush, dark plants grow in a field. Some prisoners eat the green leaves. Hmm, I'm hungry, too! I try to climb down from the boxcar to pick some leaves for myself, but the drop is too far for me.

Another young *Wehrmacht* notices my dilemma. "Let me give you a hand, son." He picks me up like a feather, and sets me down gently on the ground.

Slowly, I make my way into the field. The leaves look like spinach. I kneel down and pick some leaves, just the ones I want. Then I eat them, and they taste good.

At the very end of our train, I notice a flat car with some kind of artillery on top of it. Its presence worries me. If any of the Allied planes spot us, I think to myself, they could easily mistake us for a German military convoy.

Then the train whistle blows; the white steam from the engine escaping straight up into the air. We all get back on the train. I get a boost from the same young *Wehrmacht* who helped me down, and up I go. For the first time, the doors are not closed and locked when we pull out. It's good to see the scenery rushing by. I take a deep breath of the fresh, clean air all around me. I'm on my way out of here.

Chapter Nineteen
Feldafing

When I open my eyes, Nurse Erika is sitting by the bed.

"Pista, how would you like to meet one of the men from the company that saved you?"

"Oh, I'd love to."

"How would you like to meet their commanding officer, too, General Irving Smith of the United States Army?"

"I would, Nurse Erika. I want to thank them all."

I learn that in the morning I'll be taken to a Jewish rehabilitation facility in the town of Feldafing, not far from here, where I'll continue my recovery for a few more weeks.

Morning arrives, bright and sunny. Today I'm to leave this hospital where they brought me, literally, back to life. My joy, though, is mixed with sadness.

Since I have nothing to wear out of here but the prison uniform in which I came, the hospital staff has furnished me with a few new items of clothing: a shirt, a pair of pants, underwear, shoes, and white socks.

I sit now in Dr. Popper's office, saying good-bye. Nurse Erika is there, too, looking lovely, as always, in her crisp uniform. Today, she wears her blonde hair in a long braid.

"How do you feel this morning?" Dr. Popper asks.

"Better than ever, sir."

"You look it. So, do you think you're ready to rejoin the world?"

"Yes, I do, although I hate to leave."

"Pista, it's been a great experience nursing you back to health. We had our doubts you'd make it. To be frank, not everyone in your condition *would* have made it. But your determination and willpower kept you going."

"And your excellent care helped an awful lot, too, sir. As did Nurse Erika's." I give her a grateful look.

"Thank you," she replies.

Then Dr. Popper adds, "In case you haven't guessed, I'm officially discharging you today! Congratulations, Pista, on your excellent recovery. I want you to remember, now, to eat well, stay warm, and exercise. But don't overdo the physical activity."

"Yes, sir. I'll be careful."

Then, finally, I'm free to go! This is the moment I've looked forward to. But when it finally comes, I'm sad. The American army facility where I'm headed next is in the little town of Feldafing, not far from here, on an American army base that formerly belonged to the Hitler Youth, and is currently being used as a Jewish rehabilitation center.

Right outside the hospital entrance, an American jeep awaits me. Its driver is a handsome young GI of twenty-three or so, with reddish blond hair. He wears the standard olive drab U.S. Army uniform. He takes my small package of belongings and places it in the back seat behind us

"Please take good care of Pista for us," Nurse Erika tells the GI as he starts the motor. "He's special."

"Will do," the GI replies, giving her a wink. "OK Pista, hang on! Here we go!" The jeep's tires screech loudly, and we're off.

I turn around one last time and see Nurse Erika waving at me. I wave back with one hand, hanging onto the side of the jeep for dear life with the other. I can't help feeling wistful when the hospital where my life was saved vanishes from view.

"Pista," I'm Sergeant James Cox. "You can call me Jim," says my driver, interrupting my thoughts. "I'm in the company that pulled you out of that boxcar, although I wasn't one of the ones who did it."

"Whoever did it, I'm grateful to all of you. Thanks, Jim. And I'm pleased to meet you." This English phrase I pull from some distant school memory. Using his left hand to drive, Jim offers me his right. We shake. "I'm from Columbus, Ohio, in the United States," he informs me.

"I'm from Budapest, Hungary."

"Budapest, huh? I've never been there."

"It's been awhile for me, too."

Jim has a scattering of freckles, and his hair looks more reddish in the sunlight. His eyes are green, and his eyelashes a sandy color, sun-bleached almost white. His nose is sunburned pink. The most interesting thing about him, though, is that his jaws never stop moving, even when he isn't saying a word!

"Jim, may I ask you what you're moonching on?"

"Huh?"

"What food are you moonching right now?"

"Munching? You mean 'chewing'!"

"Yes! **Chew**-ing," I repeat, obediently, as if back in an English language class at school. At this, he grins, then slows down to take a corner. From inside his shirt pocket he produces a tiny package, wrapped first in foil, and then in light green paper.

"I'm chewing some gum. Care for some?"

"What is gum, exactly?"

"Try it. You'll see." I take a thin stick of gum from the package, unwrap its foil, and pop it into my mouth. It has a pleasant, refreshing mint flavor that lasts awhile. After the flavor fades, I swallow it.

"Where's your gum?" Jim asks me in a few minutes.

"I ate it."

He laughs. "Pista, you're not supposed to *eat* gum. It's hard on the digestion! You're supposed to just keep chewing it, and when you're tired of it, you spit it out."

"Oh." I've never heard of such a thing.

To demonstrate the proper the gum-chewing technique, he pulls a long strand of the stuff from his own mouth, stretches it out straight in front of him into a long, thin thread, and then folds it back, carefully, into his mouth. He offers me another foil-wrapped stick. "Here, Pista, try again."

In a couple of minutes, I pull my own gum out of my mouth, slowly, from behind my teeth, and stretch it out as far as possible in front of me, without breaking it. Then I fold it back into my mouth just as he did.

"Excellent! *Now* you're a gum chewer!"

Hmm. I've just had my first "taste" of American culture. I think I like it!

Meanwhile, Jim continues driving with only one hand. It feels like he's going at least one hundred miles an hour as we absorb every bump, crack, and crevice in the plentifully pot-holed dirt road. Slowly, I get used to the fast pace and bumpiness, and relax my white-knuckled grip.

Our drive takes us through some rich farmland. Along the way, we pass many burned out German tanks and overturned trucks, and much abandoned military equipment. The road takes another sharp turn as we pass a sign announcing our destination: "FELDAFING."

"Here we are. The compound you're about to see will be your new home, for awhile at least," Jim informs me.

Driving further into the compound, we soon come upon a group of two-story buildings.

Jim next explains, "These buildings used to be a training camp for the *Hitler*

Yugends (Nazi Youth). After the war ended, all Nazi activities were outlawed, and this camp was taken over by the Americans. Now we're using these facilities to house thousands of Jewish survivors, like you. Nice turnabout, huh, Pista?"

I grin. "I like it."

Jim stops the jeep outside a large cement block structure labeled "Administration Building." We both jump out of the vehicle, and Jim escorts me inside.

"Wait here," he says, threading his way toward a particular desk, one of many. Here, he hands some paperwork to a uniformed clerk on duty.

I glance around. The staff here is entirely American, and mostly male. All of the personnel wear drab army uniforms. The waiting room is busy. Typewriters click, papers crackle. I find a vacant chair and sit down.

Within a few minutes, Jim finds me again, and declares, "You're all set, Pista! Just wait here a few minutes. I'm told the general wants to meet you."

That's right! I'm about to meet General Smith, just as Nurse Erika told me yesterday. Suddenly, I'm nervous. "Thank you, Jim," I add, rising again. We shake hands.

"It's been fun," he tells me. "Best of luck with everything. Oh, here's a little souvenir of our trip here together." He hands me the rest of his package of gum.

"Thanks, Jim. You're swell."

He laughs. "Where'd you learn the word 'swell' Pista? I'm starting to think your English is more advanced than you're willing to admit."

"I heard it in an American movie."

"I should have known. So long, fella. Take care of yourself." And with that, he heads out the door.

I haven't time to even sit back down before a stained glass door just past the desks and typewriters opens. Another GI emerges and calls my name. The open door bears the name *General Irving Smith, Commander,* in gold leaf letters. I follow the soldier into an area that leads to another closed door. He knocks.

"Come in!" calls a deep voice.

The soldier opens the door. A distinguished looking American general, with a shock of white hair, stands tall and erect behind an impressive looking desk.

The white-haired man smiles warmly at me. "Come in, son. I'm General Irving Smith. I've been wanting to meet you ever since my troops found you on that ill-fated train. Dr. Popper told me about your miraculous recovery. Won't you have a seat?"

"Yes, sir." I sit down, suddenly nervous. "I, er, want to thank you, sir, for saving my life, or, I mean, I thank your men. . ." I can't believe how I'm stammering around in English all of a sudden! My nearly effortless English of only a few minutes ago seems to have left me now, right along with Jim.

Seeming not to notice my awkwardness with his language, General Smith replies, "You're very welcome, young man." He picks up a pipe from his desk and lights up.

I sit there like a stump, unsure what to say or do next.

"How do you feel?" the general asks me, taking a puff.

"A little tired, sir, but otherwise, good."

He walks around from behind his desk and offers me his hand. "I officially welcome you to Feldafing."

We shake hands.

"Sergeant Brown!" the commander calls.

Another soldier steps in and stands at attention. "You called me, sir?"

"Yes, Sergeant. At ease. Take this young man and assign him to his quarters."

"Yes, sir."

"Pista, I'll talk with you later. Now go with the sergeant and enjoy the facilities."

"Thank you very much, sir."

He winks at me as the sergeant and I exit his office.

The sergeant takes me first to the *Magazine*, and I'm outfitted with underpants, leather shoes, socks, shirts, jackets, pants, towels, toothpaste, toothbrush and soap. I'm even allowed to choose some of my own clothing. Such delicious freedom! And everything fits me properly, not anything like my old "one size fits all" pajama-like prison uniform.

An American Red Cross worker, a young woman with auburn hair, appears now to show me to my room on the second floor. She has sparkling brown eyes, the merriest I've ever seen. Ah, women! I drink in her physical beauty, making up for lost time. Seemingly oblivious to my admiration, she's pleasant and helpful, and puts me right at ease.

Inside my new dormitory, I take a quick inventory. No bunks! The beds and mattresses all have white sheets and clean blankets. And, sitting on the bed assigned to me is a huge white box with a big red cross painted on its side.

"That's a gift for you, Pista," explains my pretty young guide.

"Thank you, ma'am." Suddenly I am uncharacteristically self-conscious and shy, for the second time within about half an hour! Wow! Something about these Americans really takes your breath away!

The big white box is tightly and carefully sealed. I slide my fingers beneath one of the side flaps to rip it open, but *ouch!* My muscles still aren't strong enough to tear it open on my own.

My lovely Red Cross guide says warmly, "Let me help you, Pista." From her pocket she produces a nail file and, with the point, scores the gummed tape down the center. "This should do it."

"Thank you," I tell her, a bit embarassed at needing such help from a woman I'd prefer to impress. I guess she won't be considering me as the strong, manly type.

Inside the box I find several Hershey bars, peanut butter, and small cans of corned beef. I crow with delight at every new article, and then hand each item to her, one by one, so she can examine it herself. Evaporated milk, strawberry jam, cheese, even a small canned ham! I can't help thinking that back at Muhldorf, only a few miles from here, we prisoners probably would have killed each other for stuff like this. But here, it's all mine, and I'm free to eat it however and whenever I choose! Ah, what a glorious moment!

"I'm rich!" I exclaim, combing through the whole box over again and "oohing" and "ahhing" at everything a second time. "Gosh, Miss. . . what is your name again?"

She points to the name tag pinned to her blouse. "Miss Sanders. Barbara Sanders."

"Gosh, Miss Sanders, you've made me so happy with all these gifts. I'm sorry about forgetting your name." I feel myself blushing, and imagine my face probably matches the red cross painted on my gift box.

"That's all right, Pista. I understand." Next, she opens her purse and hands me an envelope.

"This is for me, also?" I ask. She nods. From the envelope, I pull out five German marks.

"That's a gift from the American Jewish Congress," she explains.

I'm overjoyed. "Thank you, Miss Sanders. You're an angel!"

"You're welcome. Call me Barbara."

"Thank you, Barbara." Then from out of the blue a colloquial English phrase comes to mind: "You're an absolute doll!"

She gives a long spontaneous laugh, and then answers, "Thank you, Pista. So are you!"

Wow! I've just flirted with her! I love it! It's so wonderful to be alive! Everything I went through was worth it, just to experience these last few minutes.

Gorgeous, sweet Barbara Sanders leaves me on my own to unpack and catch my breath again after being in her lovely presence.

Automatically, I start to hide my goodies under my mattress, when I feel a strange hand tapping me on the shoulder. I turn around quickly, anticipating something unpleasant, an expectation left over from my time inside the Muhldorf camp. Instead, I see a gentle looking young man with dark hair and eyes. He appears three or four years older than I.

"You must be Pista," he says in Hungarian. "Welcome. I'm George Nemes. They told me you'd be arriving."

"Yes. I just came here from the hospital in Seeshaupt."

"You must be a rescued prisoner, like me. You don't have to hide things under your mattress anymore. I did the same thing when I first got here. But it's unnecessary."

He points out a good-sized locker on the other side of the room. "Keep your clothes and valuables there; they'll be safe."

"Thank you, George," I mumble in relief, hardly recognizing my own voice.

"Would you like me to show you around here?" he asks.

"Yes, if you have time. I'd appreciate that."

"My pleasure." Companionably, he takes my arm and leads me outside.

First he points out the building that houses the dining hall, and then one where movies are shown. A third is Sick Bay. I shudder at the words.

"Don't be frightened," he tells me, noticing my reaction. "This Sick Bay is like a real hospital, not just a warehouse for corpses."

Clearly, he and I share some similar experiences.

Next, I see some soldiers working on the road nearby. I wrinkle my forehead, puzzled, and ask, "Who are those men?"

"They're German prisoners of war, doing their work detail," George explains. "They were captured by the Americans, and now they're being supervised by those armed guards you see."

It's hard for me to grasp that the soldiers in German uniforms are the *prisoners* now, and *I'm* free! What a strange life this is!

As it turns out, life at Feldafing during the next few weeks, while I complete my recovery, is the most carefree I've ever lived. Soon, my weight is up to 125 pounds. I feel good. I'm even beginning to laugh freely again. I make many friends here and even go fishing with a homemade rod, shaping a safety pin into a hook. It's fun to catch fish again, but I don't eat them. All my meals are provided here, and the food is good, too. So I give my fish away to some German children playing nearby. Even as I do so, I can hardly believe the irony of it all—*me,* giving food away, and to *Germans,* no less! Incredible!

Not a day passes, though, that I don't think of Mother. Now that I'm getting strong and healthy again, I resolve to find her.

I start with the Red Cross itself, and then various other agencies nearby. Within each of these, I search through lists and lists of names: Hungarian, Polish, Czech, and many others. I hop on trains and visit out-of-town agencies, too. Everywhere, the results are the same: no one has any information about my mother, where she's been, or where she might be now.

Finally, an American-Jewish organization directs me to J.O.I.N.T. (Jewish Organization International) in Feldafing. The woman at the desk there is gray-haired, with steel-rimmed glasses. She asks me many questions.

I give her all the facts I know of Mother's disappearance.

"Her maiden name?"

"Marmorstein."

She transfers this information to the typewriter.

"Chances are slim you'll find her this way," she says, "but it's worth a try. I'll distribute the information you just gave me to all our agencies in Europe. If we hear anything, we'll contact you where you're staying in Feldafing. Meanwhile, if you'd like, go down the hall to the first door. In that room you'll find all the lists of survivors available at this time."

"Thanks." In the small room, crowded with file cabinets, I find overwhelming documentations of the dead from Auschwitz, Dachau, Belsen, and many other, smaller camps—all without my mother's name.

After two or three weeks of hard searching at numerous agencies and offices, I need a break. I feel run down, tired, and discouraged. So I follow the advice Dr. Popper gave me before I left the hospital: rest when you're tired and eat well. I also take time out to see a few movies, and even a play performed by local talent. Finally, George and my other friends persuade me to go to a dance one Saturday night.

When we enter the dance hall, the band is playing a beautiful melody.

George introduces me to several girls. I'm sure they are Holocaust survivors.

"Betty, meet Pista. Pista, this is Betty, and her friends Marika, Agi, and Klari."

I can feel my face start to flush.

"Hi," I say, shyly.

I've never had any first-hand experience with girls, except for the lovely kiss Nurse Erika gave me when I left the hospital. I'm too shy to ask any of them to dance with me. So I stay in the background and enjoy watching the others have fun.

Then, out of nowhere, Agi grabs my hand and leads me onto the dance floor. She's about my height, with dark hair and long, beguiling lashes.

"I don't know how to dance," I protest.

"Just listen to the beat!"

"What beat?"

She doesn't answer, but just pulls me closer to her, the closest I've ever been to a girl. It's a strange but nice feeling! I forget my awkwardness and enjoy it.

I'm discovering how pleasant a girl's company can be. Back at the dormitory that night, I keep George awake, querying him about Agi.

"How old is Agi?"

"Sixteen or seventeen."

"I think she likes me."

"Oh? Did you kiss her?"

"Well, I. . ."

"Did you or didn't you?"

"I did!" I pop up into a sitting position. "In fact, she stuck her tongue right in my mouth!"

At this, George hoots with laughter.

"What's so funny?"

"You should have seen the expression on your face!"

"How would *you* feel if a girl stuck her tongue in your mouth?"

"I'd love it."

"So they all do it?"

"Maybe not *all*. But the ones who know the score probably do."

"What score?" I'm thinking of soccer, or maybe American baseball, but he couldn't mean either of those.

"I mean. . . score. . . like the ones who aren't virgins."

"What's a virgin?"

"Pista, have you never made love to a girl?"

"There weren't a great many available at the camp I was in."

"The ones who've never made love are virgins."

"Is Agi a virgin?"

"Why don't you ask her? Now good night!"

Goodness, I've so much to learn. The time at the camp not only damaged my health; it also interfered with my basic education. I'll have to catch up as soon as possible! Tonight, I don't even experience my usual lingering nightmares. Instead, I dream of girls, lots of them. Beautiful girls!

A few days later, George and I decide to travel to Munich, about 40 miles from Feldafing. Maybe I can pick up some leads there to help me find Mother. The train ride is comfortable—not at all like being stuffed in a boxcar with eighty other prisoners. Instead, there's just one passenger assigned to each soft, upholstered, seat.

I still tremble, though, at my memories of the camp at Muhldorf, even during my waking hours. It would be horrible to wake up from this marvelous dream and find myself back in the Dying Room. I have to be certain I'm not just dreaming. I look around quickly—nobody is watching, so I pull a hair on my arm. *Ouch! It hurts!* I know now I'm not dreaming.

Munich, like all of Germany, lies in ruins: broken walls, destroyed buildings, rubble, and debris everywhere. Upon arrival, George and I board an old streetcar and find a place to stand on the rear platform. We're informed upon boarding that the car will not stop until reaching the downtown area. No wonder—there's nothing to stop for, only ruins.

Finally, downtown Munich is in sight. George and I jump off the streetcar with the little package of lunch we've brought with us. We see people walking around, mothers wheeling baby carriages, children playing in the park, cars and bicycles whizzing by. Everyday life continues, despite the devastation all around us.

At the J.O.I.N.T Agency we see many other people of all ages and nationalities, all of them looking for their loved ones. I check every list I can find. Thousands of names. . . but none of them is Mother's.

Tired from our morning's work, George and I find a quiet park with benches. Seated in the warm sunshine, we unwrap the sandwiches we've brought along for lunch.

I still have a few of the German marks Miss Barbara Sanders gave me along with my Red Cross welcoming package, so I buy a large red apple from a street vendor. I wipe it on my sleeve until it shines. It's been a long time since I've eaten fresh fruit. Salivating at the mere idea of it, I open my mouth and sink my teeth eagerly into the delicious treat. But then I must stop in mid-bite; it's just too painful. My gums are bleeding! Quickly, I find a nearby fountain and rinse my mouth several times until the bleeding stops. Then I wash the apple, cut it into small pieces with my loyal pocket knife, and share it with George.

Later that day, we return to Feldafing. I'm refreshed, but still without a clue of Mother's whereabouts. On the trip back, though, I reach a decision. I must return to Budapest as soon as I can. There's no more time to waste. I'm well enough to travel now, and I've delayed my homecoming long enough. Mother would do the same, most likely. If there is anyplace I'm likely to find her, it's there.

The next day, at the Feldafing American Army facility, I return to the Administration Building that processed my paperwork upon arrival and request documents for travel purposes. They send me to see General Smith again.

General Smith greets me warmly. "Come in, Pista. Have a seat." He reaches for his pipe and points to a chair. "What can I do for you?" He sits sideways on the top of his desk.

"I'd like to get a travel document, sir, so I can return to Hungary."

The general takes a long puff from his pipe, then slowly exhales. "Son, the Communists are taking over Eastern Europe. Should I help you return to the Eastern Sector, I'd be betraying you, a young orphan who's already free. Pista, how would you like to go to the United States instead?"

Thoughts of Jim the friendly GI, chewing gum, Hershey bars, and even the tiny Statue of Liberty I once carved for the *Wehrmacht* guard at Muhldorf rush through my mind. "I'd love to," I reply.

"Great! I'll arrange it! And I'll even make sure they'll find a nice family you can live with."

"It's been my dream for a long time to go to the United States, sir, but there's something else in the way right now."

"What's in your way, young man? Let me help."

"When my family arrived at Auschwitz, my brother and I were separated from our mother. I haven't seen her in going on two years. I've visited every agency for miles around; she's not on any published list. I need to return to Hungary right away and try to find her."

"Pista, many people. . ." He bows his head and falls silent, deciding not to complete his sentence. I know what he's started to say. But he's right; I don't want to hear it. Instead, he says, "I'll tell you what—sleep on it. Come back tomorrow and we'll discuss it further."

My heart sinks. What he really means is, "Travel papers to America, yes. Travel papers back to Hungary, no." I'm on my own.

As I stand up to leave, General Smith rises from his sitting position on the desk. We shake hands. "Thank you for taking the time to see me, sir," I tell him.

After dinner that night, I pack a knapsack, a map of Europe, and every ounce of determination I have.

Chapter Twenty
Back to Budapest

At 10:30 the next morning, without saying any of the proper good-byes to those who've treated me so kindly, I slip off like a hobo, knapsack in hand, to the tiny Feldafing railroad station. Soon I arrive inside its sheltered waiting room. This lobby is empty of travelers, except me. A uniformed attendant perches behind a glass-paned ticket counter. I sit down on a nearby bench. The attendant sizes me up. Already I feel ill at ease, almost like a runaway criminal.

I glance around, trying to feel and act nonchalant. The wall clock says 11 a.m. Slowly, I get up and approach the ticket booth. My shoes clomp noisily on the stone floor, creating a series of sharp echoes that pierce the silence. The attendant, a white-haired man in his 60s, sniffs under his bushy white mustache when I present myself at his window.

"Will the train to Munich be on time?" I inquire, doing my best imitation of a seasoned young traveler.

Mustache pulls out an old fashioned pocket watch. "She'll be here in thirty minutes, at 11:30. Right on time!"

"Thank you, sir." I return to my bench, attempting a relaxed saunter.

At 11:30 sharp, I hear a distant whistle, followed by the rumbling of an approaching train. Soon the engine itself rolls past the waiting room window, hissing steam as it slows to a halt. I pick up my knapsack, go outside, and board the nearest coach. Except for me, it's empty.

I take a window seat and make myself as comfortable as possible. Soon the train pulls out and gathers speed, first sending out a long whistle, but soon making only the steady humming sounds of wheels against rails.

"Tickets, please!" The conductor stops at my seat.

"I'm a Jewish orphan, and don't have a ticket," I state flatly.

The conductor moves on without further questions.

I still have a few of the German marks the Jewish organization gave me in Feldafing for pocket money. I won't have to worry about food: wherever I can find a Jewish agency or Red Cross, food and shelter will be provided to me for the asking.

I unfold my map and check the route I'm to follow. Munich, Schwandorf, Pilsen, Prague, Bratislava and Budapest. To accomplish this, I'll need to cross (illegally) the American and Russian zones, as well as the

German and Czech borders.

I can only guess at the challenges ahead as I traverse, for the first time, a whole series of unfamiliar zones, each of them off-limits, in the legal sense, to anyone lacking the proper travel documents. Before our family's involuntary odyssey to Auschwitz, I'd not traveled outside Hungary at all, and never alone. Now all sorts of questions without answers buzz around inside my head. What I wouldn't give to have Andris with me right now!

Sitting here alone, I reflect on all the ways I miss him. Back home, having Andris around always made daily life much more bearable, from studying hard school subjects to the bullying we faced. Whatever the obstacles, Andris always managed to breeze through life, it seemed, a golden boy with the world at his feet. As with our father, anyone who ever really knew him forgave him his heritage. By the time we were forced to leave school, for instance, Andris had even his most anti-Semitic teachers in the palm of his hand, practically weeping over his departure.

After all, who can resist a star, even a Jewish one? You could despise all other Jews, but still you had to love Andris. I was never jealous, but merely in awe and content to coast along in my older brother's larger than life shadow.

Somewhere along the way, though, he must have prepared me for life without him. For now, deep down, I know I can make this trip alone, even if I'd rather not. *"I'll complete this journey in your memory, Andris,"* I tell him now. *"Yes, I'll make it to Budapest in one piece, somehow, for both of us. I'll see Mother again, and hug her and kiss her almost to pieces, as you would if only you could."*

My most serious concern, though, remains the recent Russian occupation of the whole Eastern Sector. I really don't know how I'll get through Czechoslovakia without travel papers. I'll simply have to trust that when the time comes, I'll be able to figure out what to do. With this troubling reality fixed firmly in my mind, I doze off, uneasily, to the steady rhythm of the train as it speeds toward Munich.

I wake when the train jerks to a halt, signaling my arrival. I rub my eyes, stand up and stretch, clomp down the steps, and make my way to the same Red Cross agency I visited a couple days ago with George. Fortunately, it's right near the Munich station . There, I spend the night sleeping on a portable army cot.

Early the next morning I wash up, grab a bite of breakfast in the Red Cross kitchen, and head back to the railroad yards.

Over twenty pairs of railroad tracks greet me at the station, some with boxcars, some with passenger coaches, and many others with detached engines scattered everywhere. Suddenly, I'm in a quandary. On which of these trains should I stow away to get to American-occupied Schwandorf, the first of my series of illegal destinations?

A railroad worker, his cap pulled down below his eyes, climbs out from under one of the boxcars. He grins at me. "Beautiful morning, isn't it?"

"Yes."

"And where are *you* from?"

"I'm a Hungarian Jew, trying to get back to Budapest. Right now, I'm looking for a freight train to take me to Schwandorf."

The friendly fellow thinks a moment, and then says, "Follow me!"

We cross more rows of tracks. Finally, he points to several boxcars. "There's your train. Or most of it."

"Thank you."

"My pleasure. Your train leaves tonight."

I select one of the newer looking boxcars and climb aboard. The car is empty, except for an abundance of straw on the floor. I build myself a comfortable nest in one corner and then lie down and fall asleep. My hunger pains wake me again around noon.

Leaving my hiding place, I tramp back over to the Red Cross, now teeming with myriad international refugees. A group of seven young men stand around in the food line, talking amongst themselves in Hungarian.

"Is this the line for lunch?" I ask them.

"Ah, *Magyar ember!*" says an extremely tall one among them, spontaneously hugging me. I feel like a dwarf beside him. He appears nearly seven feet tall! "Where are you from?" he inquires of me, looking straight down into my eyes.

"Budapest. How about you?"

"I'm from Kolozsvar."

"What's your name?" I ask.

"I'm Sandor. But my friends call me Giant," he answers, sheepishly.

I laugh. "I can see why," I observe. "Most of us *Magyars* don't grow *quite* as tall as you. I'm Pista Nasser."

We shake hands.

"Hey guys!" Giant yells, getting the attention of the rest of their group. "Look! I've found another *Magyar ember*, Pista Nasser."

"Hi! Nice to meet you," I greet the other six, shaking hands with everyone.

Along with Giant, my other new friends' names are Otto, Arpad, Ferenc, Attila, Rudi, and Erno.

By the time we all get through the lunch line and finish eating, the friendship amongst us blossoms, and we find much in common as displaced Hungarian refugees. It feels especially good to be with peers from my own small, distant country, and to speak my own language again. I'm glad for their invitation to join them on their trip back to Hungary.

But just then, Giant inquires casually, "Pista, you have all your travel papers in order, don't you?"

Oh well, I think, I've been discovered after all. Certainly they'll dump me now, and I'll be on my own again. I clear my throat and reply, "No, Giant, actually, I couldn't get any. I was staying at an American military base, and it was impossible."

"What will you use for identification, then?" asks Rudi.

"I don't know. I've decided I'll cross that bridge when I come to it." Now I hold my breath and wait for one of them to take the lead in booting me from their group. How could I blame them? After all, I'd be nothing but a liability.

Instead, to my utter amazement, all I hear in reply is Giant saying, "Let's get a map, then, and plan out our itinerary."

At this I brighten, and resume breathing normally. "I already have a map," I announce. "In fact, our whole trip is planned, all the way to Bratislava and the Hungarian border! I've even picked out our own boxcar."

"Wow, this is the kind of service we've been needing!" says Otto. "A travel agent and a tour guide, all rolled up into one!"

Everyone laughs. Soon, I lead the way across the tracks to "our" boxcar. After climbing aboard, all eight of us settle ourselves cozily in the plentiful straw.

Amazing! I tell myself. Just this morning, I'd been wishing for my brother. Now, within a few hours, I have seven!

Clank. . . the car jerks suddenly forward. Slowly, the train moves out. We're juggled back and forth numerous times. Finally, the whistle blows, and we're chugging off to Schwandorf.

Almost immediately, I sleep. When I wake again, the train moves at a modest speed. Two of my new buddies sit inside the open door, their legs dangling outside in the cool breeze. I stand up inside the boxcar and stretch, arching my back, until I feel all the bones crackle. How good it feels right now to be alive, healthy, and on my way home!

"Come over here, Pista, and sit down," Erno suggests. "It's fun riding like this."

I join him and Arpad. Then, settling in, I take a deep breath, drinking in the fresh air. Ahead, I see the engine laboring around a wide curve, spouting smoke. Then the wind's direction changes suddenly, and we all receive a mouthful of smoke, plus soot in our eyes. Ouch! Quickly, I stand up and move away from the door. About then, the train slows to a stop outside a small red brick station.

This particular station teems with white-helmeted American MPs.

"I wonder what they're up to?" I ask aloud, an uneasy feeling in my stomach.

"I don't know," Erno replies, "but it looks like they'll search the train."

Before I can even think the next thought, Giant grabs me by the neck. "Look! He's hiding here. We got him." My heart's in my throat, but everyone else bursts into laughter. "Don't worry, Pista," Giant reassures me, seeing the horrified expression on my face. "We won't let you down." God, I hope not!

Now my heart's really pounding as the MPs open every boxcar on both sides. Papers are taken at one door, while the opposite door is guarded by a separate MP, making sure no one hides within any of the boxcars.

Three white-helmeted MPs advance toward our party, looking stern.

"Everybody to the front door!" one of them orders. "And have your travel papers ready for examination!"

My buddies assemble at the front door.

Giant bends over and whispers into my ear, "Stand behind me, Pista, with your legs spread apart, just like mine. I'll cover you from the front."

Erno, standing in the front row with all seven sets of travel papers, hands them over, in a single stack, to the officer.

"Is everyone here at the front door?" the officer asks, directing his query to the MP at the back door.

The one at the back door peers inside of our boxcar carefully, making sure no one hides there. He sees us all standing together, but fortunately, does not count us. "Yes, sir," the MP finally replies, "they're all there at the front door."

Meanwhile, the officer at the front door counts the documents, glances up at everyone visible, hands everyone's papers back to Erno, and moves on to the other boxcars. *"Thank you God."*

I don't think I have much blood remaining in my face, or much of a heartbeat left, either. If the rest of my trip's going to be like this, I don't know if I can stand it! But I must.

When I calm down and catch my breath again, I shake Giant's hand.

"Whew! That was close. Thanks, Giant, for saving my neck!"

He smiles down at me. "I'm happy to help you out, Pista. We're all in this together, you know, going home to the same place."

Then I tell the group, "Thanks, guys." They all just smile and say, "You're welcome," and shrug their shoulders, as if having done nothing. I'm lucky to have such great friends, and with steel nerves, too.

By the time we arrive at Schwandorf we're starved, and we hurry off the train to find the local Red Cross. After eating our fill, we walk around, sightseeing. There's not much to see; Schwandorf, like all of Germany, has been devastated.

We spend the night at the Red Cross shelter. The next day promises to be tough for me. I must sneak into the Russian sector, crossing the border from Germany into occupied Czechoslovakia. Tomorrow's precise destination, if I can make it across the border, is the Czech city of Pilsen.

Early the next morning. we consult the train schedules and learn that a train leaves Schwandorf station for Pilsen at 2 p.m.

We board the passenger train's last coach. Our car is crowded and smelly; the afternoon weather is hot. Passengers perspire freely, soaking their clothes and mopping their foreheads.

Right on time, our train begins to chug and chuff. Through the open windows, I occasionally catch a much needed breath of fresh air.

Eventually, we near the dreaded Russian sector. Anxiety overwhelms me. *"How I wish I had the right travel papers now!"*

The train jerks suddenly a couple times, probably just the Communist crew taking over the engine from the previous crew. Slowly, the engine continues laboring along for a few more minutes, and then grinds to an abrupt stop. Glancing out the window, I see the station, and then a huge sign: YOU ARE NOW ENTERING THE RUSSIAN ZONE. I also see my first Russian soldier ever, running along the platform beside the train. He looks tough, with a submachine gun slung over his shoulder. A shiny red star is pinned on his cap. He also sports a red band on his sleeve, meaning he's a member of the Russian Military Police.

Then more Russian soldiers appear, as if from nowhere, and board our coach. Praying for a miracle, I glance at my friends. They're all sitting stiffly inside the coach, as if frozen to their seats, looking anxious. Even Giant, the most easy going member of the group, looks worried now.

Then the moment I've been dreading arrives: the Russian soldiers begin examining the travel papers of every passenger in our coach. Instantly, I develop sharp stomach cramps from pure nervousness and run for the toilet. Locating the WC just in time, I recognize the back of a Russian soldier's uniform as I sneak inside and lock the door tightly behind me.

An instant later, someone rattles the door knob.

"I'm coming," I call.

I hear a curse in Russian, followed by a frenzied pounding on the outside door of the WC. I'll have to open up right this instant, with my pants only halfway on, I realize. But when the Russian soldier sees me half undressed, he seems to grasp my predicament, and his anger subsides a bit. Still, he gestures for me to come out and step into the aisle. I'm afraid my time on this train is coming to an end, fast. I yank my pants back up and get ready to present myself to the authorities and be thrown off the train.

Outside the WC again, less than five feet ahead of me, stands a Russian military policeman toting a submachine gun. His legs are spread apart, and he blocks the aisle while the travel inspection is going on. His back is turned to me.

Next, I hear a sudden commotion from somewhere else inside the car. Apparently, someone else lacking papers has been caught trying to sneak across the border. The Russian who just ordered me out of the toilet now pushes me aside to rush to the aid of his fellow inspectors. He even squeezes past his comrade still blocking the aisle.

I disappear back into the toilet, but this time I leave the door open, making it appear there's no one inside. Standing behind the door, I scarcely dare to breathe. Next, I hear some sort of scuffle a few compartments away, loud cursing, and the slow, dragging footsteps of someone being forcibly escorted off the train. I don't dare move a muscle.

Seconds, and then minutes, pass with agonizing slowness. I hear the Russians noisily re-boarding the train from a door somewhere near the WC. Sounding excited and anxious, they exchange words, yelling up and down the aisle to various other members of their inspection team. Then the door of the WC, where I still huddle, motionless as a statue, is abruptly pushed open, hard, against me. Help! A Russian is coming in!

That's when the train whistle suddenly blows. My surprise intruder stops just short of entering, hesitates a second or two, and then, with a loud curse, slams the door shut from the outside and stomps off down the aisle.

Soon the train begins moving again. I collapse onto the toilet, a trembling wreck, shaking like a leaf from head to toe. My stomach cramps have disappeared, but I'm drenched in sweat from all my anxiety.

When I finally manage to walk back to where my friends sit, with my legs still shaking like jelly, everyone in our group is flabbergasted to see me.

"Where *were* you?" asks Giant. "We thought the Russians had kicked you off the train for sure. Here," he pats a seat, "sit here by the window. You look done in."

I tumble like a sack of loose grain into the proffered seat.

"You were lucky just now," Giant tells me. "The Russians caught an SS man. If they hadn't been so involved with getting rid of *him*, I'd hate to think what might have happened to *you*!"

Even in my exhausted state, the irony of what's just taken place sinks in: of all things, a German SS inadvertently helping a Jewish concentration camp boy escape across an illegal border to rejoin his family!

Erno says, "Well, Pista, congratulations! The worst is over! You've now made it through the Russian zone."

"Thank God," I reply, wondering to myself if I'll ever relax again.

For a long while, I stare out the window, still in a daze, as the train speeds past dozens of destroyed villages and burned out farmhouses. Then, determined to get my close call off my mind, I unfold my map and study it. "It looks like Pilsen's another seventy kilometers from here," I announce to the others.

"That should take us about an hour and a half, then," says Attila, seated beside Erno opposite Giant and me.

As we near Pilsen, the scenery begins to change. Farms are replaced by scattered residences as the train slows its speed. Then a sign reading PILSEN whisks by our open window.

"I see the station coming up," Giant says.

Pilsen is world famous for its beer industry, and I'm eager to see it. When we enter the city, we find people sitting on park benches among well-groomed surroundings and flower beds. The destruction is less evident here than in the German cities we've seen. Walking down the square, we spot a group of pretty girls. We stop to flirt, but there's not much response from them. We still have some fun. The Jewish organization here treats us especially well. After a nice dinner, we even see a movie.

The next morning, we board a train to Prague, the Czech capital. This beautiful old city is mostly undamaged from the war. We haven't much time, though, to look around. Soon we must catch another train to Bratislava, right on the Czech-Hungarian border.

All eight of us stand around on the platform of the overcrowded Prague station.

"Listen, guys," I say, "it looks impossible for all of us to board this train."

"Let's spread out," Erno suggests, "and every man for himself."

I'm only half listening, since my mind is already at work on a scheme. Time is running out for us; the train will leave soon, either with or without the eight of us aboard.

"Giant," I say, motioning to him, "stand here against the train. Now lock your fingers together so I can use them as a step."

"Okay." Then, from his locked hands, he lifts me up onto his shoulders. From this position, I'm even with the toilet window. I'm in luck; the window isn't locked. Quickly, I pry it open and climb inside. Next, I lock the WC door. Two of my buddies climb in easily through the window. Now, though, we're divided, with three inside the train, but the other five still outside on the platform.

Now it's Giant's turn to "board" the train through the WC. The other four still on the platform push Giant through the window, while the three of us already inside pull him in. He's halfway inside when he gets stuck. Getting Giant's huge body all the way inside the window is like pulling a trapped cork from a wine bottle.

Just then, Erno yells from below, "Hey, the train's moving!"

The three of us inside the WC get panicky, but we quickly realize there's nothing we can do. Despite my efforts, four of our buddies have been left behind, and Giant is stuck, half inside and half outside the window. I stand on the toilet bowl, pulling, inch by inch, on the seat of his pants, until he's finally all the way in.

By now, we "insiders" are packed into the WC like sardines, and totally exhausted. Giant perches on the pot, with two of us balancing ourselves on his knees. The fourth "insider" squats on the floor, his back against the door.

"What about the rest of our group?" I ask, worried, disappointed with myself for not thinking and acting fast enough to get everyone else into the train with us.

"Don't worry, Pista," they all reassure me. "Those guys will be on the very next train out of here. They'll catch up with us tomorrow morning, at the very first station inside Hungary."

Their assurances make me feel better.

During our crowded journey, we hear numerous anxious knocks on the door of the WC, which other passengers are as desperate to enter as we are to leave. Finally, we do exit the train's "facility," but not until we're all the way into Bratislava, which is still part of Czechoslovakia, but very near the Hungarian border. When we're able, at long last, to spring ourselves from the WC like a quartet of pent up jack-in-the-boxes, we're stiff and sore all over from the confinement. But that scarcely matters. What does matter is that we're here. And I can even see my beloved Hungary from across the Ipoly River as we leave the train.

No rail service exists between this part of Czechoslovakia and Hungary. Here, only the chilly Ipoly separates the two countries, creating a watery natural border. We move to the river. From where the four of us stand now, the bridge spans from bank to bank, and the river is fairly wide. As I gaze across the water to the Hungarian side, I'm suddenly filled with joy. I'm home, almost! From here, I can see willow trees, grass, and field upon field of beautiful, brightly colored wild flowers over on the Hungarian side.

Here at the edge of the Ipoly, on the brink of my homecoming, my toes kissing its cool, clear water, my memory takes me all the way back to 1938.

I'm seven years old, and it's summer vacation on a warm afternoon late in June. About a week ago, Father, Mother, Andris and I arrived here in Zebegeny, on the Hungarian side of the Ipoly River. The little village where we're staying features numerous whitewashed farmhouses and a few blue and white vacation villas. Even though this quaint village is nestled right on the Danube for good fishing, the four of us have decided to walk to the very next village, Szob. It lies right beside the Ipoly River, forms a delta, and merges into the great blue Danube. Here, the fishing is the best of all.

On the banks of the Ipoly, our favorite fishing spot is about a hundred yards south of the bridge crossing over to the Czech border. On clear days like today, I love to look across the river to the other side, and think about what might lie beyond the tiny strip of Czech landscape I can see from here.

Before they start fishing this afternoon, Father and Andris build a campfire, while I chase butterflies and collect bluebells and Margueritas. I love to surprise Mother with them.

She's sitting beside the fire now, watching Andris and Father fishing a short distance away. With my hands, I sneak up and cover her eyes from behind, asking her, "Guess who, Momma?"

She laughs. "Andris?"

"No, it's not Andris. He's fishing. Guess again."

"Then it's Father!"

"No, silly. He's fishing, also."

"Then it must be my little Pista!"

"Right!" I say, uncovering her eyes, and then running around to shower her with kisses and place my carefully gathered bouquet of Margueritas and bluebells on her lap.

"Pistukam, what beautiful flowers! Thank you." She hugs and kisses me. I run away, delighted, to search for more for her.

Awhile later, Mother opens up a large hamper of food.

"Pistukam, go get the fish Andris and Father have caught, so I can start lunch."

I run off, hopping and skipping, singing my favorite nursery rhyme, "Egyedem-begyeden, tenger tanc.. . ." I arrive at the river bank. "Andris," I yell, "Mother wants the fish now!"

"Shhh!" Andris silences me. "Quiet, or you'll scare the fish away."

Now I stand behind him, tugging on his checkered shirt, whispering in his ear. "Momma wants those fish, now!"

"Shut up, little brat"

Next, I sink my teeth playfully into his thigh, "If you won't give me those fish, I'll bite you."

"Be quiet! I just got a bite."

"If you don't hand over those fish, you'll get a bigger bite from me."

Father glances over at us from beneath his white canvas hat.

"Come on, boys," he says, "something tells me lunch will be ready soon." He gathers up the fish he and Andris have caught and carries them to Mother.

The picture fades as I continue gazing, as if hypnotized by my own thoughts, into the gently flowing water. I'm standing alone now, weeping quietly as I gaze across at the far shore of the Ipoly on the Hungarian side where I once played so merrily surrounded by Father, Mother, and Andris.

What I wouldn't give now to have them all with me again.

Twenty-one
Homecoming

The only legal way to get across the Ipoly River is by either driving or walking over the bridge. A gate on each side stops all traffic for inspection. There is no way then, that I can just slip across without any identification papers.

Giant shakes me. "Hey, Pista, did you fall asleep?"

I quickly wipe my eyes and get up.

"I'm just thinking that the only way for me to cross the river is to swim."

"Then we'd better wait until dark," suggests Erno.

We all agree.

Night approaches and the air grows damp. About half a mile from the bridge, I undress, giving each of the three others a different piece of my clothing to hang onto for me while I swim across the river. A cool wind blows from the silently flowing Ipoly. I wear only my underpants; already I feel goose pimples spreading down my arms as I survey whatever I can of the dark river. Giant, Erno, and Arpad disappear toward the bridge. Since they'll have no problem legally crossing over the bridge, our plan is for us all to meet up again at the river bank on the other side once I've made it across.

I edge my way down to the river, careful to avoid making any noise. Then I slide quickly into the water. *B-r-r-r!* It's icy cold! I start to swim across, knowing I must take care not to allow the current to drag me down to the throat of the Danube, which is treacherous with whirlpools.

I'm halfway across when I realize I'm not swimming in a straight line, so I put more effort into fighting the current. Once, I must stop because I've swallowed water, and I lose a few precious yards. Finally, though, the eastern shore of Hungary is just ahead of me. I climb out of the murky water. I'm shivering with cold, and my teeth chatter uncontrollably. But that doesn't matter. What *does* matter is that finally, against all odds, I've made it back home to Hungary, alive, well, and ready to go on with life.

In less than half an hour, my friends find me on the river bank, just as we've planned.

"Did you have a nice swim?" Giant asks me, jokingly.

"Just lovely," I reply, my teeth still chattering. "Warm as a bathtub! Brrr, who's got my shirt?"

"I do," replies Arpad, tossing it my way. Quickly, I get dressed, my wet underpants still clinging to me as I pull on my trousers. Ah! It feels heavenly to wear my clothes again after spending so long in that freezing water.

From the river bank, we all walk a short distance in the cold night air to the Szob railroad station, where we sleep on the benches. Sometime very early in the morning, Otto, Attila, Rudi, and Ferenc must have found us there, just as the others assured me earlier, and joined us sleeping on the benches and the floor. When I wake up, the first thing I see is all seven of my friends sprawled around the area, fast asleep.

I sit up and rub the sleep from my eyes, wondering what my first day back in Hungary will be like. After everyone else wakes up, we decide to board the first train to Budapest. It's so crowded that I again become separated from my friends as we all search for places to sit. Unable to find an available seat, I settle for the connecting walkway between the two coaches. Soon, the train is rattling toward Budapest.

Glancing out the window later, I catch sight of the majestic silver ribbon of the Danube. It curves against the turn of the Buda Mountains, which are crowned by several ancient crumbling castles. Hooray, I'm on familiar ground! And the nation of my birth is even more beautiful than I remember it. How I've waited for this day, yearned for it, dreamed of it. And, finally, it's here.

I ask someone sitting beside me, "What happened to the railroad track running parallel to ours?"

"Oh, you mean those broken ties? The Nazis did it. They ruined everything! They stole crops, livestock, and even forced my family to sleep in the barn, while the SS occupied my house."

As it seems, even Hungarians who weren't deported suffered personally at the hands of the Nazis. I feel the train slow down as the historical city of Vac, just northeast of Budapest, appears. After stopping briefly at the little station there, we continue on. Now we're nearing the Budapest outskirts. I wonder what's become of my once thriving, beautiful, native city. Before the war, Budapest had been a sophisticated, cosmopolitan capital, a true jewel among European cities. I wonder, if I'll ever again see, for instance, the graceful, majestic bridges spanning the powerful blue-black Danube, or the crystal clear public swimming pools Andris and I loved as kids. The parks and museums. The little zoo on Maragaret Island, with its pure white albino peacock and other rare species. The soccer stadium, where Andris and I went with Father on weekends, to cheer on our national team and dream of our own future stardom.

I hope I won't be disappointed at what awaits me here, but fear I might. Damn the Nazis! Still, they're able to punish me, even now.

Just as I'd feared, the Ujpest station near my old home is mangled almost beyond recognition. The train stops, but I make no move to get off.

"Isn't this your stop, Pista?" my friends ask.

"It used to be, but I'm not getting off."

"Why not?"

"Nobody's home."

"Yes, of course. Sorry. Where *are* you going, then, Pista?"

"Clear out to the Eastern Terminal, the very last stop. My Aunt Manci and Uncle Bela live there, or they used to anyway. Did you guys ever hear about the Swedish houses Raoul Wallenberg set up as refuges for Jews right in the heart of Budapest?"

"No. What was that all about?"

"Wallenberg's a Swedish diplomat with economic ties to Hungary. His family's rich, apparently. He set up several "Swedish Houses," like little embassies, for Jews to live in, right in the center of Budapest. As long as the people stayed inside, they were immune from Nazi arrest. The night before we were deported, when my family and I were all together at the Budafok brick factory, my mother told me she thought our Aunt Manci, her oldest sister, and her husband, my Uncle Bela, might have been taken into one of the Swedish houses just in time."

"But how would you find their Swedish house just now?" ask one of my friends, "You never went there, did you?"

"No. I'd have no idea where their Swedish house was. Besides, they would have moved out of it again by now, I'm sure. All I can do is go back to their old apartment and see if they've moved back in."

"And if they haven't?"

"He'll cross that bridge when he comes to it. Right, Pista?" says Giant, knowingly.

I smile. "For now, I just have to hope they're there. What about the rest of you guys?"

"We're all in the same boat as you. We don't know what's waiting for us when we get home. Perhaps nobody, perhaps nothing. But at least we're all from the same village, so we can stick together. If you don't find anyone, Pista. . ."

I finish the sentence. "I just might turn up in Kolozsvar, when you least expect it."

"You'd always be welcome, Pista. You're part of our family now."

"Thanks, guys." Moved, I manage to hold back my tears, just barely.

Within half an hour, the train grinds to a halt at the Eastern terminal.

I feel my heart beating rapidly again. . . *"I'm home!"*

After I look out the window, though, I tell my friends, sadly, "Just look at this station. What a mess! It used to be so beautiful." The framework of the roof still stands, but it looks like a skeleton, with pieces of broken glass now being all that remains of the once proud Keleti Railroad Terminal.

"Sorry about how it looks, Pista," they murmur. They, of course, have nothing to compare it to, having never seen this grand old terminal in better days. Besides, they're all too busy looking wistfully at me.

"But, at least you're home," someone adds.

Then Giant says the inevitable. "I guess this is good-bye, Pista, for now, at least." My huge "brother's" shoulders tremble with emotion as he leans down to hug me.

I look into Giant's kindly blue eyes, which are now tearing up. "Thank you, Giant, for everything you've done for me. I wouldn't have made it without you, you know. And all the rest of you," I add. For my other six "brothers" have now gathered in the aisle, near the door through which I'm about to exit the train and plunge into the unfamiliar world of post-war Budapest.

I hug them all, one by one: Arpad, Rudi, Otto, Attila, Ferenc, and Erno, and then, once again, I hug Giant.

"Szerbusz, God be with you!" we all tell each other, clumping awkwardly together for a final group hug. Then, before any of them can see the tears now streaming freely down my face, I'm out the door and walking quickly away. Once outside the station, I look for No. 46 streetcar, which will take me (I hope) to my Aunt Manci and Uncle Bela's home in the center of the city.

Quickly, I find a No. 46 and hop aboard. The old yellow coaches are still in good running condition, I note, as I watch the uniformed conductor walking slowly toward me. It's hard for me to keep my balance in the swaying car. Since childhood, this trick has always been easy for me, but, now, I realize, I'm out of practice.

"Tickets, please," says the conductor.

"I'm a Jewish refugee, just arrived home from Germany. I'm sorry, but I've no money, sir."

"Welcome home, young man," the conductor answers. "You should go to the Jewish Agency in Lehel Square, and they'll issue you a free travel pass. They have shower facilities, too, and food and clothing available."

I smile. "Thank you, sir."

Then I realize I must look a sight by now. I've neither showered nor changed my clothes in days, except for "washing" my underpants during my freezing swim in the Ipoly. If I can help it, I don't want my aunt and uncle seeing me as I now look. So I decide to avail myself of the Jewish Agency's services first. After all, I'll need a travel pass in any event, and perhaps the agency's other services as well, should my aunt and uncle not be at home.

Within a few minutes, the streetcar takes a sharp turn, and the conductor yells out, "Lehel Ter."

"Thank you, sir," I call to him as I jump down onto the cobblestoned street, and take my first look at Lehel Square for the first time in well over a year. Some damage is evident here and there, but to my relief, the whole square is almost as impressive and beautiful as I remember it. "Maybe the Nazis didn't destroy *everything*," I tell myself. The same large, stately buildings still border the well kept square. Statues of important Hungarians still decorate the grass-covered islands. Flowers bloom everywhere, and people sit around leisurely on scattered wooden benches. Some read; others just daydream or gaze at the busy traffic.

I cross the street with the green light. The signals work! How wonderful!

Then I see a sign in large red lettering, painted recently onto one of the old buildings just off the square: JEWISH ORGANIZATION INTERNATIONALE. I step inside the old building, which has a large entry way and office doors inside that lead in all directions.

"Information," I read on a placard on top of a desk near the entrance. The brunette behind the counter is pretty. Why do women look so different to me than before? Did they change since the war, or is it just me? Suddenly, I find myself looking at all the pretty ones as potential girlfriends, even if they don't know it. And it's fun!

I'm too shy to say anything to this beautiful girl except, "I'm a Jewish refugee, just arriving home. Where would I go inside here for clothing and a travel pass?"

"To Room 5, right across the hall," she answers, cheerfully. "And welcome home! What's your name, by the way?"

"Pista."

"Hi, Pista, I'm Margit." She gives me a dazzling smile.

"Nice to meet you Margit," I mumble, looking down, shyly. Hmmm, maybe she likes me! What do I do next? Too flustered to make a move, I simply murmur to her, "Thank you for the information, Miss."

"Sure, Pista! Please let me know if you have any questions!"

I *must* brush up on my social talk right away, I tell myself as I wander down the hall. I've been out of circulation too long, and I've missed meeting some very important people. . . women!

After I'm cleaned up, outfitted, and given enough Hungarian *forints* to last me a couple weeks on my own (hopefully, I won't need them), I re-cross the square and board another Number 46 streetcar.

This time, when the conductor comes along to take my ticket, I display my newly minted travel pass. "Very well, son. And welcome home!"

So many strangers glad to see me. Now, to find some relatives.

I wonder if anything about my now spruced up appearance would still scare Aunt Manci and Uncle Bela. I remain 20 pounds underweight, and my complexion looks awfully pale. But the haircut I got a few days ago, when still in Germany, looks fine, and courtesy of the Jewish Agency off Lehel Square I'm clean and wear new clothes. Even if I don't yet look my best, I should make a presentable appearance.

When I exit the streetcar I walk the short distance to *Szt. Istvan - Krt. 20,* the luxurious, elegantly appointed building where my Uncle Bela and Aunt Manci (the wealthiest members of our family, courtesy of Uncle Bela's thriving dental practice) live, or lived. My heart's pumping faster than ever as I draw nearer. Will they be there, or won't they? And if they *are,* how can I ever begin to tell them everything that's happened?

To my pleasant surprise, my aunt and uncle's building still stands, without any apparent damage to its exterior. Uncle Bela's dental office has always been on the second floor, part of a huge apartment he's occupied for years, both as a resident and a dentist.

Inside the doorway, I scan the glass enclosed directory for his name.

There it is, just like always! *Dr. Scheiner Bela!* (We Hungarians often refer to individuals by their last names first.) I don't bother ringing for the elevator; I simply charge up the stairs as fast as I can. As a patient, I used to hate coming here; as a nephew I loved it, since there were always delicious pastries, courtesy of my Aunt Manci.

At the top of the steps, I take a deep breath, straighten my clothes, put on a pleasant smile, and press the doorbell. Then I step back and wait.

No answer.

Thirty seconds pass.

I press the bell again, letting the ringer sound for a longer time inside the flat.

Silence.

Next, I try a series of loud knocks, which I can hear echoing inside the empty inner hallway.

Clearly, they're out. Or perhaps they're no longer here. I wonder what to do next, and where to go. I guess it's back downtown on to the Red Cross to eat and sleep.

Disappointed, I turn and begin making my way down the steps again.

I'm almost half a flight down when, very faintly, from somewhere deep inside, an unfamiliar female voice calls, "I'm coming!"

I turn and race back up the steps.

"Who is it?" the strange voice inquires.

"Um, my name is Pista."

"Who?"

"Pista Nasser."

"Nasser?"

"Yes, Pista Nasser. I'm a nephew of Dr. And Mrs. Scheiner. Am I in the right. . . ?" I've never before heard this voice. Has another family moved in? I wonder.

"One moment, please." Now I hear the footsteps retreat.

What's going on? I wonder. Are my aunt and uncle here or not? To whom could the unfamiliar voice belong?

Soon I hear a different set of footsteps approach the door, this time quicker, sharper ones. They stop, abruptly, just inside the doorway. This person, whoever it is, doesn't even bother looking through the peephole before saying, irritably, "I don't know who you are, but I'm in no mood for cruel jokes. Please go away! Leave us alone!"

Aunt Manci's voice! **"Aunt Manci, Aunt Manci!"** I'm hollering loud enough for all of Budapest to hear. **"It's me, Pista. It really is! Just look through the peephole, Aunt Manci, please! You'll see me!"**

A pause, followed by a sharp intake of breath behind the door. **"Oh! Roszi, LOOK!** *My God, it is Pista!* **Roszi, its my nephew, Pista, back from. . ."**

And then, before I know it, the front door flies open, and right there stands my beautiful Aunt Manci, in the flesh! Slightly behind her and to one side stands a plump, pleasant faced young woman I've never seen before, dressed in the plain uniform of a maid. This, I assume, is Roszi,

"Pistukam! Pistukam!" Aunt Manci cries, looking as lovely as ever, and very much like my own mother. She hugs me with all her strength. **"Oh, thank God, Pistukam! You** *are* **back!"**

And just then, when I've begun thinking all my surprises for today must be over, poor surprised Aunt Manci faints dead away!

Weak as I still am, I'm not yet robust enough to support her full weight in my arms. I let her down, gently, and then dash to the closest bathroom to find a wet towel.

When I return, towel in hand, I wipe her forehead gently with the cool cloth, and kiss her closed eyelids. "Aunt Manci, Aunt Manci," I repeat softly until she wakes up again.

When she opens her eyes, she says, "My God, Pistukam! I wasn't dreaming. It's *you*!" Shortly thereafter, she stands up again, with my help. Then we hug and kiss some more.

"Let me look at you, my darling," she says, frowning. "You've lost weight, and you're so pale."

"I know, Aunt Manci. Maybe that's why you must have thought I was a ghost at first," I say, trying to make light of my pallor. "But I'm fine, really, just a bit tired. And *you*! You haven't changed, Aunt Manci. You're still as beautiful as ever. More beautiful, actually!"

"Pista, darling, you're too generous with your compliments."

"No I'm not. It's true. But where is Uncle Bela?"

"As always, he never tells me where he is going. But he should be home soon. Right now, though, let's talk about you, angel. Poor dear little one, where *were* you all this time? How did you *get* here? And where is your mother? Oh, my! So many questions!"

"You mean my mother isn't here? She isn't anywhere in Budapest? You haven't seen or heard from her?"

"No, darling. You're the only one who's come back, so far. Let's go into the family room, dearest." She takes me by the arm and leads me there. "Rozsi!"

she calls to the maid, who's apparently gone back into the kitchen.

Rozsi reappears.

"Rozsi," Aunt Manci tells her, excitedly, "this is the one we were afraid would never return. He's my youngest sister's son, the younger of her two boys."

At this, Rozsi nods, a sad look briefly crossing her face. "I'm very happy to meet you, Pista," she says, shyly. "Welcome back."

"Thank you," I reply. "It's nice to meet you, too, Rozsi."

"Pista," my aunt explains, "Rozsi has been living with us since last year, and helps me with the housework. Please, Rozsi, bring us in some coffee with whipped cream, and some pastries!"

"Yes ma'am."

I turn to my aunt. "Goodness, Aunt Manci, you haven't forgotten!" Once again, I'm moved nearly to tears, as I've been so often lately. "How could I ever forget what my *favorite* nephew loves most? Pastries, especially the ones with marzipan!"

"You have a good memory, Aunt Manci." Have I heard her right? Aunt Manci never in her life played favorites between Andris and me. Childless herself, she adored us both equally.

"She knows about Andris already," whispers a voice inside my head. *"But how?"*

"Aunt Manci, I have something very sad to tell you. It's about Andris. . ."

"Yes, darling, we know. You don't have to speak about it, if you don't want to. For weeks now, the *Magyar Nemzet* has been publishing the names of the deceased from various concentration camps. When we saw Andris's name on the list from the Muhldorf camp, we gave up on you, too, I guess. I'm sorry we did. That was wrong of us."

"That's all right, Aunt Manci. I would have bet on Andris myself. What about Mother, though? Has there been *any* word. . .?"

"None, darling. You and Andris were the last to see her."

I begin thinking things I'd rather not.

Rozsi brings in some delicious looking pastries, including an old favorite of mine with marzipan filling, accompanied by iced coffee with freshly whipped cream.

"Thank you, Rozsi," I tell her, as I watch her set a plate in front of me on the coffee table. She has a nice walk, I notice, as she disappears again into the kitchen.

Then Aunt Manci says, "Relax, Pista. Sit and enjoy your pastries. I'm going to call all the relatives on the telephone now, and let them know you're here!"

"Sure, Aunt Manci." Just then, Buki, their fox terrier, comes bounding through the door. He stops abruptly, and comes over cautiously to sniff me.

"Buki!" I cry, as delighted as a child to see him. Spontaneously, I grab the pure white dog and press my face against his wirey whiskers, as if to kiss him "hello." To my surprise, though, my furry old friend actually growls at me. Quickly, I set him down again. "Good boy, Buki. It's me, Pista. Remember me?" At the sound of my voice, which he seems now to recognize he slowly calms down. Soon enough, we're old buddies again. All it takes is a little coaxing and half my favorite marzipan-filled pastry!

Awhile later, I stand up, stretch, and wander into the room Uncle Bela uses as his front office. Here, Aunt Manci talks on the telephone. Buki follows me now, cheerfully wagging his short tail.

"I'm telling you, Miki, Pista *is* here, and alive! Hurry over! We'll have dinner at seven-thirty, okay? Great! See you soon. Bye-bye!" After hanging up the phone, Aunt Manci turns to me. "Pista, I've just talked to Miki, Musi, Pali, and Karoly. *Everybody* will be here for a big reunion tonight!"

"That's great! Thank you, Aunt Manci!" It will be wonderful to see my uncles again, the three on my mother's side, Miki, Musi, and Pali, but especially Karoly, my father's youngest brother, and my personal favorite. Besides everything else we have in common, Karoly and I are now the only two living Nassers.

Shortly thereafter, Aunti Manci and I hear the front door open wide, and then hear it close again. "Manci, I'm home!" Immediately, I recognize Uncle Bela's stern, raspy voice, in the hallway.

"Go on, Pista," Aunt Manci pushes me toward the door with a mischievous smile. "Surprise him!"

"Okay," I whisper, softly.

"Bela," she says, "we have a guest here." She manages to keep her voice completely even, as if some downstairs neighbor had merely stopped by to say hello.

Uncle Bela and I reach the living room door at the exact same time. He looks at me, and then takes a step backward, as if to double-check what he thinks he's seen. Then, having apparently assured himself it's really me, he raises both his arms in a welcome salute, and rests his hands firmly on my shoulders.

"My God, son! You *are* alive!" Then he hugs me.

My aunt's husband is a robust man, urbane, polished, and very well educated.

Despite all this, I've always felt a bit distant toward him. I've never once seen him kiss or hug my aunt the way he hugs me now. I respect him, but I don't really like him. I'm sorry I feel this way, since I couldn't possibly love my aunt more than I do.

One by one, my four uncles arrive. First comes Karoly, having returned recently from military service in the Hungarian army, one of many young Jewish men who were drafted for hard labor on the Russian Front. During his time in the Hungarian military, he had to wear a yellow armband, signifying that he was Jewish. Despite his own ordeal, Karoly still looks dapper and handsome, as always: very much a younger version of my own father.

"Pistukam!" As he hugs me tightly, his eyes brim with joyous tears.

"Oh, Karolykam!" I kiss him on the cheek, beginning, now, to weep myself. With him and Aunt Manci standing here, side by side in the same room, it's almost like seeing my mother and father together again. Almost.

Uncle Bela sits down in his favorite chair. "Karoly, Pista, come, sit down," he says, beckoning us toward the sofa.

Karoly and I sit down on the beautifully upholstered green velvet sofa and begin filling each other in on all that's happened this past year. "I've just gotten our jewelry store back from the government," Karoly reports proudly. "I reopened it from shambles. The Nazis took everything. I live in the back of the store now. I made the back room into a little apartment for myself."

"I'm sorry you had to start from scratch. I'm not surprised, though, given all that the Nazis were capable of." As soon as the words of this sentence leave my mouth, I wish I'd never spoken them. The phrase "What the Nazis were capable of. . . capable of. . . capable of. . . capable of. . ." ricochets around inside my head, accompanied by my hideous mental image of baby Peter's last seconds. Together, they threaten to drive me mad this very minute. *"Please, Uncle Karoly,"* I say to myself, *"don't ask me about baby Peter. I don't want to have to lie to you, but I could never tell you what I saw. Never!"*

"Pistukam, do you know what happened to my Bozsi and our little Peter?" he asks me right then, as if on cue.

"We were together until Auschwitz, but then we were separated," I blurt out. There. I've managed not to lie to him. As I say this, though, I can't bear to meet Uncle Karoly's eyes. When I do look his way a few minutes later, I see tears sliding down his cheeks.

I'm relieved when the doorbell rings again, announcing the arrival of my other three uncles on my mother's side: Miki, Musi, and Pali. They give me a chance to shift my attention elsewhere.

But once my other three uncles greet everyone and sit down in the living room, everyone's questions fly at me from all directions, like pingpong balls being batted at just one small target. Some of their inquiries reopen fresh wounds, although I know that wasn't their intention.

Just when I'm sure I can't endure even one more question, Rozsi comes to my rescue. "Dinner is ready and served in the dining room," she announces to all.

Everyone rises and moves eagerly toward the dining room. When I see the huge dining room table, crammed with food—roasted duck, braised potatoes, pickled red cabbage, casseroles, wine, and white bread, I really do think I'm dreaming. What I would have given, during those seemingly endless working days at Muhldorf, to have had even one mouthful of what I see before me tonight. I would not have believed, then, that I'd ever live to eat this well again.

We seat ourselves around the table, and everyone immediately digs in, passing one another heaping platefuls of this and that. I eat with the gusto of a starving young wolf. Finishing off a big piece of duck, I comment, "Aunt Manci, you're the best cook in the world. Next to Mother, of course."

This having popped spontaneously from my mouth, everyone's eyes are instantly upon me.

Smoothly, Uncle Bela breaks the silence by rising from the table, wine glass in hand, and declaring, "A toast to Pista!"

"To Pista!" everyone echoes, in unison. After clinking glasses all around, we drink up.

"Speech!" Uncle Musi says. Shakily, I stand up while Rozsi refills all our glasses.

"I'd like to make two toasts," I begin. "First, to all of our loved ones who can't be here tonight: May this occasion prove to them that their lives were not lived in vain, and that their memories will live forever, as long as we keep on smiling. And thank you, Andris, for the strength you've given me, so I could make it here tonight."

At this, I tremble with emotion. Uncle Bela offers me his handkerchief so I can wipe my eyes.

When I regain my composure, I continue. "The second toast is for the living. Thank you all for coming here to be with me tonight. It was the thought of seeing you again, especially here in Budapest, around this table, that helped me stay alive when dying would have been easier." I pause, with tears in my eyes. "And. . . and Mother, wherever you are, please come back to me!"

By the end of the evening, I've never felt quite so loved by so many, or quite so exhausted, physically, mentally, and, most of all, emotionally.

When I finally bed down for the night inside the plush, velvet-covered bed Aunt Manci and Uncle Bela offer, I'm asleep almost instantly. Drifting off, I'm vaguely aware of Aunt Manci watching over me, anxiously, like a mother hen. Several times during the night, she shakes me gently awake from my nightmares.

"Turn over, darling. It's just a bad dream. You're home now, with your loved ones."

Back at Muhldorf, my daily life was a nightmare, and my nightly dreams are pleasant by comparison. Now that I'm safe, the real nightmares begin coming fast and furious, every night. Mornings, often drenched with sweat and only halfway rested, I often recall Nurse Erika's words "Don't fear the nightmares, Pista; they're part of your healing process, and thus necessary. Use the daylight hours to analyze them, write about them, and help you lay your demons to rest." In the months to come, though, each time Aunt Manci shakes me awake, I wonder anew how long it will take for my past and my present, my reality and my dreams, to mesh comfortably again, if ever.

Chapter Twenty-two
Renewing Family Ties and Acquaintances

The next morning, after a bacon and egg breakfast fit for a king by Muhldorf work camp standards, I travel by streetcar to see for myself what's left of our family's jewelry store. Last night before dinner, Uncle Karoly invited me to visit there, warning me that the place had changed a lot, but not for the better. Today I do my best to approach my "homecoming" to our Istvan Street jewelry store after more than a year with an open mind. Yet every block of the old neighborhood stirs up bad memories within me. I hate admitting it, even to myself, but in my time away, I've grown bitter toward those who've robbed my family and me.

Along the way, I also recognize the now boarded up jewelry shop of the old Jewish man who had been found murdered inside, probably by the SS. Then I see the street corner where I fought off a bully, just days before Andris and I were sent to work at the Martinovits factory.

When the trolley turns sharply onto Arpad Street, I recognize the storefront that once was Mr. Szolosi's big, thriving children's clothing shop. And on the opposite side of the street, a few doors down, is where Mr. Laszlo Brichta, my fellow Muhldorf inmate benefactor at the *Magazine*, and recoverer of my lost diary, had run a highly successful shoe business.

Then, here I am: Number 42 Arpad Street, the outside of our lovely old residence. From where I stand on the streetcar, the pale yellow building is completely undamaged and looks as lovely and impressive as ever. Its stuccoed exterior still glistens merrily in the sun, just as if nothing had ever happened.

But in fact, *everything* has changed. According to Uncle Karoly, another family lives in our old apartment now, with no connection to the past, present, or future of any of us Nassers. As I stare at the exterior of the stately, elegant building Mother, Andris, and I were forced to vacate so abruptly, I can't help wondering what became of the many and varied personal possessions we had to leave here. The family now living there probably eats off our dishes. Maybe they even wear our clothes. Who knows? Maybe it's better not to know, but to just get on with life. Still, seeing our old home again, where our family once lived so happily, is harder to bear than I thought.

The trolley continues on toward nearby 13 Istvan Street, where my uncle has recently reopened our jewelry store. Equally disheartening, I realize immediately upon entering, is the sad fate of our shop, owned and managed by our family for three generations. I was to be fourth, most likely inheriting it from Father and Uncle Karoly, since Andris wished to be a doctor instead. Stripped by the Nazis of all its inventory, furnishings and other equities, nothing remains now but the shop itself, a little bit of merchandise, and the good Nasser name.

Uncle Karoly has little for sale these days except for those items he managed to squirrel away from the Nazis, and a few articles acquired on a shoestring after his return home from his Hungarian army service.

My uncle's description of the shop last night was accurate; the place looks almost bare when I enter. Where the grandfather and cuckoo clocks once stood, there are empty walls. The once fully-stocked glass showcases have only a few pieces of merchandise inside them. On the opposite side of the store are enough work spaces for four watch repairmen; but only one of these is filled.

Uncle Karoly himself, though, is busy waiting on the single customer inside the store. "Pistukam," he says, "I'll be with you in a minute."

"Sure. Take your time. I'll wait for you in the back room."

I take the chance to look around again, opening first the stained glass door leading into a dim hallway. The right side of the wall contains numerous shelves, from ceiling to floor. Empty boxes are scattered here and there on them. Straight ahead, I recognize a huge, steel-plated, reinforced door. This is the back entrance of our shop, leading to a garden and to the washrooms.

To the left side of the hallway is another door. I open it. A big, square steel-barred window lets in ample light, which streams across a sofa bed with an old Persian carpet beneath it. This is our old back room, formerly used as a general storage area, where Uncle Karoly now lives. A polished game table, featuring light and dark brown inlaid squares in its center forming a chessboard, is the centerpiece of the room. Here, at this very table, but in a different place, Uncle Karoly had taught me to play chess when I was seven years old.

I lie down on the sofa for a brief rest. Still recovering from my year of involuntary exile, I realize I'm already tired, although I've done almost nothing today but eat breakfast and come over here on the trolley from Aunt Manci's. Before I know it, I'm dozing on the soft, comfortable sofa. I wake instantly, though, when I hear my uncle's voice.

"Pista!"

I jump to my feet. The door opens, and Uncle Karoly appears.

"I thought you'd be hungry by now. I didn't want to wake you, but you've been asleep for over two hours."

Over two hours! I rub my eyes and shake my head in disbelief. Here I'd just gotten up from an eight hour sleep to come here, only to go back to sleep again as soon as I arrive!

"I'm sorry, Uncle Karoly. I guess I'm pretty dull company. I came to visit you, and instead I slept the morning away."

"Pistukam, stop. Obviously, your body and mind are still recovering. If you let your body have the sleep it needs now, it'll stop needing so much pretty soon. You'll see."

"Thanks for understanding, Uncle Karoly." I hope he's right.

"C'mon, sleepyhead. Time for lunch." He produces his wallet. "Here are five hundred pengo; go buy us some lunch. Do you remember where the butcher shop is?"

"Of course." I button my jacket to go out.

I walk to the butcher shop and buy us both some Csaszar meat, a Hungarian bacon-type delicacy, but very meaty. At the bakery shop I purchase two big Csaszar rolls. Then I trot over to the marketplace and select a plump, delicious looking kosher pickle for each of us at what was always my favorite stand. I'm happy that quite a few of the old shops and stands I've always liked still remain. But others are gone—they're boarded up or simply vacant. Still others seem now to be owned and run by people who are strangers to me.

Returning to the store, I proudly display my purchases. What a lunch we have! It's just like old times. Almost.

Immediately afterward, almost without realizing it, I lie back down on the sofa and snooze another few hours.

"Pis. . . ta, Pistukam."

I open my eyes, amazed. I can hardly believe I've been sleeping *again*.

"Time to get up. It's almost five o'clock!"

I sit up and rub my eyes, realizing sheepishly that I've slept the day away and barely even talked to Uncle Karoly. "I promised Aunt Manci I'd be home by 6:00," I mumble.

"Don't worry, you'll make it."

"I'm sor. . ."

"Pista, please, don't apologize. I don't want to hear 'I'm sorry' anymore, okay?"

"Okay."

"You know, Pista, I've been meaning to tell you something. Now that you're older, you're looking very much like your father. He had so many wonderful qualities. His punctuality, for example, was legend."

"I guess he didn't oversleep, then, like I do."

My uncle ignores me. "Someday, Pista, I'll buy you a watch so you can carry on your father's habit of being on time everywhere." With that, he gently pinches my cheek.

"Uncle Karoly, the way I'm going, I'll need a really loud alarm clock for that, not a watch!"

"You have something else of your father's, too, Pista."

"His lack of energy?"

"No. His sense of humor."

"Thanks, Uncle Karoly." We embrace for a long time before I say good-bye.

Walking back down Istvan Street to the trolley stop, I find myself gazing into all the store windows and carefully examining the people on the streets in search of familiar faces.

Suddenly, I recognize a man about forty years old walking by. He has a round face and a pleasant, steady smile.

"Mr. Gombas!"

The man turns and stares at me, puzzled.

"I'm Pista Nasser, Andris's brother. I believe you used to be his Latin teacher?"

"Oh yes, Andris Nasser. A brilliant young man! How is he doing these days?"

I gulp. "He. . . he died."

"No!" Now Mr.Gombas just stands there, as stiff as vellum, staring at me incredulously with his mouth wide open, as if I've just told him some unbelievably inappropriate joke.

"I'm. . . I'm afraid it's true, sir. Andris died a few months ago, in a concentration camp in Muhldorf, Germany. I was there." Now I can't stop my eyes from filling, again, with tears.

Silence. Then he says, "I'm so sorry, Pista."

"Thank you, sir. I thought you should know." Quickly, I wipe my eyes with a hankie Uncle Bela loaned me for times like this.

Neither of us says anything else for a few moments. I stare at my shoes. Finally, Mr. Gombas breaks the silence.

"Pista, will you be registering for classes this year?"

"Yes, sir. In a few weeks."

"Good. I'll see you in school then. God be with you, son." With that, Mr. Gombas hurries away, gazing down at the ground now, his habitual smile gone.

Soon it's August. Realizing I'll have very little free time once school begins (especially with my having missed an entire year of classes) I step up my search for Mother. Every afternoon I visit a different agency in downtown Budapest in an effort to locate her. My search has yet to produce any leads, but I refuse to give up.

September arrives, still without news of mother. I'm starting to worry. I haven't shared my concerns with Aunt Manci, but I sense she feels the same.

I'm less tired now and have stopped nodding off every minute, thank Heaven! This is a big relief, with school starting so soon. I'm sure I'd be expelled in short order if I didn't stay awake during my classes. I've also gained ten pounds since arriving, with only ten more to go until I'm at 140 again. Actually, I should probably weigh 150 instead, since I grew two inches at Muhldorf, incredible as that seems. It must have been in my genes, because it sure wasn't thanks to the food I ate.

Today I must register for the upcoming school year. When I jump off the streetcar bringing me from Aunt Manci's to the *Konyves Kalman Gymnasium*, my heart and mind are flooded with all kinds of incomplete thoughts and emotions. It feels strange walking down these old familiar halls without Andris beside me, especially on registration day. But where else should I be? Both Father and Andris would want me to finish *gymnasium*.

Still, I'm sad as I enter the red brick building and climb those wide marble steps Andris and I used to race up together.

Today I'm early, just as I'd planned to be.

First, I make my way to the registration office, a required ritual for all new and returning students. I clear my throat, straighten my tie, and open the door.

Assembled behind a long table are Mr. Gombas; Mr. Kardos, my Latin teacher; Mr. Szerdai, algebra; Mr. Toros our school's headmaster, and many others, most of them familiar to me, but some of them new since I was last here.

When he sees me, Mr. Gombas rises and extends both his hands in welcome. "Good morning, Pista, and welcome back."

"Good morning, Mr. Gombas," I say.

Then he tells everyone, "Here is Pista Nasser. I told you fellows he was back!"

"Yes, yes! This would be *little* Potyi, of course!" says Mr. Kardos, who'd been another of Andris's Latin teachers.

Before I even know it, tears are suddenly running down my cheeks. I doubt Andris would approve of my spontaneous emotional display in front of all these teachers. But I can't help it. *"I'm sorry, Andris. I blew it!"*

Mr. Gombas invites me to sit down. Try as I might, I can't stop sobbing. I'm feeling my brother's absence more keenly than ever.

"It's all right, son." Mr. Gombas tries to comfort me.

I pull out Uncle Bela's handkerchief, into which I now blow my nose.

"Welcome home, son," the headmaster, Mr. Toros, says, breaking the gloomy silence. He extends his hand.

Quickly I rise, walk over to where he sits at the end of the table, and shake his hand. Then everyone else at the table follows suit, shaking my hand in greeting.

After I register for my classes, the headmaster says, "Pista, please come to my office with me." I follow him down a long hallway, and he opens a familiar door. On the wall, side by side, dominating the office, hang two large pictures I've never seen in here before. The one on the right is of President Roosevelt of the United States. The one on the left is of Josef Stalin, the Russian leader.

Mr. Toros gestures me toward a chair, and then closes the door. "Pista, today we've registered you in the 5th grade. I know you've lost a year because of the Nazis. Let's see how you do by the end of the school year. If you have better than average grades, I'll see about helping you get permission from the Ministry of Education to complete the 6th and 7th grades in one year."

"Thank you, sir. I'd appreciate that."

Within the Hungarian school system, we have twelve grades of school in all, just as in the United States, but our grades, though equivalent, are numbered differently. From ages 5 through 8, students first attend four years of elementary school. Then, at age 9, students enter the *gymnasium*, where they go for another 8 years. At 9, you are considered to be in the first grade. By the time you're 17, you're in the 8th grade (which would be the 12th grade by United States standards.) After graduation from the *gymnasium* and receiving a baccalaureate degree, you may (depending on your grades) either enter the university or take up an apprenticeship or trade.

Since I'm 14, I should now be in the 6th grade, except for having missed an entire year of school. What Mr. Toros offers me now is a chance to catch up next year, provided I do well enough in the 5th grade this year. I'm thrilled! Before coming here this morning, I had no idea such an opportunity even existed.

When Mr. Toros stands up again, he nods toward the two looming portraits. It seems he's waiting for me to comment on them, although I'm not sure what to say. I opt for "Those pictures are new, sir, since I last saw you."

"That's right. There's a lot that's new since you left. I couldn't help noticing how you've been staring at these portraits. May I ask why?"

"I'm not sure, sir. I suppose it's because I haven't ever seen them in here before."

"Do you know who the two men are?"

"The one on the right, Franklin D. Roosevelt, is the President of the United States. The picture on the left is of Josef Stalin, the ruler of Russia."

"That's right. Seemingly, two allies, but not for long."

"Yes sir," I reply, hoping he thinks I understand his meaning, even though I don't.

Then Mr Toros clears his throat and says, "You can go now, young man. I have a feeling the future will hold a lot of happiness for you, to make up for all the sadness and difficulty you've experienced."

"I hope so. And thank you for everything, sir."

After leaving school, I walk over to Uncle Karoly's jewelry store, only ten minutes away. It's a nice clear day. I think of my studies and the rough tasks ahead of me this year if I hope to complete the sixth and seventh grades together next year.

I cross the wide, cobblestoned street, and then stroll beneath the shady trees in Istvan Park. Near the park entrance I stop a moment at the huge stone monument honoring numerous soldiers from Ujpest who lost their lives in the first World War. Under the letter "N" is the name "Elemer Nasser," my father's eldest brother. Seeing my uncle's name engraved here is yet another reminder that I'm now the younger of only two living Nassers, Karoly and me.

The next few weekends are filled with dinner invitations from relatives and soccer games with Uncle Karoly. One lazy early October afternoon, following one such match, Uncle Karoly and I sit together inside the jewelry store, behind the counter.

"Legally and ethically, I'm obliged for your financial needs," my uncle says. "I've talked this over with Manci and Bela."

Involuntarily, I screw up my nose at the mention of Uncle Bela.

"I guess you don't care for Bela, huh?"

"To be honest, Uncle Karoly, I don't know how someone as good-hearted as Aunt Manci stays married to him."

"I know, Pista. But he's still your uncle, and deserves your respect. After all, he's taken you in."

"Don't worry, Uncle Karoly. I'll always show respect to the old goat, even though I don't like him much. He's just not warm, like you and Aunt Manci."

"I know, but he is the way he is. No one can change him, Pista."

"I know."

"Anyway, speaking of your living with them, I wanted to tell you that, aside from my paying for your room and board with him and Manci, which I'm doing now, I'll see to it that you have pocket money."

"Thanks, Uncle Karoly! You know, you're not just my father's brother; you're my best friend."

"And you're mine. I love you like my own son. . ." His voice trails off, and I know he's thinking now of baby Peter. Perhaps he's wondering what really happened to the baby, or imagining what might have been: birthday parties, soccer games, a *bar mitzvah,* a wedding someday, followed by grandchildren. To think of all the joy snatched from my uncle in one horrific instant. He tears up now, and watching, I feel sad and helpless. That awful lump travels toward my throat again. With effort, I stop myself from crying, too. *He must never know.*

"Pista, don't call me Uncle anymore, okay? From now on, just Karoly."

"All right. Karoly it is. By the way, Karoly, I love you very much."

The front door opens just then, and a customer appears. That gives me an opportunity to flop down on the back room sofa for a nap, which I still occasionally need.

I can't have been sleeping long, though, when a series of screams wakes me.

I scramble to my feet and peek, through the stained glass door, into the shop. A drunken Russian soldier waves a revolver around wildly. I count six people inside the store altogether, including Karoly.

Quickly, I slip out the back entrance, locking the door, and then steal quietly around to the front of the store. Next, I pull down the corrugated metal security blind outside and lock everyone in. I hope the Russian, knowing he's trapped now, will somehow come to his senses and put away that revolver. I know it's a risk. He could easily shoot someone in the time it will take me to get the police over here.

I sprint toward the nearest policeman, who directs traffic at a nearby intersection. He summons a nearby Russian military policeman, and the three of us rush back to the store. When we yank up the metal blind, all six individuals are still in there, alive and well, and just where I left them. Uncle Karoly, meanwhile, has done an admirable job of keeping everyone calm. The drunken Russian soldier is arrested and carted off to jail.

Uncle Karoly rewards me for my "heroism" by placing a new watch on my wrist. "Pista, I really appreciate your quick thinking. You may have saved all our lives. No one had any idea what that Russian soldier might do next. I've wanted to give you a watch for a long time. As it turns out, now is a good occasion." With that, he tightens the leather band around my wrist. "This isn't an expensive watch, but it keeps good time."

"It's the most wonderful watch in the world, Karoly," I tell him.

This fall, Karoly also donates a large silver trophy to the Ujpest Sports Club, to be awarded annually to the club's best all-around athlete. The name of the award is engraved in fancy script: *The Peter Attila Nasser Award, in memory of Karoly Nasser's infant son, whose fate is unknown to him.*

Unknown to him, yes, and thank God! But *I* know baby Peter's fate, and I am the only living Nasser who does. I must always keep it that way. Again I envision the baby's head bashed against that boxcar wheel. I remember how Nurse Erika advised me to talk the worst of my memories out of my system. But this *one* memory, my *very* worst one of all, I must *never* discuss with any family member.

Will it haunt me, privately, forever? If it must, it must, for I'd sooner die than have Karoly know.

Chapter Twenty-three
Back to School

For awhile now I've hoped that when school began, I could simply slide back into my old familiar routine, almost as if I'd never left. But alas, such simplicity is not to be. Too much has changed all around me, not to mention all the changes within me.

I must now take classes with younger pupils. True, I've missed lots of work and need to make it up. Ironically, though, I feel even older than students my own age. It's hard relating to my new classmates or making friends with them. They seem like babies to me. Academically, though, some of them know more than I do.

Harder for me, still, are the constant daily reminders of Andris: the obvious grief of his former teachers; the questions and comments, however innocent or well intended, of his former classmates or teammates; even the athletics trophies on display in our main hall, many of which he helped win.

Often while I'm at school, I'll catch myself expecting him to appear from around a corner, or to join me dashing down some hallway to our respective classes.

Who else but Andris could possibly understand the strange and horrible times I've experienced, and how my year "abroad" has wizened me, prematurely, in ways I could never have imagined? Who else could possibly fathom all I've lost, not just in terms of family, but physically, emotionally, and spiritually as well?

Then one day, as if in answer to all these questions, I see, coming toward me on the school grounds, an old friend: Janos Markus. Janos, or Jancsi, is one of the few other Jewish students here. His father had been an Ujpest doctor and a friend of my own parents.

"Jancsi?" I call as he draws near, knowing it's him, yet almost not believing it. He appears pale, like me, and still has big hollows in his cheeks from too much weight lost.

"Pista?"

"Yes!"

We embrace, without saying another word. When we finally break apart, neither of us knows what to say first. Finally, Jancsi asks me, tentatively, "How's your family, Pista? Andris, your mother. . .?"

I tell him.

"I'm sorry," he says, simply. "My whole family was wiped out, too. I myself was imprisoned in Bavaria, in a work camp near Muhldorf called Wald Lager."

"You're kidding! I was in the Muhldorf camp myself! Horrible place! I worked right alongside some guys from Wald Lager, on this big cement project. I wish I'd known you were so close. Not that it would have done any. . ."

I don't bother finishing my sentence. I don't have to.

"Where are you staying now in Budapest?" he asks.

"With my aunt and uncle in the city center. They went into one of the Swedish houses, so they weren't deported."

"Same with me. My aunt and uncle in the city center weren't deported, either. Too bad we don't have some classes together. They put me back in the fifth grade, by the way. I hate it."

"Same here. I feel like I'm in kindergarten again. Remember when we both used to feel so smart?"

He laughs. "Yeah. That seems like a whole other lifetime."

I agree.

We exchange addresses and telephone numbers. After that, I feel better. There *is* someone here who will understand all I've been through. After our first time getting together, though, Jancsi and I seldom speak about our respective concentration camp experiences. We're too busy making up for lost time and planning for the future. Still, it helps me a lot just to know he's around, and I think he feels the same way.

As my schoolwork begins in earnest, my family commitments narrow to just Aunt Manci and Uncle Bela, and Uncle Karoly, of course.

Within just a few months, snow covers the ground, dressing up Budapest in a glittering white blanket. I've settled into my student routine and adjusted, at least as well as possible, to my quiet new life with Aunt Manci and Uncle Bela.

One Saturday afternoon, the warmth of the fire roaring in the big fireplace keeps Buki the fox terrier curled up on a nearby cushion, and me watching the snowflakes as they fall to the ground outside the window. Aunt Manci reads in her favorite chair.

"Aunt Manci," I ask her, "who are those people who just moved in upstairs?"

"An architect and his family. I don't remember their name. Someone told me they have two daughters."

"How old?"

She smiles. "I don't know, Pista. I've never even met the family."

"Have you heard anything about them?"

"Just that the father works downtown. The daughters are supposedly quite pretty."

"Oh? What do they look like?"

She smiles. "Pista, something tells me you could describe those two girls quite well yourself."

I blush.

"You're blushing, Pista. Am I right?"

"Umm, I would say, uh, you're, er. . . you're right. Yes. In fact, one of them smiled at me today. It was the older one, I think. She has golden brown hair. She's slender, with light blue eyes."

"You must have gotten pretty close then, dear, if you could see she has light blue eyes."

"Not as close as I'd like."

"Then why don't you just go up and introduce yourself?"

"You mean just go up there? Uninvited?"

"Why not?"

"Well, um, it's just. . ."

"You're nervous about introducing yourself to two young girls? After all you've been through?"

I shrug. "Well, this is different."

"Pista, let's face it. In this life, if you want something, you have to pursue it. The things you want aren't going to just walk up to you and present themselves."

I know she's right, but that doesn't make my venture up the stairs a few hours later any easier for me. Halfway up, my courage nearly deserts me, but I force myself to continue. Soon enough, I'm all the way up the steps. Help!

Here at the top, I see a light shining through the stained glass kitchen door. I hear voices, and feminine sounding giggles. They seem to be enjoying their conversation. I wonder what they're talking about?

Straightening my shoulders, smoothing my hair, and taking a deep breath, I steel myself, and then knock.

"Who is it?" a sweet sounding female voice calls.

In my calmest, deepest voice, I reply. "It's Pista. The dentist's nephew from the apartment below you." I hope I sound suave and confident.

Now I hear approaching footsteps, and then the slow opening of the front door. *"Yikes! Whatever made me come up here? Where's a nice trap door to fall through when a fellow really needs one?"*

Then, all at once, the tall, slender, light-eyed girl from this afternoon stands before me. My, she's beautiful!

She laughs, a lovely, lilting laugh. "Well," she says, "don't just stand there. Come in. I'm Vera Koranyi." Her sparkling eyes are smiling. They're hazel, actually. We shake hands.

"And may I ask the reason for your visit?" she asks, coyly, once I've stepped inside.

"Well, Vera, I could give you a lot of reasons, but the main one is that I wanted to meet you." There. Now I've said it, and I'm still alive!

"I'm glad you came, Pista. Please come meet my mother and sister."

I close the door. Vera's mother, a woman with gray hair, and the younger sister sit at the table drinking coffee.

"Pista, this is my mother, and my sister, Marta."

"Pleased to meet you," I say, shaking hands with both. Marta is more my age, but for some reason I prefer Vera.

"May I get you a cup of coffee?" Vera asks me, sweetly.

"Yes, please, with a teaspoon of sugar."

Our eyes meet. At that instant, I feel something indescribable deep down. Could this be love?

Mrs. Koranyi suggests a toast "to a wonderful new friendship."

I return the toast with a restrained, "To our lovely new friends and neighbors," although I'd rather have said, "To the beautiful siren who lives overhead and is shaped like a guitar."

We all smile agreeably and clink our coffee cups. So far, so good.

For the next hour or so, we drink our coffee and make small talk. They're impressed that I attend the prestigious *Konyves Kalman Gymnasium*. I avoid topics like the war, Muhldorf, or anything else unpleasant. I make them all laugh a few times. When Vera sees me to the door an hour or so later, I ask her, "Are you free on Sunday afternoon?"

"Yes, I'm free."

"Would you like to go to the park with me, Vera?"

"Yes, Pista, I'd love to."

"I'll come by for you at 2:00."

"I'll be ready."

Ah, sweet success! I float back downstairs on a cloud.

Sunday afternoon, I take Vera skating, and then for a long walk. By the end of our first date, I'm madly in love! Now my days fly by as if they have wings. I'm hardly even aware of the passing of time. The emptiness in my heart these past two years, caused by all my hardships and losses, is being filled again, finally. What a wonderful feeling, to be wanted, cared for, caressed, and by someone so beautiful, too! Soon, I'm the envy of my friends. But I don't care about that. My only real wish is to belong to someone, to love and be loved, like before the war. It's icing on the cake that Vera is so pretty.

Soon, though, I'm spending more time with Vera than with my books. Why not? She's much more interesting, and a lot more attractive!

One afternoon, when I least expect it, Uncle Bela corners me. "We need to talk, Pista," he says. He looks and sounds angry, although I can't imagine why.

"Yes, Uncle Bela?"

"Pista, it seems to me you're ignoring your main responsibilities. You *must* get the best grades in school if you want to succeed in life. Now this is no threat, but I'm going to tell you this only once: if your next report card shows poor grades because of your involvement with Vera, I will not be responsible for you in the future. Do we understand each other?"

I give him a curt, "Yes."

Feeling irritable now, I take Buki for a walk, keeping him on a short leash and dragging him along. When I realize I'm almost choking the poor dog, I suddenly feel ashamed of taking out my anger out on an innocent animal. To make it up to him, I pick Buki up and carry him home. On the way, he licks me all over with gratitude.

Despite Uncle Bela's ultimatum, my friendship with Vera continues to blossom. I hardly crack a book, but when I'm at school, I manage to soak up and remember, virtually by heart, every word my teachers say.

A couple days after the fall term ends, I stand in the living room looking out the window. I'm hoping Vera will walk by so I can look at her.

Aunt Manci reads in the glow of the fireplace. It's a lazy, relaxed late afternoon, just the kind I like. Just then, Uncle Bela comes bursting in from his office. Before either Aunt Manci or I can even say hello, he starts right in on me: "Wasting your time again when you could be studying, Pista? When are you getting your report card, by the way?"

"I got it a couple days ago."

Then he turns to Aunt Manci. "See? I *knew* it! I *told* him that damn girl would make him fail in school! All right, Romeo! Show me that damn report card of yours, now!"

"Yes, sir." My throat's a little dry, so it sounds like my voice is quaking with fear. Great! I disappear into my room and pull my grade sheet out from under the mattress, where I've hidden it, waiting patiently for just this moment. Returning to the living room, I hand my report card humbly to Uncle Bela, and then back away to get the best possible view of his reaction.

"Manci, listen to this," he intones, without even bothering to first read the report card himself. "Didn't I *tell* you this would happen?" Now Uncle Bela takes a deep breath, and, straightening his posture like a criminal judge about to deliver an unpleasant verdict, begins reading aloud to Aunt Manci, in a scornful voice: "Latin—B; Geometry—A; Chemistry—A; History—A; Geography—A; German—B."

"But Pista's grades don't sound that bad to me, Bela," Aunt Manci interrupts him, gently.

Realizing, now, what he's actually been reading, my uncle's face turns beet-red, and his nostrils flare in anger. Flinging my report card onto the piano, he stalks back into his office.

Aunt Manci tries to apologize. "Poor darling. Bela must have upset you."

"Not as much as he upset himself, I'm afraid."

"And now he's in his office fuming because a fifteen-year-old boy made an ass out of him."

"As far as I'm concerned, Aunt Manci, I've already forgotten the whole thing." I take out my pocket comb and run it through my curly hair. "I'll be upstairs with Vera, if you want me. I'll be home by 10:30." I kiss my aunt goodbye.

"Have a good time, darling," she calls after me. "And congratulations on your excellent grades!"

"Thank you, Aunt Manci!" I call over my shoulder, opening the front door. Then I charge up the stairs, two at a time, to see my beautiful Vera.

Chapter Twenty-four
Bad News

Despite my ongoing involvement with Vera, my grades remain high throughout the school year. Consequently, I have an excellent chance of getting permission from the Ministry of Education to complete both the 6th and 7th grades in one year next year.

One Saturday morning, Uncle Bela and I, having declared a truce, eat breakfast at the dining room table. We make polite small talk as Aunt Manci putters around the kitchen. Suddenly, the doorbell rings. Rozsi has today off, so I answer it. It's the mailman, who hands me all the letters in his hand except one, for which Aunt Manci must sign. I call to her in the kitchen to come sign for it. After the mailman departs, I inquire, "Where's that stamp from, Aunt Manci?"

"Sweden. It's from your Great Uncle Zsiga, your maternal grandmother's brother, and my first cousin."

"May I keep the stamp when you're finished?"

"Of course."

We both return to the dining room, where Aunt Manci sits and reads her mail, choosing the Swedish letter first.

Meanwhile, Uncle Bela and I resume our efforts at conversation. He's always comfortable discussing his dental practice, so I decide to ask him how to fill a tooth, although I have no real interest in learning.

Just as I thought, Uncle Bela is delighted to explain the whole process to me, step by tedious step. "First, Pista, one deadens the patient's nerve, locally, taking great care that the area is completely numb."

I nod, feigning keen interest. "After numbing the area, how long should the dentist wait to begin drilling?"

"On average, seven to ten minutes. But of course it depends on the patient, the amount of anesthetic used, and the area to be worked on. Also, the dentist must always consider. . ."

We immediately cease our discussion upon hearing a sharp intake of breath, followed by a poorly stifled sob, from Aunt Manci.

"Aunt Manci?"

"Darling?"

"What's wrong?" Uncle Bela and I ask her in unison, the one time, ever, that we're thinking the same thing.

Before she can reply, tears fill Aunt Manci's eyes, turning them bright blue. Then tears roll down her cheeks onto the starched linen tablecloth. Quickly, she rises and goes to grab a cloth napkin from the kitchen, into which she blows her nose.

"Aunt Manci, please, tell us what's wrong. Maybe we can help."

"Oh, Pistukam!" she manages to say. More sobs, much louder now. I run to my room and retrieve one of Uncle Bela's hankies, of which I've now "borrowed" at least half a dozen. Upon returning, I hand it to my aunt.

By now, Uncle Bela hovers over Aunt Manci, looking as concerned and helpless as I feel.

"Aunt Manci, please tell us why you're crying. Is it something you read in that letter?"

"Y. . . yes."

"What does the letter say?"

"Pista, Pista. . ."

"May I please read the letter myself, Aunt Manci?"

"N. . . no, Pista. Please don't."

"Why not?"

"Pista, it's about your. . . m-m. . .mother," she finally blurts out, and then buries her head in the handkerchief, sobbing uncontrollably.

Without asking further permission, I snatch the letter from her trembling hand, rush into the living room, hurl myself on the sofa, and begin reading:

My dearest Manci,

I am writing to you with some very sad news about your youngest sister Georgia. A Swedish friend of mine, Magda, with whom I attend synagogue, recently told me of a young woman she knows who lived in the barracks with Georgia at the Bergen-Belsen concentration camp. According to this young woman, Georgia came to Belsen from Auschwitz in a work detail, but contracted a serious case of typhus shortly before the liberation. She died at Bergen-Belsen exactly two weeks after the liberation.

Before writing you this letter, I wanted to be sure this information was correct, since I know, from your letters to me, that you've waited several months now with no word. Yesterday, I visited the Red Cross office here. A case worker did some research for me, and found Georgia's name on a list of deceased sent recently from Bergen-Belsen. This, unfortunately, confirmed the news I've given you.

Manci, please give Pista my deepest sympathy. He was just a baby when I last saw him, so I know he wouldn't remember me. Please tell him, though, that he is in his Uncle Zsiga's thoughts and prayers.

Your loving cousin,

Zsiga

As I finish reading the letter, there are no words for what I feel. I'm shocked, grieved, and angry. Moreover, I can't even believe the news. Yet I know, deep down, that it's true.

How I've hoped and prayed, even convincing myself all this time, that Mother was simply delayed, lost, or recovering in a hospital somewhere, and making her way home, slowly but surely. How I've refused, vehemently, to believe otherwise, all this time, even for a second.

Mercifully, Aunt Manci does not disturb me as I lie sobbing in my bedroom. I lose all track of time. Maybe this isn't real, I tell myself. Perhaps I'm just having my worst nightmare yet. I'm not dreaming, but I wish I were.

"Oh, God, no! NO, NO, NO!" I scream into my pillow. Why did I struggle so hard to survive? I wish I were dead now, with the rest of my family.

Exhausted from weeping, I hear a soft knock on my door. A gentle female voice whispers "Pistukam? May I come in?"

I sit up, sniffing loudly. "Yes."

Vera appears inside my bedroom, and sits down on my bed, stroking my hair and kissing me. I cry myself loudly to sleep beneath her soothing caresses. When I open my eyes again in about a hour, I expect she'll be gone, but she's still there. I sit up, and she kisses me again. Then I search for a handkerchief, but she gives me hers.

"Pistukam. . . I'm so. . ." Now *she* chokes up, and it's my turn to comfort her.

I tell her of Andris's smile, and his final request that he and father be able to look down and see me smiling.

"Pistukam, I promise you that I, too, will always help to keep you smiling, as best I can."

"Oh, Vera, thank you so much for saying that. I'm so lucky to have you."

"Not as lucky as I am to have you," she answers.

"Vera, how can I thank you enough for being here with me, during my worst time?"

"I wouldn't want to be anywhere else."

During the hot summer months ahead, Vera's company helps me continue to heal. Afternoons, when it's hottest, we often go swimming in the various public pools around the city. Our favorite is the multi-tanked Palatinus, located on beautiful Margaret Island only a short distance from our building.

When I return home later that evening, Aunt Manci greets me with an official looking envelope from the Ministry of Education. Impatiently, I rip it open as she stands there, awaiting the news of my petition to complete two grades in one.

The letter reads: *"Dear Mr. Nasser: This is to inform you that your request to complete the sixth and seventh grades during the 1947-48 academic year has been reviewed by our board and approved. We wish you good luck in your upcoming endeavor."*

As I explain to Aunt Manci, this means I'll need to pass my exams for all thirteen subjects of the sixth grade by January, and then an equal number of exams for the seventh grade in June.

"Can you handle all that in one year, Pista?"

"Sure," I reply, sitting down on the couch beside Buki, who gazes at me, lovingly. "Buki, do you think I can handle it?"

"Woof!" Buki replies, wagging his stubby tail enthusiastically. With that, he rolls over onto his back, waving all four feet in the air, so I can scratch his belly.

"See, Auntie? Buki knows I can handle it. Have you ever known him to be wrong about anything?"

"I can't say I have, Pista."

So that settles it, my aunt and I agree.

Once school starts again in September, though, my academic marathon proves difficult. My days and weeks are filled with endless studying each night, far into the night, and even on weekends. When bedtime finally rolls around, often, by then, it's well into the morning of the next day, I'm completely exhausted. I have no choice, now, but to spend much less time with Vera than either of us would like.

Late one Sunday night, just after taking my shower, I say goodnight to Aunt Manci and Uncle Bela, who both still turn in at a reasonable hour, and then return to cracking my Latin book.

A few minutes later, I'm sitting at my desk memorizing irregular verb conjugations when I hear a loud thud, and then a scream.

"Pistukam!" comes my aunt's frantic voice through the wall.

I jump up from my desk and dash toward their bathroom, the direction of the scream. There, Aunt Manci kneels helplessly over Uncle Bela, who lies flat on his back on the floor, unconscious.

"Aunt Manci, stay here with him while I go for help. I'll be right back," I yell over my shoulder as I throw on my overcoat and charge down the block to the home of one of Uncle Bela's colleagues, a heart specialist. In less than ten minutes we're back. Quickly, the doctor gives Uncle Bela an injection, but it's too late.

He's dead.

As befitting a man of Uncle Bela's professional stature, his funeral is big, expensive, and attended by many members of Budapest's professional class, including his two brothers, both prominent attorneys. I can't help but notice, though, that little real mourning occurs at the funeral, including my own. I compare this funeral to that of Father three years ago. Father, although less wealthy, was genuinely loved by his family, friends, and business associates alike. Aunt Manci does shed some tears today, having now lost her companion of many years. She has not lost a husband, though, in any but the most official sense. That she lost long before today.

Ironically, my first term grades arrive in the mail the very morning of Uncle Bela's funeral. Even on a day like today, with so much else to occupy her mind, Aunt Manci is curious about how I've fared academically. She hovers nearby as I open the envelope. Every grade for all 13 subjects of the 6th grade is an "A" And I've been promoted from the 6th to the 7th grade in less than four months.

"See, Aunt Manci? Buki was right when he said I could do it."

At this, Aunt Manci says. "Congratulations, *Pistukam. I* always knew you could do it, even before Buki said so. I'm so proud of you. And I know that many people looking down today are proud of you, too," she adds, tearfully.

Silently, I offer even Uncle Bela my thanks. After all, it was he who gave me the determination to prove him wrong about my grades and future prospects.

Chapter Twenty-five
Good-bye

Vera and I talk much of the future. We make plans. . . make them and then change them. But one thing is clear: we see ourselves married someday.

Yet it's increasingly hard for me to imagine continuing to live much longer in Hungary. Before the war, I always assumed I'd spend my life here, like so many generations of Nassers before me. Why not? Back then, we had everything: family, friends, success, and prosperity.

But now Mother, Father, and Andris are dead. Aunt Manci is growing older, but she's healthy and self-sufficient, having been left very well off by Uncle Bela in his will. Karoly runs the jewelry shop, but there's not enough business to bring me in on it, and there won't be for many years, if ever. Meanwhile, the specter of Communism looms like a thunder cloud over all of Eastern Europe. Hungary is no longer the place my parents knew, or even the same place I knew growing up.

I've been thinking a lot, lately, about General Irving Smith's offer, back in Feldafing, to help me emigrate to the United States. With so much unfinished business here in Hungary, I couldn't possibly have accepted the offer then. *Then*. Now, however, my business here is finished, and I find myself yearning to leave the ancient land of my ancestry and birth.

But what about Vera? Even if I talked her into accompanying me, even if she *could* somehow accompany me, how would I provide for her in a strange new country?

Despite my confusion, I'm convinced of two things. First, I love Vera and want to marry her. Second, I must leave Hungary. My quandary over how to reconcile these is a source of continued agony.

I find palliatives, but not solutions. Since childhood, for instance, I've loved working with my hands, especially whenever it involves building or repairing something. I'm fascinated with how anything mechanical works. My particular joy (and greatest challenge) is the small details, for which I have an unusually good eye. Maybe its hereditary, or even genetic, with so many forbears in the jewelry business. I guess if I were a painter, I'd be a miniaturist.

Now, as a hobby that helps calm my mind, I take up building miniature glider planes. This soon gets old, though, so I switch to model boats, which are more intricate and thus offer greater challenge. The boat I work on now, my largest and most ambitious so far, even features a movie theatre, with tiny seats and a picture projected on the screen.

One morning I'm working away on my boat in Aunt Manci's kitchen, the door shut, when I hear a knock.

"Come in," I call, preoccupied.

Vera appears, hugging me from behind as she inspects my handiwork over my shoulder. "Hello, love. That looks great," she whispers, her warm breath tickling my ear.

I laugh. "Thank you, darling. But it's not fair of you to ambush me right now, with both my hands full."

She nips at the top of my ear. "That's the whole idea," she says.

"I see," I reply, laughing again. I decide, to take a chance and remove my hands from the two pieces I've been pressing together for awhile, waiting for the glue to dry.

Fortunately the glue holds on its own. "I need a break," I tell Vera, getting up and stretching. "It's a beautiful day outside. How'd you like to take a walk along the Danube with me?"

"I would."

Outside we cross the wide, tree-lined boulevard, arm in arm.

"Pista," Vera asks as we stroll along, enjoying the late winter sunshine and the soft breeze against our faces, "what are you going to do when you finish your double school year?"

"Depends on my grades."

"That's not what I mean. How about *us*?"

"We'll get married, of course. Someday." How can I tell her about my desire to emigrate? What will she think? Where would she see herself fitting into a scenario like that? Or will she just dump me? I don't know how to even begin telling her what's on my mind, and I fear that even when I do, it will come out all wrong.

"Pista, how will you earn a living once we're married?"

"I'll become a professional man of some sort. Most likely, I'll start a business designing or repairing something. That seems to run in my family, and hopefully I've learned something watching my father and uncle all these years."

"That sounds like a wonderful idea, Pista."

"Whatever I do, I'll take good care of you and our family, Vera. And let's face it, I *can* do just about *anything* with my hands." Taking advantage of the double meaning here, I give her waist a playful squeeze.

She laughs. Just then, she pulls me over to a store window displaying dolls of all shapes and sizes. She wants to look at the dolls themselves, but I notice something altogether different, a sign in big letters: WE REPAIR DOLLS OF ALL KINDS. In the very next window, a man sits at a bench repairing a doll, as if to demonstrate.

"I could very easily do what that man is doing," I tell Vera.

"Do what? What man?"

"Repair dolls by hand, like the man at this window. See? In fact, you've just given me an idea for a business I can start, with absolutely no initial investment!"

That same evening, I make up a big, eye-catching sign, featuring thick block letters in all different colors: DR. PISTA'S DOLL HOSPITAL. I REPAIR DOLLS and BUY BROKEN PARTS. This I place downstairs, just outside the main entrance to our building. The many Passers-by won't be able to *help* noticing it!

My advertisement works well. After attracting my first clients, business builds rapidly by word of mouth. Soon, I'm so busy I have to take in a partner, Aunt Manci.

She's delighted to have something new to learn, and learns very quickly. And like my mother, her sewing skills and her eye for detail are both superb.

With my initial profits, I buy a Leica III camera and a gold Shaffhousen watch for myself, and some gifts for Vera, Aunt Manci, and Uncle Karoly I couldn't have otherwise afforded. It's nice to have money. Ah, the feeling of success!

Hmmm. Maybe it wouldn't be so bad, after all, to stay right here in Budapest. I could keep building up my business, buy a little shop eventually, get married. . .

But as usual, just when I'm finally enjoying a little peace of mind, fate throws me a left hook.

When school ends Monday afternoon, Jancsi shares a trolley ride home with me, as usual.

"I'm emigrating," Jancsi announces out of the blue, once the trolley's been moving awhile.

"Huh?" He's never even spoken to me of this before. "Emigrating? To where?"

"Either Australia or Canada. I'm still trying to decide. All I know is I want a fresh start, away from here, away from my memories, and *especially* away from these damn Communists! I didn't survive two years in a concentration camp just to come home and settle for this."

I nod, thoughtfully. "Can't say I blame you, Jancsi."

"What about you, Pista? Do you plan to hang around Budapest and watch the Communists take over—look on as they make mincemeat of your doll business, or anything else you try to build up for yourself?"

"Look, Jancsi, I want out as much as you do. But I've got something holding me here."

"What? Airplane glue?"

"Hardly. I'm in love."

He nods slowly, more serious and respectful now. "I understand, Pista. I'd have a hard time leaving, too, if I had a girl like Vera. Fortunately for me, I don't."

Silence.

"Pista," he begins again in a couple minutes, "it's not right for me to try swaying you one way or another, and I won't. You have to decide on your own. But for whatever it's worth, I wanted to let you know that the Canadian Jewish Congress in Budapest is taking immigration applications from Jewish orphans." He produces a folded piece of paper. "Here's their address, in case you want to look into it."

"Thank you."

We arrive at our stop, say good-bye, and go our separate ways. That evening, Vera and I stroll along the Danube again, and then spend a lovely evening at her apartment, which only deepens my dilemma. Alone in my bedroom that night, I open Jancsi's folded sheet of paper, and find myself staring at the address, as if hypnotized. Here's my ticket out of here, I say to myself. In my heart of hearts, I'd love to emigrate to Canada if given the chance. Sure, it's not the U.S., but it's close enough, and I could easily move there from Canada. I realize I've just been handed a second chance at freedom, and when I least expected it. I'd be a fool to pass it up this time. But I can't admit that fact. Not just yet. Not even to myself.

After school the very next afternoon, however, I find myself, as if propelled by some invisible force, hastening downtown toward the Canadian Jewish Congress agency, clutching Jancsi's folded piece of paper as if my life depended on it.

"I'd like to apply for immigration to Canada," I announce in a firm voice to the woman at the front desk there. She's heavy set, with dark eyes and heavy eyebrows. Abundant hairs also grow on her upper lip, like a man's mustache.

She raises her bushy eyebrows. "How old are you, young man?"

"I turned seventeen in February."

"Are either of your parents alive?"

"They're both deceased, ma'am."

"Fill out this form, then, and answer *every* question. It sounds to me like you *will* qualify, since you're under 18, with neither parent living."

"Thank you, ma'am."

I sit down on a creaky chair nearby, and, using the side of my school briefcase for a hard surface, complete the lengthy application form right then and there, answering each question thoroughly, and in my best handwriting. Then I walk back to the front desk and hand my completed application form to the thick-browed woman.

"You should hear something within the next couple of months, if not sooner," she informs me.

I thank her again and turn to leave.

I really don't know how I'll tell Vera about this.

Meanwhile, my 7th grade final examinations loom ahead. Between now and then, I'll need to study like never before if I hope to pass them all.

The first of May rolls around quickly. It's a holiday, replete with a grand May Day parade, clearly visible from the third floor balcony of Vera's apartment. She and I stand there now, gazing down at what is actually just a Communist show of force, thinly disguised as holiday fun.

"Look, Vera, here comes the parade," I say, as soon as I hear the loud marching and military music starting to drift our way.

The first "exhibit" we see is a streetcar bearing numerous red flags and banners. Big pictures of Communist leaders are plastered on all its windows. Another huge banner that stretches across the side of the streetcar proclaims:

THIS STREETCAR WAS BLOWN UP WITH THE MARGARET BRIDGE INTO THE DANUBE BY THE RETREATING NAZIS! THE HUNGARIAN SOCIALIST REPUBLIC REBUILT IT FOR THE WORKERS' BENEFIT!

The procession flows on in that same spirit, with endless marching soldiers and brass bands. At times, the blaring music almost splits our eardrums. Hundreds of white-shined factory workers carry signs bearing Communist slogans, like *"DOWN WITH THE IMPERIALISTS!"; " LONG LIVE STALIN!";* and *" THE FACTORIES BELONG TO THE PEOPLE!"*

Gazing at the elaborate spectacle, I'm dismayed and shocked, but not all that surprised. I realize, sadly, that not much has really changed since the days of Nazi Hungary, only the time we're in and the uniforms worn by our oppressors. Some of today's eager parade participants and attendees may even be those same individuals who, not long ago, carried Nazi emblems and cried, *"Heil Hitler."*

Even more disturbing to me is the newly organized *Communist Youth,* with its numerous children and teens smartly clad in bright, impressive uniforms. This politically charged movement has now replaced the mainstream Hungarian *Boy Scouts,* just as *Hitler's Youth* had done only a few years ago!

Then I think about how, even as Vera and I stand here, factories are being nationalized daily, along with major privately owned stores and companies. I even forsee the day when our jewelry store is again confiscated, this time by the Communists.

Jancsi's questions to me on the trolley a few weeks ago keep repeating themselves within my mind: *"What about you, Pista? Do you plan to just hang around Budapest and watch the Communists take over?"*

Had Father and Mother foreseen the dangers of Nazism in the mid thirties, before it was too late, I know they would have packed up and left Hungary, for their children's sake, whatever the cost to themselves. Knowing what I know, seeing all I've seen, how could I now possibly do less for my own future children?

Next, I recall General Smith's statement to me at Feldafing, right before I sneaked back to Hungary: *"Pista, if you go back to the Eastern Sector, to Communism, I would feel responsible for abandoning an orphan."* And, finally, I hear the echo of Headmaster Toros's remark that day in his office about Roosevelt and Stalin: *"Two allies, but not for long."*

Father, Mother, and Andris can't advise me. But there's no doubt in my mind what they'd do in my situation—if only they could.

As the parade draws to a close, finally, I hear yet another voice inside my head, Andris's. Gently but firmly, he insists, *"Pista, now that you've made up your mind, you need to tell Vera of your decision. It wouldn't be right to wait any longer."*

"Okay, Andris. But help me. I don't know what to say, or how to say it."

"I'm right here with you, little brat.".

Taking a deep breath, I turn to Vera, taking both her hands in mine. Quietly, I say, "Dearest, I'm going to have to leave Hungary soon, and that means leaving you, too. But only for the short term. I'll send for you as soon as I can, once I get settled in America. I've thought it through, and I just can't marry here and start a family, not with everything I've been through, not with what I see happening here day by day. I don't want any children of mine experiencing the things I did, or facing no future because their father ignored the handwriting on the wall."

"Pistukam, I love you with all my heart. But I've known for a long time it would be impossible for you to stay here. As soon as you learned of your mother's death, I knew your days here were numbered. Hungary is like a coffin to you. I don't want you to try living in a coffin for my sake. So I'll wait for you, and when you're ready, I'll come to you."

"Thank you so much, dearest."

One day late in June, Vera appears in Aunt Manci's kitchen to help me finish my latest model ship.

"Pista, just think," she remarks. "You'll soon be boarding an ocean liner built just like this one!"

"I sure hope not. You want it to sink?"

"You're always joking, you clown. Besides, I'm sure you're unsinkable. I've been wondering, how big is Canada, anyway, compared, say, to Hungary?" And where is Canada, exactly?

"Good question." I've always been good at European geography, but my knowledge of Canada is sparse. After all, I'd never thought I'd be moving there.

I take Vera by the hand and lead her into Uncle Bela's old office, where his expensive globe still sits atop his highly polished desk.

Vera spins the globe around, slowly. "Here's Europe. . . Germany. . . Austria. Is this little spot of pink Hungary?"

"That's us," I say. "Now, find Canada."

She spins the globe around again and stops at Canada. "Wow! That's a big hunk of land you're going to, Pista. Don't get lost, okay?"

*Bzzzz. . .*The doorbell rings and I answer it. It's our mailman.

"Hello, Mr. Katona," I say. Anything special today?"

"As a matter of fact, yes. A registered letter for you, Pista Nasser. Sign here." He hands me a pen.

I sign my name, close the door again, and return to Vera, who's still spinning the globe, but now rather listlessly.

"What's wrong, darling?"

"I'm just thinking of how far away you'll be."

"Not for long, dearest."

"What's in the big envelope? Is that your passport already?"

"No."

"What is it?"

"A letter." Why does she have to be sitting right here, right now? Fate is making this as hard as possible for us both.

"Why don't you read it to me?" she says, trying to sound brave.

"All right." I rip open the letter, take a deep breath, and begin: *"Dear Mr. Nasser: We hereby officially inform you that on the sixth of July, nineteen forty-eight at six o'clock P.M., passage has been booked for you on the express train to Paris, France. Your passport and all your documents are to be picked up at this office on the twenty-seventh of June, nineteen forty-eight at nine o'clock a.m. Luggage instructions and itineraries will be given to you at the same time. Congratulations and good luck!'"*

After I finish reading the letter, the silence is dreadful. I swallow hard and look over at her. "Oh, honey," is all I can say as I hug her tightly.

She pulls away from me a moment, long enough to gaze directly into my eyes and declare, with heartfelt conviction, "Remember, Pista, this is for both of us, and our future, so we can bring up our children in freedom."

In June, I pass all my exams for the 7th grade, making me eligible to receive a baccalaureate degree in only one more year. But since I'm leaving, I must forego this long cherished goal. Mother, Father, and Andris would be probably feel disappointed that I'll not receive my baccalaureate, since we greatly valued education in our family. But they would understand, I'm sure.

Thus, I'll arrive in North America with a first rate education from one of Hungary's top preparatory schools. The education I've already received, even without finishing the degree, roughly equals a Canadian or U.S. bachelor's degree. But I'll have no piece of paper to prove it. I'll make do without it, though, somehow. I always have.

My final weeks in Budapest fly by, with much to do, many good-byes to say, and not enough time for any of it. The day before I leave, Vera and I go on an outing to Margaret Island with her family. Her mother gets chilled by the surprisingly cold evening air, so Vera and I volunteer to return to their apartment for her sweater. Round trip, it's an hour's walk.

We both welcome the break. As soon as we're out of sight, I hail a taxi. Only minutes later, we're back inside her apartment—all alone there, for the first time ever. We sit on the edge of her bed, holding hands. Then we seal our love with close hugs and long, intimate kisses, but nothing else, though we're both painfully tempted. I've too much respect for Vera not to wait until we're together again, permanently. And should anything interfere with our being reunited, I've left her her virginity.

That night I toss around in bed, unable to sleep. Tomorrow is July 6th, and I'll leave for Paris. My bags are packed and my papers in order. There's simply no turning back now.

The plan for tomorrow afternoon, before I leave Budapest for Paris on the 6 p.m. train, is for Karoly, Aunt Manci, Vera and me to have a last farewell dinner at the Gundel Gardens in the City Park. From there, we'll all take a taxi to Nyugaty Terminal, where they'll see me off.

Everything is in order, so I should be able to just close my eyes and go peacefully to sleep. But I can't. For a long while, I've been preoccupied that my emigration might in fact end my relationship with Vera—not in any romantic sense, but rather, for political and bureaucratic reasons, unless I can somehow get her out of Hungary. Already, though, the Communists have restricted nearly all emigrations from here, save for exceptional cases like my own. Vera, with her family alive and well, obviously would not qualify for any of the special programs designed to help Jewish orphans make a fresh start in the free world.

Finally, toward morning, I fall into a troubled sleep.

"Pistukam!" A gentle hand shakes my shoulder. I force my eyes open, feeling as if I closed them only a few minutes ago.

Aunt Manci bends over me. "It's 10:00! Time to get up. You were out like a light."

Slowly, I rise from my bed, stumble toward my bathroom, and take my last morning shower, ever, at Aunt Manci's. Combing my sleep-tousled hair before the bathroom mirror, I see a young boy's face smiling back at me. Curly black hair, dark eyes, a mischevious look. It's hard for me to believe that the youthful face gazing back at me is really mine; my expression gives no clue at all of the hardships I've suffered. I stick out my tongue at my reflected image, and have to laugh at how well that silly childish gesture still fits me. Andris was right when he used to call me "little brat." Despite all the *gravitas* that's been kicked and beaten into me so early, I still look, somehow, like a carefree kid. If only I *felt* as young and light-hearted as I *look*, even just a little bit.

Rozsi has prepared a delicious breakfast for Aunt Manci and me in honor of my departure, but, I barely taste it although I praise it lavishly and force myself to eat much more than I want.

For our final afternoon at Varosliget, Vera appears from upstairs later in the afternoon, wearing a beautiful new yellow cotton dress with a tiny orange flowered print in the material. Her full, lovely lips are painted red. Her naturally rosy cheeks don't need any makeup. I rush into her open arms, but to my surprise, she turns her face away.

"Don't mess up my lipstick yet." she begs me, prettily. "Let's save it for the goodbye."

"Oh, all right," I growl, pretending to sulk. She laughs.

Soon Karoly arrives, looking especially dapper for the occasion.

Next it's time for me to hug Rozsi good-bye. "Thank you so much for everything," I tell her as we embrace. "I'll miss you, Rozsi. Please take good care of Aunt Manci for me."

"I will, Pista," she promises. "And best of luck to you, always." She wipes away a tear.

Then Karoly and I grab various pieces of my luggage and head downstairs, with Aunt Manci and Vera just ahead of us. Outside, we hail a cab. Karoly tells the driver, "Gundel Gardens, please!" And with that, we're off.

It's 3:45 when we arrive at a plush restaurant in beautiful Central Park, right beside the zoological gardens. Inside, I slowly drink in all the beauty of my surroundings: the lovely garden, the well-manicured bushes, the flowers creeping up trellises; the gaily decorated white gazebos reserved for diners like us, celebrating special occasions.

Oh, God! I can't bear to think I'll not see any of this again.

The maitre d' greets us and leads our party to our table, which, as it turns out, is inside one of the specially decorated white gazebos, just for our special occasion. Karoly, Aunt Manci, and Vera must have planned all this, I realize. As we sit down, I feel like some sort of prince.

After everyone is seated, we set about scanning the extensive menu. After we all order, we talk and talk about everything except, of course, my impending departure.

The elegant waiters wear red coats, and each one has a white napkin slung over his arm as he serves us.

"Stuffed roast veal for the young lady; roast duck for the young man," the waiter who brings us our food intones, placing each plate carefully before its recipient. Once everyone is served, he bows, wishes us all "*bon appetit,*" and disappears.

I pluck a red carnation from the elegant bud vase sitting on our table, and place it in Vera's hair. "Promise me you'll press this flower and preserve it until we meet again."

"I promise."

Silently, I wonder when that will be.

Soon a gypsy violinist arrives and takes a position near our table. The bittersweet melody he plays seems just right for the occasion. It begins, "*Csak egy kislany van a vilagon.*" (There is only one sweetheart in this wide world.) Then, lipstick or not, I find Vera's lips, and, seizing the moment, we kiss, again and again.

After we finish our meal, and having lingered as much as possible over dessert and coffee, the dreaded hour arrives: 5:00 p.m. We must now depart the restaurant for the railroad terminal; my train to Paris leaves in exactly one hour.

Right at this moment, I'm certain I'd undo everything I've set into motion up to this point, if only I could. I'd remain here forever, precisely in this Eden-like spot, with my lovely Vera by my side. What more does a man really need for happiness?

"It's time to go now, little brat." I close my eyes a moment, and see Andris, smiling at me, encouraging me. *"Don't worry, runt. Everything's going to be fine. You'll see.*"

As we all stand and exit the beautiful gazebo, I wonder, for the first time ever, if my brother's words are indeed correct.

When we arrive at the railroad terminal, it teems with people, as always. Over the loudspeaker we hear: "*The Paris express on track number two is ready for boarding. Time of departure will be 6 p.m., on time.*"

It's already 5:40 according to the huge station clock.

Then Aunt Manci breaks my melancholy as Vera and I stand, silently gazing into each other's eyes. "Pistukam, you'd better board the train now if you want to get a good seat. You've got a long trip ahead."

"I know, Aunt Manci," I reply, without moving an inch. I don't want to get on the train, not just yet. Maybe I can pretend, for another second or two, that

I'm not really going anywhere.

"I'll run ahead and pick you out a window seat," Aunt Manci finally says. "Karoly, you come, too."

"Good idea," Karoly replies, following her.

When we're alone again, Vera puts a hand on my arm. "Pista, put down your suitcase. I want to take your picture."

I straighten my white shirt jacket.

"Smile," she says. I do so, with effort. She clicks the camera.

"Pista!" Now Aunt Manci is calling me. I turn around and see her leaning out a window three coaches away, waving to us. Karoly is with her, and he, too, sticks his head out the window and waves. When they look away again, Vera and I slip into one another's arms and kiss, one long, final time.

Next, we board the train together, arriving slowly at my compartment, where Karoly and Aunt Manci still wait. I place my two suitcases, one by one, on the big shelf just above my seat.

Soon the loudspeaker booms the words I've been dreading: *"Non-passengers must depart the Budapest-Paris train immediately. Passengers, last call to board the train."*

It's 5:55. I stare at Vera, memorizing her clear eyes, her rosy cheeks, her even white teeth, her full lips, her gentle but mischievous expression. God, how I'll miss her! Silently, I take her in my arms one last time, not knowing whether I'll ever see her again.

"It's time to go now, little brat. Be brave!"

Vera whispers in my ear, "Pista, I'll love you for all eternity." How I yearn to tell her she's sweet and charming and means everything to me. But when the time comes for my parting words, I'm as tongue-tied as a mute.

Then Aunt Manci breaks in again, hesitantly, self-consciously, clearly wishing not to have to interrupt us. "Vera, darling, and Karoly, we have to get off."

In a daze, I manage to let Vera go. Then I kiss Aunt Manci and Uncle Karoly good-bye. I'm numb. None of this feels real. Maybe that's for the best; otherwise, I doubt I could follow through with it.

Now I'm alone inside my compartment, waiting for the three of them to walk around and appear, again, outside my open window. Soon there they are, gazing up at me, their eyes full of love and tears.

Karoly shouts, "Don't forget to write, Pista."

"I won't. I love you all very much."

"Be good Pista," says Aunt Manci. "Make us proud of you."

"I will, Aunt Manci."

"All aboard!"

"Time to go, little brat! This is the toughest part. Be brave!"

Now the sudden high pitch of the steam is almost ear shattering. The engine's wheels start up. Slowly, the train begins to move.

Outside my open window, Vera still grasps my hand tightly, fighting back her tears. Her walk quickens right along with the faster movement of the train, and then it turns into a slow run. She continues clasping the tips of my fingers, running faster and faster now, faster than I ever knew she could. I can still see her rosy cheeks, her golden brown hair, her. . .

Finally, the speed of the train forces us to break our grip. The distance stretches between us until her very outline shrinks to nothing.

"I love you, Vera!" I whisper, gazing back her way long, long after I know I can't see her.

Epilogue

In 1950, I was prevented from reuniting with Vera by the Iron Curtain. Vera Koranyi, who was my first love, whom I met at fourteen after returning from the concentration camp at Muhldorf. When I left Budapest for Canada in late 1948, our plan was for Vera to join me there as soon as possible after I became established in the new country. Meanwhile, we exchanged dozens of letters around 1950, though, the political situation in Hungary grew very grave, and the Communists made it impossible for anyone to leave. This eliminated even the tiniest ray of hope of Vera's joining me in Canada. After much hesitation, and many sleepless nights spent mulling over our predicament, I wrote Vera that I thought it is best for both of us to go on separately with our lives, given the now insurmountable barrier the Communist had erected. She never replied, and I never heard from her again. I did hear from her mother, Mrs. Koranyi, who wrote back and expressed her gratitude for my honesty in allowing Vera to continue with her life in Hungary. After that, Vera and I lost touch. When I finally returned to Budapest, many years later, after the Iron Curtain fell, I was unable to locate Vera, her family, or anyone else who I knew or had known them. But ever since the evening of July 6, 1948, when I last saw her, Vera has continually occupied a special place in my heart, and always will. God bless you, Vera, wherever you are!

About the Author

In 1948, the Canadian Jewish Congress brought Stephen to Canada. He soon found an opportunity to use his artistic skills in a ten-year career as a diamond-setter.

In 1955, a chest x-ray revealed a spot on his lung, which was diagnosed as tuberculosis. Stephen was quite sure that the spot was accumulated cement dust, deposited during his days in the concentration camp. The doctors confined him to a hospital for an entire year. Stephen's own diagnosis was the correct one, he does not, and never did have, TB.

Stephen moved to the United States in 1958. He had learned cooking skills as a Boy Scout prior to the war. He purchased and opened a restaurant. Later, he sold insurance and securities, eventually becoming a member of the Pennsylvania Life Insurance Company Hall of Fame. He then worked for a real estate company, heading his own office. Subsequently, he worked as a decorator for Sears for 15 years until he retired.

Stephen and his wife Francoise, a retired nurse, currently reside in Las Vegas. At age 72, Stephen remains as dynamic and creative as ever. He is a speaker for the Holocaust Survivor Group in Las Vegas. Both he and Francoise enjoy playing tennis, snow skiing, snorkeling, hiking, attending theatre and duplicate bridge. Stephen has built a complete HO gauge model railroad layout by hand, an endeavor that consumed over 600 hours. He is an avid artist, specializing in oils, and now working with watercolors.

Stephen has two married children, Daryl and Michele, from a previous marriage. He enjoys his three grandchildren Andrea, Andrew, and Chelsea and two great-grandchildren.